DIVORCE

SHAKTI BOOKS is devoted solely to publishing studies on Women. The aim of the several series under this imprint is to provide documentation, analyses, interpretive comment and research findings on all aspects of the various issues related to women, from the standpoints of anthropology, sociology, history, politics, economics and social history. Emphasis will be placed on the Third World experience and contributions invited from academicians, professionals with field experience, social scientists and scholars. In those areas of social concern where formal data are scanty or unavailable, informal but fully authenticated studies will be considered as part of a holistic treatment of a complex and, in many ways, still undefined subject.

SHAKTI intends to publish a body of work, multidisciplinary and unaffected by bias, that will serve as resource material and as a reference point for further enquiry.

The following books have been published:

Feminism in a Traditional Society: Women of the Manipur by Manjusri Chaki-Sirkar

Women's Oppression: Patterns and Perspectives by Susheela Kaushik

The Face Behind the Mask: Women in Tamil Literature by C.S. Lakshmi

Tyranny of the Household: Investigative Essays on Women's Work Edited by Nirmala Banerjee and Devaki Jain

Status and Position of Women in India: With Special Reference to Women in Contemporerary India by Kiran Devendra

DIVORCE

Its Causes and Consequences in Hindu Society

S. POTHEN

SHAKTI BOOKS

SHAKTI BOOKS
a division of
Vikas Publishing House Pvt Ltd
Regd. Office: 5 Ansari Road, New Delhi 110002
Head Office: **Vikas House, 20/4 Industrial Area, Sahibabad 201010**
Distt. Ghaziabad, U.P. (India)

Printed at Chetna Printers, A-27/2-A, Shastri Marg, Maujpur, Delhi-110053

FOREWORD

THIS book "Divorce: Its Causes and Consequences in Hindu Society" is an attempt towards an examination of the etiology and consequences of a social problem which is causing serious concern to sociologists all over the world. Carrying out research in an area which is very sensitive is both a gigantic as well as a delicate task. In this work, the author has exhibited all the professional abilities required for research. She has an inquisitive mind, the required perception and above all, perseverance and industry which contribute not in any mean measure to success in field research, particularly in this area of Family Sociology.

In addition to the documentary evidence from the judicial courts, the author had discussions with parents, relatives, friends, neighbours and co-workers of the respondents, whenever possible, and, all these sources provided very valuable information which is given in the book.

Divorce was fairly an unknown phenomenon among the Hindus before the passing of the Hindu Marriage Act, 1955, and the Special Marriage Act, 1954. The Amendment in 1976 is an improvement on the previous legislation relating to marriage and makes divorce easier. The main attraction of the Amendment is its broader base for staking a divorce claim. All grounds available for a judicial separation are now available for a divorce. Hindus can now expect a divorce on the ground of desertion or cruelty of their spouse. The definition of "desertion" has been widened to include wilful neglect, so that a wife, who is living with her husband but is neglected and uncared for, will be able to petition for a divorce on the ground of her husband's desertion. Secondly, a single act of infidelity will now be sufficient for the aggrieved spouse to earn a divorce. The most publicized change, however, relates to divorce by mutual consent.

This study brings to light the fact that the process of divorce among the Hindus has been accentuated after the passing of the Amendments in the Act in 1976. Another interesting fact that has emerged as a result of this study is the high incidence of divorce among the *Brahmins* and in joint families. Still another interesting finding is that most of the women who went in for divorce were not employed at the time of seeking for divorce. Her study, like other studies, proves that early years of marital life are more prone to marital disruption in our country too.

Contrary to the general belief in our country, dowry did not play a major role in marital conflicts, tensions, and ultimately divorce among the Hindus.

This book by Dr (Mrs) Sosamma Pothen is a significant contribution to the growing literature in the field of Sociology of Family. I am sure that the book will be very useful and valuable for the social scientists, social workers, administrators and policy-makers.

I wish this book a great success.

Professor & Head, Department of Sociology
Bharathiar University

C.M. ABRAHAM

PREFACE

DIVORCE is related to 'marriage' and 'family' which are the most important institutions of the human society. Divorce is the legal dissolution of marriage, and, it has great socio-cultural implications. Divorce is also viewed as a social invention, and a socially devised means of dealing with marriage failure. Divorce is almost a new concept among the Hindus, for, the characteristic quality of Hindu marriage was that it was a union for life. The Hindu woman has been asked to put with all sorts of repressions and suppressions in the name of the honour of family and for the good of the children. It was generally argued that if legislation was allowed to interfere with the sacrament of marriage, the institution of marriage will break down. It was in this background, that, the Hindu Marriage Act, 1955, was passed with several amendments, particularly the 1976 Amendment, making a provision for divorce by consent also.

The impact of legal dissolution of marriage on the institution of family and the total society is a matter of difference of opinion. According to some, divorce is the most practical index of family disintegration. Divorce is also recognised as a serious social problem. However, it can safely be said that divorce is one of the many signs of family disintegration and it represents the final one.

Divorce has far reaching consequences with regard to persons, social institutions and communities. The alarming rate of divorce in Western countries indicates the same. While it is reported that one-third of all marriages in the United States end in divorce, some latest surveys have shown that married people basically are opposed to the concept of divorce.

The rate of divorce in India is relatively low. It has several reasons. Yet, recent legislations are likely to help in the increase of the rate of divorce. Modern education has inculcated in the Indian woman a sense of her own identity, which, in turn, has undermined her capacity to perpetuate her marriage at the cost of her self-respect. The ideals and values relating to the Hindu marriage are changing rapidly and it is no more viewed as an eternal bond predestined by the gods.

The legislation on marriage and family pertaining to the Hindus is relatively recent. One has to investigate and see how the members of the Hindu society are taking advantage of the legislation especially on divorce; what are the processes and problems in relation to divorce litigations and what are the effects of the decrees of dissolution of marriage. The public is also becoming more aware of the legal provisions of divorce as seen in newspaper reports.

The aims of the present study are to find out (*i*) the marital adjustments before divorce, (*ii*) major causes of divorce, (*iii*) the consequences of divorce on the socio-economic status of the divorcees, (*iv*) what happens to the children, and finally, (*v*) patterns of remarriage.

Our hypotheses are that (*i*) the urban Hindus in India are taking advantage of the legislations made by the Government, especially the Hindu Marriage Act, more particularly the provision for divorce, (*ii*) there are adverse and far-reaching consequences of divorce, (*iii*) most of the conflicts which lead to divorce spring up in the early years of marriage, (*iv*) children are the worst sufferers of divorce, and (*v*) remarriage of the divorced spouses especially of the males is taking place in considerable number. Most of the these hypotheses have been tested and found correct. With regard to the children, however, we find that because of the traditional joint family structure of different types, even among the urban Hindus, children are taken care of by the parents of the divorcees, and, therefore, their physical care is not too adversely affected, although the personality development of the younger children is much hampered. The advantage of the joint family system in traditional societies like India to take care of the children of the divorced parents has been pointed out by Kingsley Davis, Elliott & Merrill and others, too.

Some of the most important suggestions, I would like to make are: (*i*) spread of social education about various aspects of marriage, sex, family, availability of legislation, etc., (*ii*) family courts, with specially qualified and trained male and female judges, (*iii*) control of misuse of the provisions of the legislation for divorce, (*iv*) better and greater efforts for reconciliation, (*v*) Marriage and Family

Counselling Bureaux and (*vi*) more studies on the subject as the present one may be treated as a pioneer study.

It has been experienced that studies of the type undertaken has to surmount great difficulties particularly in the matter of data collection. Unless and until people are better enlightened, they would not bother to give any data. Likewise, the courts, municipal corporations, State governments and Central Government should collect and maintain primary data concerning divorce as done in the United States and elsewhere.

I express my heart-felt gratitude to Professor V.C. Tongia my esteemed guide and supervisor for the research study. I must express my sincere thanks to Prasanna Menon, M.A. (Sociology) who accompanied me during my visits to the divorcees, their families, and others in order to collect data.

I am thankful to my husband, Dr K.P. Pothen for his valuable suggestions, encouragement and guidance.

I must thank my young children for their patience and cooperation for bearing my absence from home for long hours in connection with the data collection for the study of divorce.

My sincere thanks to all my respondents who, willingly or unwillingly opened their hearts to me and shared with me their bitter and painful past experiences. I must apologize for calling back to their minds sorrows and pains, sense of personal failure and shame, forgotten and hidden in the depth of unconscious mind.

Above all, I am grateful to Almighty God for His mercy on me for enabling me to undertake such research work, along with my work as a teacher of Sociology and household responsibilities.

SOSAMMA POTHEN

CONTENTS

Chapter 1

INTRODUCTION AND METHOD OF STUDY

GENERAL INTRODUCTION

HUMAN society is made of groups. Of all the groups human beings have formed, none can be thought more important than the family. It is a group as ancient as man himself. It is a multi-functional group which satisfies basic physical, mental and spiritual needs of human beings. In marital relationship alone, two human beings enter into a complete physical, mental and spiritual union with each other. The highest of human ideals, values and qualities namely, love, devotion, cooperation and sacrifice are found in the family. It is a universal institution as well. Marriage and family are ancient institutions and around them have grown up deep and powerful sentiments and traditions. Family is the institution which forms the basis of every other institution on the face of the earth. It is in family that the expectations of society first impinge on the infant forming his habits, setting his standards and defining his roles, thus preparing him for later roles in the community and the society. Importance of family as a fundamental social unit and the role of family in determining the character and structure of society are accepted by all. Family is intrinsic to human life and society. It is an institution founded on the laws of nature. It is also an association supporting and supported by every civilization, sanctioned by law, esteemed by knowledge, blessed by religion and wisdom, extolled in its highest achievements by literature and art and endowed with specific attributes by all forms of economy. In spite of evolutionary and revolutionary disruption, the institution of family has witnessed all the assaults made upon it and has survived as a witness to its own indispensability in determining the character and structure of society and man.

This important institution is formed on another institution, namely, marriage. Whereas all other animals enter into mating relationships, human beings go through a procedure of marriage to establish a family. In most societies including Hindu, marriage is considered as a permanent life-long and sacred union. When we examine the scriptures, we come across many passages to support the view that marriage is union made by God himself and hence none should break it. In the *Holy Bible*, it is written : Man must not separate, then, what God has joined together.[1] In Hindu texts, a still more intense view is expressed. For a Hindu, marriage is a sacrament and hence unbreakable. It is a union not only for this birth, but for all the births to come; in other words, immortal, interminable, eternal.

In spite of all these dicta and slogans supporting the indissolubility of marriage, there are factors, internal as well as external, working to undermine the stability of marital ties. Such a situation is termed as marital maladjustment or disharmony, which may be manifested in various forms, divorce being the final. In this book, an attempt is made to analyse the phenomenon of divorce among Hindus in the light of an empirical study conducted by the author.

CONCEPT OF DIVORCE

The word 'divorce' in English is derived from the Latin word *divortium* which again is derived from *dis* which means 'apart' and *vertere* which means 'to turn.' Divorce is the dissolution of the tie of marriage.[2] So, divorce is the turning away of partners from each other. It truly is a complete turn from the way of life the couple had so far.

Divorce in the proper and strict sense of the term means complete rupture of the marital bond, the persons divorced returning to their original state of being free to marry. Divorce is the word we use to mean the legal ending of a marriage. In the legal language, it might appear as a simple phenomenon, but in practical life its implications are massive. Divorce 'represents the end of the hopes

[1]St. Mathew's Gospel, Chapter 19:6 (*Good News Bible*).
[2]*Encyclopedia Britannica*, Vol. III, Cambridge, 1910, p. 334.

that two people had for each other; it is the certificate that their relashionship failed.'[3]

According to the Hindu Marriage Act, 1955 (amended upto 1976), "any marriage solemnized, whether before or after the commencement of this Act, may, on a petition presented by either the husband or the wife, be dissolved by a decree of divorce"[4] on the grounds mentioned therein.

The concept of divorce may be understood as different from such terms as (*a*) separation, (*b*) desertion, and (*c*) annulment.

(*a*) *Separation.* Separation may be an informal preliminary step toward divorce, a temporary expedient to lessen the immediate conflict, or a legally recognized decision to live separately without divorcing. Marital separation means that the mates are deprived of normal marital association, affecting their health, security and happiness. For the children, there is the loss of daily love and counsel of one parent. The divorced and the widowed may remarry but the separated may not. Provision is made for 'judicial separation' under the Hindu Marriage Act, 1955. Some of the grounds for judicial separation as laid down in Section 13 (1) & (2) of the Act are adultery, cruelty, desertion, conversion, incurable disease and renunciation of the world.

(*b*) *Desertion.* Desertion, as the term is ordinarily employed, means, "the irresponsible departure from the home on the part of either husband or wife, leaving the family to fend for itself."[5] Several studies have shown that deserters are husbands from the lower economic groups. Desertion is an evasion of marital responsibilities and hence, we have no way of ascertaining its true extent. A large share of desertions are never brought before any public agency. Many wives apparently feel the stigma of being abandoned and prefer not to report about their husbands. Since divorces cost money, and many deserted women are financially unable to bear the cost of court proceedings, they do not attempt to get relief through court.

[3]Sanctuary, Gerald and Whitehead, Constance, *Divorce and After*, Victor Goliancz Ltd., London, 1970 (flap).

[4]*Hindu Marriage Act, 1955* (*Act 25 of 1955*), amended up to 1976 by the *Marriage Laws Amendment Act. 1976*, Section 13 on "Divorce."

[5]Mabel, A., Ellioitt & Francis, E. Merrill, *Social Disorganisation*, Third Edition, Harper & Brothers, New York, 1950, p. 411.

Many of the consequences of desertion are similar to those of divorce, for, the family may be permanently dissolved. Desertion, however, presents a few special problems. Emotionally, the wife and children often suffer much more severely than in the case of divorce, for desertion entails a humiliating rejection of the spouse. It also carries with it a lack of certainty. Will the husband return? Is it possible he has met death unnoticed or unnotified? These and other countless questions plague the deserted wife. The children feel especially hurt by a father or mother who cares so little about them as to leave them without support. The wife and mother in the family often finds herself in serious economic straits. If the husband goes for good, his departure may signal a more favourable outlook for the family.

Desertion is popularly known as "the poor man's divorce."

According to the studies of the Family Location Services, in the United States of America, some of the prominent causes for desertion of the husbands are:

(*i*) marital incompatibility,
(*ii*) immaturity of one or both the partners,
(*iii*) mother-in-law interferences,
(*iv*) alcoholism,
(*v*) gambling,
(*vi*) money worries,
(*vii*) modern woman's spirit of independence,
(*viii*) cruelty, and
(*ix*) lack of interest in the home.

Desertion as a ground for divorce (as also for judicial separation has been recognized in section 13 (1) (b) and section 10 (1) of the Hindu Marriage Act. The term desertion has been defined in the Hindu Marriage Act, in the recently added explanation to section 13 (1) of the Hindu Marriage Act. This explanation added by the Marriage Law (Amendment) Act, 1976, read as:

> The expression 'desertion' means the desertion of the petitioner by the other party to the marriage without reasonable cause, and without the consent or against the wish of such party, and includes the wilful neglect of petitioner by the other party to the marriage and its grammatical variations and cognate expressions

shall be construed accordingly.

Legally, for the act of desertion to exist, there must be both the factum of physical separation and the *animus deserendi* or intention to desert, and both the necessary ingredients must continue through the statutory period.

(*c*) *Annulment*. Annulment is a court decision that the marriage contained some legal flaw (coercion, fraud, unwillingness to consummate the union, nonage, bigamy, etc.).[6] Nimkoff defines annulment as "a legal action that invalidates the marriage on the ground that it never legally existed and should not have occurred."[7]

When a judge issues an annulment decree, his purpose is to return the couple to their previous status, with their pre-existing rights, re-established, as if the marriage had not taken place, Annulment is a judicial declaration that no valid marriage ever existed between the parties in question. In the United States, the most common grounds for annulment are nonage, mental incapacity, force or duress, consanguinity or affinity, insanity, impotency, conviction of a felony, and prior undissolved marriage. In general, these grounds coincide as would be expected, with the causes for which marriages are prohibited. The three most common causes are: (*i*) fraudulent representation, (*ii*) bigamy, and (*iii*) under legal age.

The Hindu Marriage Act has provision for nullity of marriage. Section 12 of the Act lays down that any marriage solemnized whether before or after the commencement of the Act shall be "voidable and may be annulled by a decree of nullity" on grounds such as impotence, unsoundness of mind, recurrent attacks of insanity or epilepsy, obtaining of consent by force, fraud, and pregnancy by some other person at the time of marriage.

Thus, it would appear that there are differences between separation, desertion, annulment and divorce. Divorce has come to mean the process by which a marriage, recognized as valid, can be revoked in the life-time of the partners who then revert to single status and are free to remarry. In separation, the spouses are

[6]William, J. Goode, *Family Disorganization, in Contemporary Social Problems*, (ed.), Robert K. Merton, & Robert A. Nisbet, London, 1963, p. 401.

[7]Mayer, F., Nimkoff, *Marriage and the Family*, New York, 1947, p. 623.

legally recognized as living in separate households but are not free to remarry since they retain their marital status. Desertion is the voluntary withdrawal of one marriage partner from the other without the latter's consent, while nullity is the legal recognition that a marriage had not in fact been valid.

HINDUS AND DIVORCE

The social milieu in which the Hindus lived for ages is not accustomed to the concept of divorce, although Narada, Kautilya, Manu, and others permitted separation between the spouses in certain extreme cases such as (*i*) impotency, (*ii*) unrevealed physical diseases or defects, (*iii*) bad character, (*iv*) fallen from caste, and (*v*) mutual enmity.[8] Valvalkar clearly states that divorce is not known to the Hindu institution of marriage.[9] A married partner, more particularly a woman, was expected to undergo any hardship in order to salvage her marriage. The Hindu writers seem to be partial and lenient towards men right from the beginning. Strict fidelity and devotion was demanded from a woman, whereas a man could marry again even in the life-time of a wife. Writers of later days even debased womanhood. Women were pictured as lesser human beings with only low desires and goals. Sexual enjoyment was said to be the sole aim of a woman's existence. The sex urge in her is so great that she will cohabit with any man irrespective of age or appearance. If she is chaste, it is because she has not found the proper man, place and opportunity. A woman is depicted as a temptress who contempts and seduces any man, even the most learned one. The woman was created for infatuating man and hence there is nothing more heinous than woman. Through centuries, Hindu women were suppressed, fettered and ill-treated for no fault of hers. Even when she led a life of absolute devotion, sincerity and bondage, to her husband, and his relatives, even when she sacrificed every pleasure and willingly underwent hard penitences and punishments, for her husband's and children's sake, even when she followed him right up to the funeral pyre, Hindu womanhood was derided, looked down upon and treaded upon. It is little wonder that any attempt to change the

[8]P.H. Prabhu, *Hindu Social Organization*, 1963, pp. 190-192.
[9]P.A. Valvalkar, *Hindu Social Institutions*, 1939, pp. 145-199.

nature of Hindu marriage was violently opposed by fickle arguments like if legislation was allowed to interfere with the sacrament of marriage, the institution of marriage will break down. Vast majority of the Indian men, so much used to the idea of a humble, devoted and long-suffering wife, were not prepared to risk a change even mentally.

IMPACT OF DIVORCE IN GENERAL

Legislations permitting divorce and separation will have far-reaching consequence in any society. This is particularly so in a country like India where no divorce was permitted by law, more so, among the Hindus who have a traditional life.

The impact of legal dissolution of marriage on the institution of family and the total society is a matter of difference of opinion. According to Derrett, divorce cases reflect a sick society, not a healthy one.[10] Horton and Leslie feel that divorce and desertion are widely recognized as problems. They are not problems in all soeieties, as they do not exist in all societies.[11] According to Burgess and Locke, who have been pioneers in the study of Family Sociology, "the most practical index of family disintegration for research purposes is divorce."[12] Mowrer has also mentioned that "family disintegration first impinges itself upon the attention of students of social problems in the form of the disruption of marriage relations expressed in divorce and desertion".[13] Fonseca who made a research on the subject under the guidance of the eminent sociologist, Professor G.S. Ghurye, came to the conclusion that "it can be safely asserted that separation, desertion and divorce as they represent various degrees of dissolution of the family are generally not favoured in Indian society".[14] This is possibly due to the adverse effects of divorce.

At the same time, some other social scientist has pointed out that "family dissolution is an imperfect index of family disorgani-

[10]J. Derrett, M. Duncan, *The Death of Marriage Law,* Epitah for the Rishis, Vikas Publishing House, New Delhi, 1971, p. 187.

[11]Horton, Paul B. and Gerald B. Leslie, *The Sociology of Social Problems, New York*, 1960, Chapter 7, Problem Families & Family Problems.

[12]E.W. Burgess, H.J. Locke, *The Family*, 1950, p. 627.

[13]E.R. Mowrer, *Disorganization—Personal and Social*, 1942, p. 474.

[14]Mabel Fonseca, *Counselling for Marital Happiness*, Bombay, 1966, p. 21.

zation. According to this writer, "divorce is an imperfect index of marital disorganization, because, there may be disorganization without divorce."[15]

For instance, divorce was very difficult to obtain in England prior to liberalization of the laws in 1857, and again in 1937. When the divorce door is closed, marital disorganization may be unconspicuously endured. On the other hand, a couple with high expectations of marital bliss but relatively little marital disorganization may seek divorce as an exit from marriage. That marital disorganization is often not extreme is shown by the frequency of reconciliation, dropping of divorce suits and remarriage to the former spouse. Marshall Clinard has stated that:

> although many persons regard divorce as the only index of family disintegration, it is but one of the many signs, since it represents the legal dissolution of the marriage, it certainly is the final one.[16]

Here, it may be pointed out that perhaps the viewpoint of Marshall Clinard is acceptable to the present investigator. At the same time, we should not underestimate the seriousness of the subject, in view of the fact that divorce in any society has far-reaching consequences, with regard to persons, social institutions and communities. The alarming rates of divorce in Western countries indicate the same. More than 390,000 divorces in the United States in 1960, virtually affected the lives of 780,000 adults and their 460,000 children in many instances permanently.[17] Again, divorce generally hurts and when that pain affects more than 15 million Americans, they are justified in regarding the situation as something of a national health emergency. As a result of a nation-wide survey of marriage in the United States, it is pointed out that "although one in three American marriages now ends in divorce, most married people basically are opposed to the

[15]David L. Sills, (Ed.), *International Encyclopedia of the Social Sciences*, Vol. 5, Family: Disorganization and Dissolution, New York, p. 314.

[16]Marshall B. Clinard, *Sociology of Deviant Behaviour*, Holt Rinehart and Winston Inc., New York, 1965, p. 436.

[17]Carter and Flateria, *Trend in Divorce and Family Disruption in Selected Studies in Marriage and the Family* by Robert Winch and Louis Goodman, 1968, p. 564.

concept".[18]

As elsewhere, certain redeeming aspects of divorce in India would be that it would help to liberate the women and in reorganizing the family. Instead of dragging a miserable family life, it is better to secure a divorce. Certain studies in India have shown that the Hindu women are in favour of legislation in respect of divorce. Mrs. Hate found that out of 805 cases in her survey, 498 were in favour of the law of divorce, and 160 were against it. Mrs. Desai found 383 women in her study (47 per cent) in favour of divorce and 398 (49 per cent) against it. Those who favoured divorce did so as they had to bear one or the other of afflictions such as maladjustment in marriage, bigamy, a drunken, whimsical, cruel or immoral husband, supersession by the husband, excessive sexual indulgence on the part of the husband when the woman is physically incapable of conceiving.[19] The study of Rama Mehta has shown that modern education has inculcated in the Indian woman a sense of her own identity. There is evidence in her of a personal desire to live fully and express herself fully, preferably within marriage, but not exclusively in it.

Several social legislations in India (especially of very recent times) have furthered the women's movement in India and added to her stature both economically and socially. Important ones are:

(*i*) The Child Marriage Restraint Act, (Amended upto 1978);
(*ii*) The Hindu Married Woman's Right to Separate Residence and Maintenance Act, 1946, now repealed by the Hindu Adoptions and Maintenance Act, 1956;
(*iii*) The Hindu Succession Act, 1956;
(*iv*) Dowry Prohibition Act, 1961; and
(*v*) The Hindu Marriage Act, 1955 (with its Amendments up to 1976).

Women today no longer occupy a subordinate position in the family as they did at one time. This is especially true in the urban areas. The policies and programmes of the Central and State Governments in India, the activities of several private organi-

[18]Anthony Pietropinto and Jacqueline. Simenauer, *Husbands and Wives*, Berkley Books, New York, 1981, Introduction.

[19]*Cf.* K.M. Kapadia, *Marriage and Family in India*, 1959, p. 181.

zations, and a number of publications prove this. A very recent publication by Yaqin and Anwar has brought to light that there are really numerous social legal studies regarding the rights of Indian women.[20]

IMPORTANCE OF DIVORCE STUDIES IN INDIA

Sociological study of divorce is very significant in India for a number of reasons:

1. There are very few studies on divorce in the whole of India. The present researcher had written to all the major universities of India, and it transpired that the field for the study of divorce is almost, virgin. Barring a very few studies conducted on or related subjects such as the following, there has been practically nothing of sociological significance:

(*i*) Rama Mehta, *Divorced Hindu Women*, 1975.
(*ii*) Mabel Fonseca, *Counselling for Marital Happiness*, 1966.
(*iii*) Promilla Kapur, *Marriage and the Working Women in India*, 1979.

In her work, Promilla Kapur has pointed out that in India, adjustment studies, on the whole, are rare. One of the probable explanations for the absence of these studies in India may be that social science studies as such started very late in the country, and have been focussed mostly on the problems considered more important, that is, those which involve the majority of the population of the country. The paucity of studies on marital adjustment might well be accounted for, by the fact, that this problem had remained in the background, rather suppressed, on account of well-established social norms and the traditional pattern of Indian social organization. Further, the problem of adjustment in marriage had formerly been dormant, because men and women probably sought accommodation for their conflicts within the traditional framework of married life. Traditionally, a Hindu man or woman could never think of legal divorce.

[20]*Cf.* Yaqin, Anwarul, and Anwar, Badar, with a Foreword by Y.V. Chandrachud; *Protection of Women Under the Law*, An Annotated Bibliography, Deep and Deep Publications, New Delhi, 1982.

Fonseca has correctly remarked that studies in the field of interpersonal relationships in the family and interaction between husband and wife are lacking. Increased complexities in the present social setting emphasize family relationship as a challenging pattern and bring into play new forces which invite intensive research.[21]

2. Legislation on Marriage and Family pertaining to the Hindus is relatively recent. The first comprehensive legislation is Hindu Marriage Act, 1955, with its later Amendments, especially in 1976. One has to investigate and state:

(*i*) How the members of the Hindu society are taking advantage of the legislation ?

(*ii*) What are the processes and problems in relation to divorce legislations ?

(*iii*) What are the effects of the decrees of dissolution of marriage?

In this connection, the problems of children of the divorced (for instance, their custody, upbringing, education, personality development, etc) and the future of the divorced men and women (more particularly, women, their maintenance, remarriage, employment, etc.) are very important.

3. The Sociology of Family, as a distinct field of Sociology is in its infancy in India. Marital disruptions like the divorce, desertion, separation and annulment are very vital subjects to be studied in the Sociology of family. The changing patterns of marriage and family, marital adjustment, the organization, disorganization and reorganization of the family, customs and problems pertaining to family such as dowry, bride price, child marriage widow remarriage, and such like matters may also be included within the scope of family sociology. In our country, the joint family and the caste system are the two major social institutions. Here again family studies are very important.

Much of the sociological and anthropological researches in India so far have been on village communities, tribes, castes, etc. Not much research has been done on urban social institutions and their various aspects. This may be due to the fact that India is still

[21]*Cf.* Mabel Fonseca, *Counselling for Marital Happiness*, 1966, pp. 6-7.

predominantly rural. Yet, we have to inquire into the impact of urban way of life on institutions like marriage and family comprehensively.

4. Divorce is one of the most striking and predominant themes of modern literature. It has attracted the attention of many social scientists during the past several decades particularly in the United States of America. In India, daily-newspapers contain news of court decisions regarding divorce. One such report says:

> *Divorce Graph Zooms*
> More marriages are on the rocks these days. In less than five years, the divorce rate has gone up almost four times. On an average, 20 divorce petitions are filed daily in the five district courts of Delhi, dealing with cases under the Hindu Marriage Act. Sociologists, Judges and Lawyers maintain that the number has gone up since the amendment of the Hindu Marriage Act in 1976, when, among other things, a clause facilitating divorce by mutual consent was introduced.[22]

Another news item says:

> *Wife's Nose Disease Bar to Sex-Divorce Upheld*
> The Delhi High Court today upheld the divorce granted to a man by the trial court on grounds of cruelty as his wife was suffering from an incurable disease of the nose.[23]

A lengthy article with pictures of some people, who have been divorced or separated says:

> *The Divorce Syndrome*
> The sufferings of people after a divorce are many and varied. Sometimes, discovering another companion, they do not suffer at all. Sometimes, they suffer whether or not they found a new mate[24]

Yet another recent news item reads:

[22] *Indian Express*, April 17, 1978.
[23] *The Hindustan Times*, October 19, 1980.
[24] *The Sunday Standard Magazine*, February 1, 1981.

A rescarch paper entitled "A Comparative Study of Matrimonial Advertisement by Divorcees" presented at the Psychology Session of the six-day Indian Science Congress (held in January 1982) indicates that there is considerable increase in the rate of divorce in the country and more advertisements seeking remarriages are being published in the newspapers than ever before."[25]

In a very recent news item, it was stated as follows:

> Soviet Schools will introduce sex education next month as part of an attempt to give young people better preparation for married life, as part of a drive to reduce a divorce rate that now dooms one marriage in two to failure in Europe. A separate report said that Moscow city authorities were trying another method of combating divorce by introducing a marriage guide.[26] This clearly shows that even in Communist Russia, divorce is a serious problem.

METHODOLOGY

The methods that are adopted in the pursuit of a research study are very significant in order to make it scientific, unbiased, and logical. The author in the present study had resorted to some of the following methods in her study concerning divorce:

1. *Scope of Study*. By scope, we mean the ingredients or the specific areas of study. The main scope of the present study is mentioned below:

(*i*) Marital adjustment before divorce, such as the type of marriage, how the marriage was arranged, age at marriage, sex satisfaction and employment of the spouses.

(*ii*) Causes of divorce, especially with reference to the socio-economic status of the couples.

(*iii*) Processes and procedures of divorce, such as the interval between marriage and the application for divorce, the time taken for the decision of the judicial court, and other problems in obtaining divorce decree.

[25] *The Indian Express Magazine*, Sunday, January 10, 1982.

[26] *Free Press Journal*, Sunday, August 14, 1983

(*iv*) Consequences of divorce, such as personal problems, family problems, reaction of the community, employment of the divorced women, sexual adjustment, and the contacts and sentiments of the former partner.

(*v*) Divorce and children, especially, with whom are the children, how are they looked after, and the children's contacts with and attachments to the parents.

(*vi*) Remarriage, such as the incidence of remarriage, whom re-married, how the remarried partner was found out, happiness in the present union, and the children born out of the new marriage.

2. *Sampling*. How to select the sample cases for the study was indeed a difficult problem for the present researcher. At first, it was planned to include all the major urban centres of Madhya Pradesh. Later on, it was abandoned as data collection would have proved extremely difficult. Further, adequate number of divorce cases was available in the premier city of the state, namely, Indore. Therefore, cases for the study were taken from Indore. Indore is largest city of Madhya Pradesh, and it has a cross-section of the population of central India with regard to occupation, caste, culture, and the various modes of life. Indore was the capital of the erstwhile Madhya Bharat State also. Prior to Madhya Bharat, Indore was the capital of the Holkar State. According to the 1981 Census of India, the population of Indore is 8,27,071. It has the highest rate of literacy (48.98%) in the whole State. It is also known as the city of industry and commerce. A number of textile mills are located in Indore. Almost all other types of industry such as iron, drug, vegetable oil, washing soap, crockery, and timber are also found in Indore. It is also centre of transportation and communication by road, rail and air. Indore is also a centre of higher education, with about 25 colleges (arts, science, commerce, agriculture, fine arts, medicine and engineering).

The population of Indore is of mixed origin. The bulk is constituted by Malwis, (people from the Malwa region, consisting of Indore, Ujjain, Ratlam, Mhow, Dewas, Dhar, and Mandsaur), closely followed by Marwaris. Due to Maratha rule (Holkars, Pawars) for a considerable period, it has a large number of Marathi-speaking population also. Because of development in industry, education and business, it has attracted a good number of immigrants from other states and cities.

For the purpose of the present study, only those were selected in which marriage has terminated irretreivably. For this, the cases in which actual decree of divorce was granted by the judicial court, or at least an order of judicial separation was obtained and the parties are living separately for several years, so that the question of reunion does not occur, only, were selected. So, the first problem for the researcher was to locate such cases. Permission of the magistrate concerned was obtained to go through the files of the court, and all the cases in which a decree of either dissolution of marriage or judicial separation was obtained, were separated. These files themselves offered a lot of data in the form of personal information, in respect of the parties concerned, the main argument put forward by the petitioner, the response by the defendant (the other spouse), statement of the witnesses, cross-examination statements of the parties concerned, and finally, the judgment order (divorce-decree). Over 300 cases were thus located. Later, some of them were to be rejected for various reasons such as:

(*i*) nontraceability of the respondent,
(*ii*) change of address by the respondent,
(*iii*) transfer in employment,
(*iv*) migration on account of new jobs,
(*v*) remarriage, and a number of other reasons such as avoidance of stigma and criticism,
(*vi*) death, and
(*vii*) refusal to disclose the relevant information.

Therefore,, finally, 200 cases were selected for the study, consisting of 200 husbands and 200 wives.

3. *Tools of Data Collection.* The different techniques or tools of data collection are very important in a research. In fact, data is the basis or skeleton of research and if adequate and reliable data is not available, it is difficult to discover worthwhile findings. In the research relating to the present study, the following tools were made use of :

(*i*) *Judicial Court Record.* Each divorce case has a file in the judicial court. These files are consinged to the record room of the Court in bundles of several cases. After taking permission of the court, the divorce case files were seen. Much time, energy and patience were needed to locate, segregate and go through the individual case files. In the case file different papers such as (*a*) the application of the petitioner, (*b*) court notice to the respondent, (*c*) reply of the respondent, (*d*) statements of witnesses like relatives, friends and others, (*e*) statements of both parties at the time of the hearing of the case, including cross-examination, and finally, (*f*) the decree of divorce by the Hon'ble Judge are available. Thus, the divorce file of each case gives a lot of information.

(*ii*) *Schedule-cum-interview.* First, a draft schedule was drawn to elicit information from the couple. This was tested by interviewing a few couples. Thereafter, the schedule was revised and finalised. The schedules were got printed also. The schedule contains columns to record the (*a*) identifying data such as age, education, occupation, caste of the husband and wife, (*b*) family background, (*c*) details of marriage, (*d*) various aspects of marital adjustment, (*e*) divorce and child, (*f*) life of the husband and wife after divorce, (*g*) remarriage, and (*h*) other relevant data. In addition to these, lot of other details were noted to be used in case studies and explanations.

Barring a few cases of highly educated and enlightened respondents, others were very hesitant to provide all the necessary data. The researcher did not disclose to the respondents that she had seen the case files from the court. This was to enable therespondents to express their feelings and views freely and in as much detail as possible. It took some time to establish rapport between the researcher and the respondent. Further, in some cases, more than one visit to a respondent were needed. In some cases, the respondents were very emotional, reaching a point of breaking down while narrating the case. Of course, in certain other cases, all the information was readily given, impressing upon the researcher that he/she was not at fault. In some cases the respondents confessed their faults and added that they made a mistake in getting a divorce, and that they should have been more patient, understanding and careful in their relationship with partners concerned.

Thus, matters relating to marital disruption and dissolution are very personal, delicate and complex. Much care, tact and patience were exercised to deal with the respondents while interviewing them, even in very awkward and embarrassing situations. It must be admitted here that our people in India are not used to do such interviews for purposes of research or otherwise, as different from the United States of America and other Western countries where people readily disclose all such information.

(*iii*) *Case Study*. It has been experienced by the present researcher, that for the study of phenomena like divorce, case study method be one of the most useful and effective methods. In her study, aimed at discovering and analysing factors that contribute to maladjustment or adjustment in marriage of educated working women in India, Promilla Kapur prepared case studies on the basis of structured, non-structured, as well as intensive interviews.[27] Twenty typical studies are given by the present researcher, (ten per cent of the sample) which would throw light on the various aspects of divorce, including background, marital adjustment, ground for divorce, actual cause/causes, effects of divorce, (on the socio-economic status of the husbands and wives), children of the divorced couples, remarriage of the divorced husband/wife, etc. It must be mentioned here that each case of divorce is a distinct and unique one. Although certain classifications, interpretations and generalizations are formulated, every case should be treated individually. It was clearly observed that different combinations of factors caused divorce in different cases, the reactions of the respondents to their divorce were quite individualistic and their efforts to readjust also differed widely.

(*iv*) *Observation*. The researcher visited the families of the respondents and from the home environment, first hand and requisite information could be gathered. It also afforded an opportunity to meet the children, relatives and other associates of the respondents. In some cases, the researcher visited the place of work (school, office, etc.) and observation could be made there too about the behaviour and relationship of the divorcees.

(*v*) *Discussions with lawyers dealing with Divorce Cases*. A

[27]Promilla Kapur, *Marriage and the Working Women in India*, Abridged Edition, Vikas Publishing House Pvt. Ltd., Delhi, 1972, p. 37.

number of senior lawyers were contacted in their offices/homes/courts. A brief questionnaire regarding the general trend of divorce cases, the types of petitioners, their background, effects of divorce, etc., was also administered to the lawyers. It was also possible to go through the case files of some of the peculiar divorce cases, kept by them as lawyers of the parties concerned (petitioner/defendant). The various processes and proceedings stipulated by the Judicial Courts in regard to cases for divorce/judicial separation/restitution of conjugal rights from the time of the filing of the petition to the time of the pronouncement of the decree of divorce, including efforts for reconciliation, were also discussed with the lawyers. Certain legal aspects like (*a*) the grounds for the petition filed in the judicial court (as different from the real cause of the divorce, in several cases) and (*b*) the Amendments to the Hindu Marriage Act, 1955, (especially, the provisions for mutual consent) and the Sociological implications thereof, could also be freely discussed. Valuable suggestions offered by the lawyers, both from the legal and sociological points of view, were also obtained.

(*vi*) *Judicial Court Attendance.* With the permission of the court, and with the cooperation of the lawyers concerned, it was possible to witness personally the proceedings of certain divorce cases right in the court. This gave the researcher deeper insights into the divorce cases, more particularly, the legal proceedings relating to divorce.

DIFFICULTIES IN THE STUDY

The researcher had to face many difficulties in the study. Some of them are listed below :

1. Matters concerning marriage and family are quite intimate, personal, and sentimental. Marital disruptions like divorce and separation are very delicate and emotional. Outside inquiries into such phenomena are unwelcome in our society. When the researcher approached the divorcees, most of them were unhappy. They were hesitant to divulge personal information. Therefore, the establishment of rapport and collection of data was indeed a great task. In many cases, one visit was not enough; the respondents were contacted several times according to their convenience.

2. The divorcees reside in widely dispersed urban areas. Many have moved away from the original place of their residence for a number of reasons. Therefore, searching out the divorcees and locating them was a big job.

3. It appeared that several divorcees had a fear that the researcher was sent by the other spouse to trouble him/her. Because of this sort of fear, the respondents were at first disinclined to entertain the researcher, although she made it clear that it was a purely academic study, and the personal identity and other information will not be leaked out.

4. The relevant data was to be collected from multiple sources. To start with, it was a problem to get permission from the judicial court to see the divorce case files from the record room. When permission was received, she had to spend much time to see the files. The information given by the spouses was supplemented by and verified through other sources like parents, relatives, friends, neighbours, co-workers and members of their community.

5. Another great handicap was the absence of any other sociological study on divorce in India from which the researcher could take guidelines. Studies elsewhere could not be depended upon much as they have been in entirely different socio-cultural setups, e.g., studies in the USA and UK.

Thus, I would like to mention that collection of data about subjects like divorce and other forms of marital disruptions is a mountainous task, in which much tact, patience, time, energy and money are to be spent.

It may also be recorded that even in a traditional country like India, norms regarding marriage and family are undergoing tremendous changes. Divorces are becoming more and more frequent especially among urban Hindus. Therefore, there is scope for studies of this type on a larger scale.

SOME STUDIES ON DIVORCE

As indicated earlier, sociological research studies relating to marital disruptions like divorce, separation and desertion are indeed rare in India. In the United States of America, and the United Kingdom, there have been several studies during the past about fifty years. But since the type of community, the environment and the culture are entirely different, these studies cannot be of considerable use in the study of divorce among the Hindus in India. In fact, the Government of the United States of America, as well as colleges and universities in that country, sponsored, supported and encouraged numerous studies. Most of them are quoted extensively in the works of Baber, Burgess & Locke, Elliott and Merrill, Mowrer and others. Some such studies are as follows :

S. No.	*Author*	*Title*	*Publisher*	*Year*	*Remarks*
1.	Alfred Cohen	Statistical Analysis of American Divorce	Columbia Univ. Press, New York	1932	—
2.	Willard Waller	The Old Love and the New	Liveright, NewYork	1930	—
3.	WIlliam Goode	Problems in Post-Divorce Adjustment	American Social. Review	June, 1949	—
4.	E.R. Mowrer	Family Disorganization	University of Chicago	1927	—
5.	C.W. Schroeder	Divorce in a City of 1,00,000 Population	Bradley Poly. Inst. Library	1939	—
6.	W.M. Kephart & T.P. Monahan	Desertion & Divorce in Philadelphia	American Social. Review	December 1952	—
7.	U.S. Govt.	Marriages & Divorce—United States	Vit-St. Sp. Report	June, 1959	—
8.	P.H. Jacobson	American Marriage & Divorce	Rinehart, New York	1959	—
9.	Lincoln H. Ray	Patterns of Divorce in US & Australia	American Social. Review	29 Aug. 1964	—

Let us now state the details of some studies in India, which are relatively more significant to us :

1. *Divorced Hindu Woman*, **Rama Mehta,** published by Vikas Publishing House Pvt. Ltd., New Delhi, 1975.

Mrs Rama Mehta, who is also the author of works such as; *Western Educated Hindu Women* ; *Ram : A Story of India* ; *Life of Keshav* (a novel) and *India Now and Through Time* (co-author) made a "pioneering study", focusing attention on the divorced or separated Hindu women. The author does not distinguish between those who are legally divorced and those who are merely separated. According to the author, "a woman's marriage once broken, does not basically make any difference regarding her need to readjust to society and find a new place in it." The author's findings relate mainly to urban society in northern India.

The study of fifty women by Mrs Rama Mehta shows that "belief in marriage as an indissoluble union is no longer a deterrent to preserve an incompatible marriage" (preface). In her Introductory Chapter, she mentions that "the purpose of this study is to find out what is the place and the problems faced by the Hindu women divorcees in Indian society (page 1). She had selected 50 cases from two classes as follows:

(*i*) Lower middle class	25	Total—50
(*ii*) Upper middle class	25	

It took more than two years for her to collect the data. All the fifty respondents were Hindus but their caste or provincial affiliations were not taken into account. Out of the total sample of 50 women, only 13 had been divorced, 7 were contemplating taking action, and the rest had no intention of going to court. According to Rama Mehta, "a study on this subject does not seem superficially speaking necessary, considering the rate of divorce in relation to marriage in India today. However, the divorce rate is on the increase, marital difficulties being more evident now than before" (p. 5).

Some of her main findings are:

(*i*) Indian society is going through dramatic and rapid changes, affecting radically the traditional role of women.

(*ii*) The younger generation is increasingly ignorant of the ritualistic basis of their religion.

(*iii*) The women who were joint family based and who were brought up to respect and fear their related group were less capable of breaking with conventional standards of behaviour.

(*iv*) The husband-wife reiationship has become pivotal to the success of a marriage.

(*v*) Though there was confidence in the arranged marriage pattern, this pattern would have to undergo a change.

(*vi*) Secular society was more tolerant and more open for women who were divorced.

(*vii*) The Western educated women inculcated in her a sense of her own identity.

(*viii*) In spite of liberal ideas taking a firm hold in India, in the upper and lower middle class, it was clear that the position of the divorced or separated women had only marginally improved.

While, the study of Rama Mehta may be accepted as a pioneer study on divorce in India, its main shortcomings from the scientific, sociological point of view are:

(*i*) Her sample is too small. In fact, out of 50 cases she had taken, only 13 were of real divorce. However, it must be accepted that when she made her study, the divorce cases were really few, because, it is found that in urban Madhya Pradesh also, there were not many cases of real divorce until 1976, when the Hindu Marriage Act was substantially amended by the Marriage Laws Amendment Act.

(*ii*) Mrs Mehta did not care to ascertain the specific caste of the respondents.

(*iii*) Her techniques/tools of data collection were not satisfactory, because, in a delicate and intricate phenomenon like divorce, she should have inter viewed the respondents personally.

(*iv*) No where could she interview the husbands of the divorced women. To that extent, the study may be said to be just one sided.

(*v*) Even with respect to the 13 real cases of divorce, she did not appear to have seen the Judicial Court Records which could have given her much relevant information to arrive at more reliable findings.

2. *Counselling for Marital Happiness* by Mabel Fonseca, published by Manaktalas, Bombay, 1966.

This book is an outcome of the Ph.D. Thesis of Dr Mabel Fonseca (born 1935) in Sociology (1965) under the guidance of the eminent sociologist, Dr G.S. Ghurye, Professor Emeritus of Sociology, University of Bombay. The study has mainly been "an inquiry into the subtle disorganization of the family in Indian communities reflecting marital separation and domestic disorganization in our complex urban industrialized setting" (flap). To ascertain the nature and extent of disorganization, records and proceedings in 1927 suits in the Bombay City Civil Court have been examined, of which 894 form the sample of investigation, besides taking into account the recordings of 367 desertion cases from the wellknown social welfare institution, *Bapu Ghar*. According to her, "studies in the field of inter-personal relationships in the family and interaction between husband and wife are lacking. Increased complexities in the present social setting emphasize family relationships as a challenging pattern and bring into play new forces which invite intensive research." (pp. 6-7, Introduction)

The study of Fonseca revealed that as a result of the Special Marriage Act, 1954, and the Hindu Marriage Act, 1955, there were a number of wives who sought divorce and protection during the years 1954-61. Nearly two-thirds of the wives are petitioners in cases of matrimonial relief. Some of her important findings are given below:

(*i*) Separation, desertion and divorce as they represent various degrees of dissolution of the family are generally not favoured in Indian society.

(*ii*) Today, however, the transitory phase of adjustment, or rather readjustment to changing ideas, ideologies and values brought to the surface, maladjustment in some considerable number of cases. In others, it has brought to light families which were already "weak" where marital partners displayed little marital affection and there was no sharing of desires or pleasure or mutuality of affection. This has made investigation into maladjustment imperative.

(*iii*) According to Fonseca, counselling will be very useful for marital happiness. Life has become extremely complex, and demands new adjustments. In the realm of marriage, therefore, counselling has much to achieve to bring about these adjustments as near to perfection as is humanly possible.

(*iv*) The analysis of the various factors that create disruption between the spouses—whether temporary at times in the form of desertion or permanent as determined after much consideration as in the case of termination of the marriage through divorce—undertaken by the author is very useful. For instance, see the grounds (impotency, adultery, desertion, etc.) on which the petitions are filed (p. 61), and the major and complementary factors of marital discord as seen from institution cases (ill-treatment, interference, and ill-treatment by in-laws, infidelity, vice, incompatibility, etc.).

Although her study was mainly motivated for marital counselling, it is a pioneering study and the data given are really illuminating. In fact, any study on marital disruptions like desertion and divorce would involve suggestions for marital counselling as well.

3. *A Study of Divorce Cases of 1971 & 1972*, A Project Report for M.A. Social Work, by Donna Maye, 1975, Tata Institute of Social Sciences.

This is an exploratory study of 15 couples selected by a method of purposive sampling from the case records of the Bombay Civil Court. The couples were granted divorce during 1971-72. The unit of the study was the divorced couple. The main findings of the study are:

(*i*) Majority (53 per cent) of the respondents prior to marriage came from upper middle class, where the average monthly income ranged from Rs 1000 to Rs 2000 per family.

(*ii*) Majority of the husbands (73 per cent) married at the average age of 25, and the majority of wives (86 per cent) at the age of 20.

(*iii*) The areas of conflict as indicated by majority of the couples (74 per cent) were personality differences and incompatibility, whereas minority (33 per cent) stressed infidelity and unfaithfulness as prominent factors. The study revealed that since the law required certain grounds for divorce, in most cases, the real factors were not stated.

(*iv*) 30 per cent of the respondents had remarried, while 20 per cent were getting married within a couple of months.

(*v*) Majority of the couples (80 per cent) were of the firm opinion that marriage counsellors should make attempts at reaching out to the larger community by conducting premarital and post-marital guidance and counselling courses. They also felt that schools and colleges must introduce such talks and short-term courses as part of the curriculum.

Though it was a brief study, the findings of Maye were really significant.

There may be some other studies also, especially by students and teachers of institutions of higher learning in India, but then, the present researcher could not get hold of them. However, it must also be put on record that inquiries from the Departments of Sociology of various universities in India did not reveal any more studies. These included major universities like Delhi, Bombay, Chandigarh, Mysore and Schools of Social Work. It should also be mentioned here that unless and until research studies are published, the fruits of such studies cannot be enjoyed by the academicians, administrators, social workers and the general public.

Chapter 2

DIVORCE IN DIFFERENT SOCIETIES

A SHORT HISTORY OF DIVORCE

BEFORE looking into the actual practice of divorce in different communities, a short discussion of the history of divorce is not out of context.

As a social phenomenon, divorce must have been in existence as long as socially regulated marriage.[1] The earliest known legal forms of divorce regulation are those to be found in the Code of Hammurabi, which was drawn up around 2300 to 2250 B.C. According to this code, marriage was virtually a purchase arrangement in which the bride enjoyed a status little better than that of a chattel. The husband might divorce his wife at will without assigning any cause.

Among the Hebrews, divorce was a masculine prerogative. This was established by the scriptural injunction in Deuteronomy 24: 1-2, to the effect that, "when a man hath taken a wife, and married her, and it came to pass that he find no favour in her eyes, he had found some uncleanness in her, then, let him write her a bill of divorcement, and give it to her hand, and send her out of his house. And when she is departed out of his house, she may go and be another man's wife." This right to divorce his wife at pleasure was accepted among all Jews until the eleventh century.

Under the earlist Roman law, the husband had complete right to renounce his marital relationship and obligations if he so desired, but, he was subject to certain restrictions. A wife must not be repudiated without the forfeit of property, unless she were guilty

[1]M.A. Elliott, and F.E. Merrill, *Social Disorginization*, Harper & Brothers, New York, 1950, p. 418.

of adultery or drinking wine, when the the Roman law was codified into the 'Twelve Tables,' divorce for both husbands and wives was allowed. Either party was allowed to terminate the relationship upon securing a bill of divorcement.

After the advent of Christianity, Roman law was considerably mitigated by its influence. Divorce by mutual consent, however, continued until the second half of the fourth century. When Constantine adopted the Christian faith, he tried to restrict divorce by pecuniary penalties except for the following:

(*i*) Divorce was allowed to the husband in case his wife committed murder, prepared poison, or acted as a procuress.
(*ii*) Similarly, the wife might divorce her husband for murder, preparation of poison, or rifling of tombs.

In connection with the history of divorce, it should be kept in view that the three major factors responsible for Euro-American marriage and divorce legislation are generally conceded to be the following:

(*i*) Hebrew and Christian religion;
(*ii*) Roman law; and
(*iii*) Teutonic custom.

The influence of the Christian Church upon the marriage status has unquestionably been to conserve the permanent monogamic family.

DIVORCE IN DIFFERENT COUNTRIES OF THE WORLD

1. *Divorce in England.* Marriage was regarded as a sacrament by the Catholic Church and divorce was forbidden unless the Pope granted special permission which he hardly ever did.

Subsequently, the English common law recognized two types of divorce, both of ancient lineage. One was legal separation (from bed and board) without the right of marriage to another. This was controlled by the ecclesiastical courts. The other type, absolute divorce, a termination of the marriage bonds, could be obtained only in special cases and then by an Act of Parliament which cost a minimum of 500 pounds

The Protestant Reformation demanded that marriage be restored to the control of civil authorities, and, that it be regarded as a private contract which could be dissolved for just cause. This demand succeeded temporarily in England in Cromwell's Civil Marriage Act of 1653. But this Act became inoperative due to some counter-revolution and the Church of England came to control marriage by rules similar to Canon Law of the Roman Church. After 1857, the high court of London and after 1912, certain provincial courts were allowed to grant divorce with adultery as the only ground. In 1912, the Royal Commission on Divorce was appointed, which, after a five-year study of the problem, recommended that five other causes for divorce be added. But, until recently the cultural resistance supported by both the Roman Catholics and Anglican Churches, has prevented any change. In 1937, after years of struggle, led by A.P. Herbert, M.P. and dramatized by his novel *Holy Deadlock*, Parliament extended the grounds for divorce to include desertion, cruelty and insanity.

In England, Law Commission was again appointed in 1967, known as Law Commission No. 14. The Commission concluded that a good divorce law should seek to achieve two objects:

(*i*) To buttress, rather than to undermine the stability of marriage, and

(*ii*) When, regrettably, a marriage has irretrievably broken down to enable the empty legal shell to be destroyed with the maximum fairness, and the minimum bitterness, distress and humiliation.

Of these objects, the first required that divorce should not be so easy that the parties had no incentive to make a success of their marriage—to overcome temporary difficulties. It also required that everything possible should be done to encourage reconciliation. The second required that when the marriage was dead, it should not merely be buried, but buried with decency and dignity, and in a way which will encourage harmonious relationship between parties and their children in future. The solution adopted to meet these requirements was embodied in the Divorce Reforms Act, 1969, which camein to operation in England on January 1, 1971. It represented a somewhat uneasy compromise. Irretrievable breakdown of the marriage replaced the former matrimonial offences and is the sole ground for divorce. The Matrimonial Causes Act, 1973, with effect from January 1, 1974, repealed and consolidated with some minor amendments virtually all the then subsisting legislation. In particular, it replaced almost all that remained of the Matrimonial Causes Act, 1965, the whole of the Divorce Reforms Act, 1969, the Matrimonial Proceeding and Property Act, 1970, the Nullity of Marriage Act, 1971 and the Matrimonial Proceeding (Polygamous Marriages) Act, 1972, in so far as that Act applies to England and Wales. The decree of divorce severs the marital tie altogether, the parties being at liberty to remarry after such period as prescribed by the statutes.

2. *Divorce in France.* In France, divorce by mutual consent was estabilished by the Revolution, but subsequently repealed. French divorce, however, is comparatively liberal in that it can be granted for *injura grave* which covers almost any serious offence to the plaintiff. According to the new legislation which came into force in January 1976, there are three kinds of divorce, namely:

(*i*) divorce by mutual consent—joint request or request of one accepted by the other,

(*ii*) breakdown of marital life—separation of at least six years, or serious deterioration for the mental faculties of one for at least six years, and

(*iii*) divorce for misconduct.

The divorce rate of France is relatively low, and the frequency of remarriage high. This suggests that "matrimonial unions remain the normal couple-structure in France."[2]

3. *Divorce in Scandinavian countries.* Norway, Sweden and Denmark introduced divorce by joint or mutual consent in the period 1918-1922. Before that, their laws were made liberal than those of England, wilful desertion having been the common ground used. The most important change in the divorce law since 1915 came into action in Sweden on January 1, 1974. This abandoned the old grounds and substituted a single criterion for divorce, which is that one or both spouses have no wish to continue the marriage. In the case of unilateral application, and in situations where there are child-

[2]Boigeol, Anne and others, in *Divorce in Europe*, by Robert Chester, (Ed.), 1977, p. 147 and pp. 172-73.

ren under sixteen, however there are certain time-restrictions. If only one spouse applies, then, divorce will not be granted until there has been a renewed application six months later, and a similar provision applies to joint applications where younger children are involved. The rationale of these rules is to afford time for reconsideration in appropriate cases.

4. *Divorce in Russia.* In Russia, before the Revolution (1917), marriage and divorce were under religious control, but when the revolution came, a simple court procedure for divorce was inaugurated. This was abolished in 1927, by the Family Code of Soviet Russia, which substituted for it divorce by mutual consent. This new divorce law reduced to an absolute minimum the trouble involved in getting a divorce. Both parties could ask for a divorce, or either one separately, without the consent or even the knowledge of the other, the divorce being granted in either case. The fee is trifling, the procedure lasted only a few minutes, and the questions did not relate to causes, but merely such facts as names, addresses and occupations. Divorce was too easy. The peak reached in 1935, when in Moscow, there were 44 divorces for every 100 marriages during the month of May. This created much domestic chaos, and the law was changed. The restrictive measures in divorce law resulted in a remarkable drop in divorce. The Soviet Government is still concerned about the high rate of marital disruptions, and a campaign is set against the same, according to the latest information given by Mr Sergery Guseve, First Deputy Chairman of the USSR Supreme Court. The campaign stresses the importance of the family on the basis of Marx's dictum that "the family is the basic unit of society".[3]

It is also reported that the Soviet schools will soon introduce sex education as part of an attempt to give young people better preparation for married life, and as part of a drive to reduce divorce rate that now dooms one marriage in two to failure in Europe.[4]

5. *Divorce of China.* In 1878, divorce in China was compulsory, if there had been an impediment to marriage or if the wife had committed adultery. Divorce might be secured under the following conditions:

[3]*The Indian Express*, November 11, 1980.
[4]*The Free Press Journal*, August 14, 1983.

(*i*) Mutual consent; (*ii*) if the wife left home against the will of the husband; (*iii*) if the wife beat her husband; (*iv*) if false statements were made in the marriage contract, and (*v*) if the wife was barren, sensual, loquacious, jealous, distrustful or lacked filial piety towards husband's parents. The wife could not ask for divorce.

Though divorce and concubinage are male prerogative, the rates of both are exceedingly small. No exact figures on divorce in pre-modern China are available, but it can safely be said that the rate has been less than 0.5 per cent in any given population at all times. Even in the changing times of China, it is stated that "the rate of divorce in China, wherever they are known, are low."[5] In recent times, there are reports of increasing rate of divorce in China, but the authorities are making efforts to curb the same.

6. *Divorce in predominantly Catholic countries.* Some Catholic countries like Spain, Italy and Ireland do not permit divorce even now.

7. *Divorce in the United States of America.* Though American population is composed of migrants from England and other European countries, marital problems were never referred to the ecclesiastical courts. Early divorces were obtained through a special Act or legislation, and, then in more and more States, under Statutes through a Court. Each State retains jurisdiction over marriage and divorce, within its boundaries, but the provisions in different states vary. For instance, commercialization of divorce in Neveda and Florida makes quick divorce possible.

Divorce legislation in different States of USA exhibits two general tendencies: one toward lenience and other towards greater restrictions. The main legal grounds accepted for divorce in majority of the States are adultery, desertion, imprisonment or conviction of crime, cruelty, alcoholism, impotence, non-support, insanity and living apart.

A generation or two ago, divorce rate was very low in the United States. Divorce meant a scandal and divorcees were looked down upon. In 1870, there was only one divorce for 34 marriages; in 1900, the rate was one to 12 marriages; in 1940, it was one to five,

[5]Hsu, L.E. Francis, The Family in China, in, *The Family, Its Functions and Destiny*, by Ruth Nanda Anshen, Harper & Brothers, 1949, p. 82.

and in 1948, it rose to one to 4. It is estimated to be one to three at the present time in the United States.

In spite of this high divorce rate, a recent survey by Pietopinto and Sienauer showed that "most married people basically are opposed to the concept of divorce, only one spouse in five expressing the view that a marriage should be readily dissolved at the mere wish of either partner.[6]

DIVORCE AMONG THE HINDUS

In this work, we are primarily concerned with the phenomenon of divorce among the Hindus. Hence, it is worthwhile to examine the traditional Hindu view of marriage as well as divorce in detail.

The term for marriage used by Hindus is *vivaha* (Sanskrit), which means carrying away the bride. But nowadays, the entire nuptial ceremony is denoted by the term. For a Hindu, *vivaha* is something absolutely essential. Every Hindu is supposed to go through four *ashrams*. The entry to the second *ashram*, namely, *Grihasthahsram* (household stage or cycle) is through marriage alone. The ultimate goal of every Hindu is to attain *moksha* (salvation) and it cannot be attained till a male progeny is born. The term *putra* (son) in Sanskrit is interpreted as one who rescues a father from the hell. For a father, a son is ritually significant due to other reasons also. He is free from *pitru-rina* (debt towards forefathers) only when he himself gives birth to a son. A father's soul finds peace only when the last rites are performed by a son. The aims of Hindu marriage are chiefly three—*dharma* (practice of religion), *proja* (progeny) and *rati* (sexual pleasure). So, the foremost purpose of a Hindu marriage is to practise *dharma*. In *Manusmrithi* (Law of Manu) it is written, "to be mothers were women created and to be fathers men, therefore, vedas ordain that dharma must be practised by man together with his wife." *Vivaha* (marriage) is one of the *sarira-sanskaras* (sacraments sanctifying the body). Every Hindu was supposed to pass through these *sanskaras* (rituals) at the proper time and age. Marriage was obligatory for this reason also. If marriage was essential for a male it was doubly so for a Hindu female, because a male had to pass through several *sanskaras*

[6]Anthony Pietropinto, and Jacqueline, Sienauer, *Husbands and Wives* (*A Nation-wide Survey of Marriage*), Berkely Books, New York, 1981, Introduction.

(rituals) whereas, for a female the only important *sanskara* ordained is *vivaha*. The absolute necessity for a girl to get married in time is emphasized by several of the Hindu writers. A girl who continues to stay at her father's home more than three years after attaining puberty is called a *vrisala*, *sudra*, or a woman of low nature, and the father as guardian who is not careful enough to give her in marriage in time is said to be committing a great sin. If the elders fail to arrange the daughter's marriage in time, she was free to choose her own mate. *Mahabharta*, *Manusmrithi* and Vatsayana express identical views in this respect.

The Hindu marriage could be consecrated in different ways, and this we call as forms of marriage. There are eight of them. The first four namely, *Brahma*, *Daiva*, *Arsha* and *Prajapatya* were called *dharmya* (proper) and *asura*, *gandharva*, *rakshasa* and *paisacha* were called *adharmya* (improper). A marriage was legally completed only when the improper rites like *homa* (offering in the sacred fire), *panigrahana* (taking the hand of the bride) and *saptapadi* (the bride and groom taking seven steps together), all these to the accompaniment of *Vedic mantras*. "The *mantras* of marriage", says *Bhirahama*, "accomplish their object of bringing about the indissoluble union of marriage at the seventh step. The maiden becomes the wife of him to whom the gift is actually made with water. Again, till the hand is actually taken with due rites, marriage does not happen. And the rite of marriage must take place in the presence of sacred fire. *Narada* has said that once the *mantras* are recited by joining the hands of the bride and the bridegroom (*pani-grahana*), the marriage becomes binding. *Vatsyayana* has attached great importance to the sacred rites performed in the wedding.[7]

The duties of husband and wife towards each other also are described in detail by several Hindu writers. Manu has said that husband/wife should be faithful towards each other, and should always try to see that they do not get separated. According to *Thaithiriya Brahman*, "by good deeds husband and wife should become befitting each other, like oxen in a yoke they should work together for good name, they both should be of the same mind and destroy enemies, and in heaven attain undiminishing light. The

[7]*Cf.* P.N. Prabhu, *Hindu Social Organization*, Fourth Edition, 1963, Popular Prakashan, Bombay, pp. 173-74.

Dharaashastra writers say that wife's foremost duty is to obey the husband and respect him like god". A wife should be pleasant, alert, efficient, a good housewife, one who keeps the house and utensils clean and spends moderately.

Manu has said that a wife's duties are to take care of money, spend, keep things clean and arranged, perform religious duties. The wife is expected to be efficient, pleasant, spend moderately, and do things pleasing to the husband. She should massage the feet of mother-in-law and father-in-law, walk beautifully and control the sensory organs. She should get up before her husband and elders, should eat only after their eating and should sit on seats placed at a lower level as compared to theirs.[8]

The duties of the husband are also detailed. According to Manu, old parents, faithful wife and small children are to be looked after by a man, even if, he may commit a hundred wrongs for this. Manu has said that if a man does not look after his parents, wife and children, he can be fined 600 *panas* (coins) by the King. *Yanjavalky* has said that a man who does not look after his wife is a great sinner. He and Narad have said that if a man leaves his good-natured wife, who is also the mother of his sons, he should give her one-third of his property. If he has no property, he should make proper arrangements for her maintenance. *Vishnu Dharmsutr* says that a man leaving his wife should be punished as a thief.[9]

Thus, it would be seen that the ancient Hindu writers have specified the duties of husbands and wives very clearly. Strangely, in the succeeding times, the Hindu society seems to have conveniently forgotten the importance of the duties of the husbands toward the wife. On the other hand, wife's duties toward her husband have been simply over-emphasized in each generation that husbands were lifted to the exalted position of gods and wives degraded to the status of mere slaves to their, many a time, even worthless, husbands.

In the Vedic and post-Vedic literature, there is no reference to or evidence about divorce. In *Smrithis* too, marriage is considered indissoluble, and is regarded as a sacrament. Manu says: "Let mutual fidelity continue till death. This may be considered as the

[8]*Cf.* Kane, Bharatratan, Mahamahopadhyay, Dr. Pandurang Vaman, *Dharmasastra Ka Ithihas*, Vol. I (History of the Scriptures), Hindi Samiti, Uttar Pradesh, pp. 315-19.

[9]Ibid, p. 321.

summary of the highest *dharma* of husband and wife."[10] Manu speaks in another place, "Kings speak only once; saints speak only once; girls are given only once." Each of these three things is done only once. Manu goes to the extent of saying that a girl cannot be released from her husband even if he sells her or abandons her. Since the marriage is a sacred institution for a Hindu, it is irrevocable. Though some of the ancient Hindu writers mentioned certain extra-ordinary circumstances under which a separation between two spouses was made possible, we are forced to think that a true Hindu rarely made use of them. Some of the circumstances facilitating divorce are stated below:

(*i*) Concealment of the defects of the bride by her father or kinsmen.
(*ii*) Concealment of defects in the husband.

In the case of brides and grooms of pure character and high conduct, however, the question of rejection on any other account can never be raised.[11]

According to Altekar, divorces were permitted before the beginning of the Christian era.[12] To support his argument, he quotes one of Manu's statements which says that a wife is not to be blamed if she abandons a husband who is impotent, insane or suffering from incurable or contagious disease. But the abandonment does not necessarily imply divorce, because women were allowed to contract a second marriage only if the previous marriage is not consummated. Once the marriage was consummated, the union of the husband and wife was considered indissoluble. There are certain occasions mentioned by Manu, when a wife could be superseded. But even before doing so, sufficient efforts were to be made. A husband is asked to forbear a hating wife for one year. A woman was not to be turned away even in the case of grievous sins. If the wife disregards her husband owing to her insanity, disease or intoxication, she should be deprived of ornaments and abandoned for three months. Drunken, false, rebellious, diseased or mischievous wives are to be superseded. A barren wife may be superseded in eighth year after

[10]*Manusmrithi*, IX, 101.
[11]P.N. Probhu, *op. cit.*, p. 191.
[12]A.S. Altekar, *The Position of Women in Hindu Civilization*, Motilal Banarasidas, Banaras, 1956, p. 83.

marriage; if the children die, in the tenth year; and if she bears only one daughter, in the eleventh year (*Manusmriti*, IX, 81).

Kane has mentioned that even for adultery, a wife could not be abandoned[13] Gautam has said that when a woman becomes unchaste, she had to do penitences, yet, she had the right to receive maintenance. Yanjvalkya has said that when a woman loses her chastity, she should be deprived of her authority in the house; she should be given dirty clothes to wear, and just enough food for subsistence; she should be scolded and asked to sleep on the floor. After her next menstrual period, she should be considered clean. If a wife has become pregnant through adultery, she should be abandoned. Mitakshara has interpreted Yanjvalkya by saying that if a *Brahmin*, *Kshatriya* or *Vaishya* wife committed adultery with a *sudra*, but has not become pregnant, she can be received back after making remission. Leaving a wife did not mean throwing her out, but denying her rights to perform religious functions and cohabitation with her husband. Narad has written that an adultress's head should be shaved off, she should be asked to sleep on the floor, she should be provided with low type of food and clothes and she should beassigned to clean the husband's gate. Vyas also has written that a woman caught in adultery should be kept in the home, but she should be denied the right to perform religious sacraments and also the right of cohabitation with the husband. But after the menses, if she does not engage in adultery again, she should be granted again her rights as a wife. Thus, we can conclude that even adultery was not considered as a reason enough for divorce or desertion.

Narad and Parasura have allowed a wife to dissolve the marriage if the husband is found to be impotent. According to Narad, the woman is the field and the man is the seed-giver; so, the field must be given to one who has seed.[14] So, if a woman finds her husband devoid of virility, she should wait for six months and then choose another husband.

Narad and Kautilya allow a woman to seek a second husband if the first one is missing, dead, becomes an ascetic, is impotent, or

[13]Kane, Dr. Pandurang Vaman, *Dharamasastra Ka Ithihas*, Vol. 1 (History of the Scriptures), Hindi Samiti, Uttar Pradesh, pp. 322-23.

[14]Quoted by P.N. Prabhu, in *Hindu Social Organization*, Popular Prakashan, Bombay, Fourth Edition, 1963, p. 191.

has fallen from the caste.[15]

Narad adds that even if the woman is not eager to take another husband, she should be persuaded by her relatives to do so. Kautilya permitted the woman to abandon her husband if he is a bad character, or is long abroad, or has become a traitor to the King or is likely to endanger her life or has fallen from his caste, or has lost virility.[16]

Kautilya also speaks of divorce. A divorce may be obtained only in the case of mutual enmity and hatred between the husband and wife. Neither the husband nor the wife could dissolve the marriage against the wishes of the other.[17]

Kautilya is the only author who writes about the possibility of divorce, and also stresses that the marriages performed according to *Brahma*, *Daiva*, *Arsha* and *Prajapatya* forms cannot be dissolved at all.

So much about the views of different writers in Hindu civilization with regard to divorce or dissolution of marriage. It would appear that there is considerable similarity and in some respects dissimilarity in the views expressed by the writers.

There is a difference between the *Smritis* and the *Arthasastra* with regard to the indissolubility of marriage. This may be due to the fact, that the *Dharma* school or the Smritis considered marriage as a sacrament, whereas the *artha* school regarded it as a contract and this is pointed out in the *Artha* laws. When marriage is considered as a sacrament, it becomes indissoluble whereas if it is viewed as a contract, it can be terminated. Even Kautilya did not allow divorce for the first four forms of marriage. Evidently, the circle for which the *Arthasastra* was written were aware of the *Brahmana* view of marriage, but had not accepted it fully. The growth of Brahmanism which followed the Maurya period was responsible for strengthening the orthodox view, and the possibility of divorce was almost forgotten.

In the Buddhist texts, there is no reference to divorce, but there are certain stories in the *Jatakas* to support the possibility of supersession of a wicked wife. In spite of such sporadic mention of the possibility of putting asunder the marital bond, for a true Hindu,

[15] Ibid, p., 191.
[16] Ibid., p. 191.
[17] Ibid., p. 192.

marriage remained an eternal bond. The ordinary Hindu believed that when they get married, the parties are bound to each other until the death of either of them, and the wife bound to her husband even after his death. This idea that the marriage is an indissoluble one is a truely lofty one. It encouraged, persuaded and pressurized the spouses to adjust to each other in spite of differences, difficulties and problems. It enabled them to overcome incompatibility that may have existed. Thus, marriage came to be looked upon as the highest ideal and value of human life, and Hindu men and particularly women were taught to make sacrifices in order to sustain the marital bond.

The problem of marital conflict which we come across usually in the present day marriages was out of question in olden days. Authors like Manu with their elabroate writings successfully kept the Hindu women willing slaves to their husbands. Manu states, "he (husband) is the Lord and master of his wife and as such he should be worshipped by her even though he is devoid of virtues. He is the guardian in her youth as her father guards her in childhood and her sons are bound to do in her old age." Even in the end of his writing, Manu declared that women are weak and they would fall an easy prey to the seduction of man, because of their sensitive character which quickly responds to any offer to love. They have no strength of will to resist temptation. It was only the husband who possessed knowledge about *Vedas* and religious rites. Though marriage was essential for fulfilling the religious duties, the role of the wife was passive. The wife was neither capable of nor expected to contribute actively. Marriage was a religious and social obligation primarily and the individual interests hardly mattered. The authority and control exercised by the joint family and caste regulations were so rigid that it hardly allowed any flexibility to suit individual tastes, interests and expectations. All inter-personal relationships including those between husband and wife were strictly regimented to well-established patterns. Moreover, when a woman joins the traditional joint family as a newly-wed wife, she becomes such an integral part of the whole that the question of severing herself from it even in the eventuality of her husband's death becomes impossible.

Though marriage was equally binding on both husband and wife theoretically, in practical life, the burden of maintaining the marital bond fell upon women. The ancient writers cleverly manoeuvred the minds of women in such a way that they accepted their lots most submissively and devotedly. An ideal woman was expected to be a *pativrata.* This did not simply mean fidelity towards husband, but complete surrender of her entire life in his service alone. As a river merges with an ocean and loses its identity, so the wife was supposed to merge with her husband and lose her own personality and individuality. He is the centre of her life, her interests, thoughts and activities. For her to live is only through him, and, apart from him she has no existence. Her duty towards him does not cease with death. The ideal of *sati* became popular due to this line of thought. A woman who had no identity and existence of her own apart from her husband, was left only with the choice of following him even in death. With the passage of time, *sati* became the highest symbol of Hindu womanhood and many women immolated themselves on the pyre of their husbands, rejoicingly. It is rather illogical to think that such a traditional Hindu woman ever dared to take advantage of the provisions made by the law-givers for obtaining divorce. Therefore, it can safely be concluded that there is much relevance in the statements of Indian Sociologists like Kapadia and Prabhu quoted below:

(*i*) Ordinarily, divorce is not known to the Hindu institution of marriage. Husband and wife are bound to each other, not only till death, but even after death, in the other world.[18]
(*ii*) In short, marriage continues to be a sacrament.[19]

It was in this orthodox and traditional background, hesitant efforts to legalize divorce among the Hindus originated. The first legislation with regard to dissolution of marriage was probably enacted by Kolhapur State in the 1920's. The State of Baroda followed suit in 1942. The Bombay government also passed an Act in 1947, permitting divorce. Madras and Saurastra followed the example of Bombay in 1949 and 1952 respectively.

According to the 1942 Act of Baroda State, dissolution may be granted if either party has disappeared for seven years, has become a recluse, has been converted to another religion, is guilty of cruelty that might cause danger to life, guilty of desertion without

[18]P.N. Prabhu, *op cit.*, p. 226.
[19]K.M. Kapadia, *Marriage and Family in India*, Second Ed., 1959, p. 184.

reasonable cause, impotency and adultery. On the dissolution of marriage, the party is allowed to contract a second marriage, if desired, after the expiry of six months from passing the decree. The outstanding achievement of the Act is that the woman is allowed to separate from her husband whose marriage obligations are not properly fulfilled.

Under the Bombay Act of 1946, impotency, lunacy, leprosy, desertion for a continuous period of four years, absence for seven years, and bigamy are some of the grounds on which divorce is allowed.

In the meantime, a Committee, known as the Rau Committee, was appointed by the Government of India in order to examine the Hindu Women's Right to Property Act, 1937, and to advise upon the law to remove any injustice. Rau Committee issued a questionnaire and received many responses. In their report, it was concluded that "the Hindu Law is a complicated organic structure, the various parts of which are inter-connected, so that an alteration of one part may involve the alteration of others."[20] They recommended to attempt a Code of Hindu Law. In 1944, the Government of India entrusted the Hindu Law Committee with the work of formulating a code of Hindu Law as complete as possible. This Committee prepared a draft of Hindu Code and circulated it for public opinion. It also visited important cities of the country and heard views of individuals and representative bodies. The necessary changes were made in the Code. In April 1947, the Bill was introduced in the Central Legislative Assembly. The bill could not be discussed or passed due to other burning issues like Partition and Independence. There were lot of agitations and opposition against Hindu Code Bill. Yet, Pandit Jawaharlal Nehru and other Congress leaders were determined to pass the bill. The bill, however, could not be passed en bloc, but was passed in the form of different acts, the Hindu Marriage and Divorce Act of 1955 being one of the most significant among the same.

The Hindu Marriage Act, 1955 (as also the Special Marriage Act of 1954) was substantially amended by the Marriage Laws Amendment Act of 1976.

The 1976 legislation has brought about retrospectively colossal changes wiping off many of the shortcomings the statutes suffered

[20]V.D. Mahajan, *New Legislation on Hindu Law*, 1957, p. 2.

from in the earlier legislations. Still a provision for easy divorce on an irretrievable breakdown of the marriage would have been welcome, for, when the intrinsic love and affection has withered away, the empty shell of marriage should be exploded at the first available opportunity, without further bitterness. With this object in view, and to facilitate divorce when the matrimony is only a humdrum dreariness, the Marriage Laws (Amendment) Bill, 1981 seeks to introduce sections 13-C and 13-D in the Hindu Marriage Act. The interest of the children of such marriage is sought to be protected by the proposed section 13-E of the Hindu Marriage Act. A copy of the Hindu Marriage Act, as amended upto 1976 is placed as Appendix in this work. (Appendix 7)

At the end, it may be mentioned that there are three stages through which we may trace the history of divorce law of the Hindus: first, during the Vedic period where we do not find even the germ of the idea of divorce; secondly, the *Smriti* period, when the idea of divorce is put forward by Narad, and others; and the third, which commenced only in the second quarter of the present century. In the third period, with theories of individual liberty in every sphere of life, equality of sex and emancipation of women, we have discovered in divorce a remedy for the ills of inconvenient and ill-honoured marriages. We have effected a complete break with the past. It should be added here that since the 1960's, the Hindu attitude towards divorce has undergone much change as is substantiated by the data concerning large number of such cases.

DIVORCE AMONG THE CHRISTIANS

Marriage is a sacred institution among the Christians, whether Catholic, or Protestant. According to the *Holy Bible*, the first marriage of human society was performed at the initiative of God Himself. After the creation of the entire universe, the first man, Adam, was created by God. But then, Adam was alone, and, therefore, God said, "it is not good that the man should be alone; I will make him a help meet for him."[21] Thus, Eve, the first woman, was created from out of Adam, and God gave her to him. Since the woman was made out of the man, God ordained, "therefore, shall a man leave his father and his mother, and shall cleave

[21]*The Book of Genesis* (*Bible*), 2: 18.

unto his wife, and they shall be one flesh."[22] The Christain Church and Christian community everywhere consider marriage and family as the basic and most pivotal institutions. King Solomon wrote "who so findeth a wife findeth a good thing, and attaineth favour of the Lord."[23]

Even the priests are not forbidden to marry, but they are asked to lead a holy and ideal family life. For instance, St. Paul wrote, "Let the deacons (priests) be the husband of one wife, ruling their children and their own house well."[24] Sanctity of marriage is emphasized in Christian religion, as St. Paul declared, "Marriage is honourable in all, and the bed undefiled."[25]

Christian Church advocates monogamy and the practice of polygamy and adultery is forbidden.

According to the *Old Testament*, the Mosaic Law (the Hebrew Law) permitted divorce for adultery. But Christ made it very clear that Moses (the great Hebrew Leader of the *Old Testament* permitted divorce "because of the hardness of your hearts but from the beginning it was not so."[26] In other words, Christ said that divorce was permitted in olden times by the Mosaic law (law given by Moses) because of the hardness of the heart of the people at that time, and not because it was ordained so. To Christ, marriage is indissoluble, and so, no divorce be permitted, for, Christ declared "what God hath joined together, let no man put as under."[27] Nevertheless, he recognized the practical difficulty in this matter, when he pointed out, "all men cannot receive this, save (except) they to whom it is given."[28]

In spite of the fact that the Holy Scriptures of the Christians do not permit divorce, it was permitted in the course of time in the history of the church. After the division of the Church into the Eastern (Greek Orthodox) and Roman Catholic (A.D. 843), the Greek Church condoned divorce for adultery, and, more recently, for other offences. When Martin Luther precipitated the Protestant Reformation and rejected the Catholic dictum of the sacramental

[22] *The Book of Genesis*, 2: 24.
[23] *Proverbs* (*Bible*), 18: 22.
[24] *I Timothy* (*Bible*), 3: 12.
[25] *Hebrews* (*Bible*), 13: 4.
[26] *St. Mathew* (*Bible*), 19: 8.
[27] Mathew, 19: 6.
[28] Mathew 19: 11.

nature of marriage, he paved the way for the civil marriage. Nevertheless, Luther never completely divested himself of a belief in its sacramental character. Neither have Protestant Churches ever entirely relinquished the idea. Lee has correctly pointed out that:

> the Church has been preaching the indissolubility of marriage as the union prearranged by God, and many people have been and are still under the influence of the Church. Yet public sentiment in favour of easier divorce has been growing steadily.[29]

The basis of the principle of indissolubility is essentially religious; it is the idea of the sacrament of marriage, which is God-made. Yet, "the Church admits that the human will enters into the marriage."[30]

In India, the Church and the Christian Community still maintain the view that marriage is an indissoluble institution. The Roman Catholics and the Syrian Christians of South India are firm on this, while the Protestants are relatively less firm. Factors such as the following may be helpful directly or indirectly in order to minimise the incidence of divorce among the Christians in India today :

(*i*) Most of the marriages are still arranged by the parents or elders. This is so, more particularly in Kerala;
(*ii*) Marriage ceremonies are performed in the Church;
(*iii*) Banns are called in the Congregations of the Bride and Bridegroom before the marriage, so that anybody can raise legitimate objections;
(*iv*) Entries are made in the Marriage Register of the Church soon after the wedding ceremony in the Church, with the signatures of the Bridegroom, Bride, the Priest, and witnesses, with full particulars; and
(*v*) The legislation concerning marriage is still old (1872) and the movement of uniform legislation for all religious communities has not yet yielded much fruit. (For instance, the

[29]B.H. Lee, *Divorce Law Reforms in England*, Peter Owen, London, 1974 (Chapter I).

[30]W. Friedmann, *Law in a Changing Society*, Abridged Edition, University Book House, Delhi, 1970, p. 174.

Hindu Marriage Act, 1955, is not applicable to Christians).

Legislations such as the Indian Christian Marriage Act (XV of 1872), the Indian Divorce Act (Act IV of 1869) and the Special Marriage Act (43 of 1954) make provision for divorce among Christians in India. The last-mentioned legislation of 1954 is to provide a special form of marriage which can be taken advantage of by any person in India, and by citizens of India in foreign countries, irrespective of the faith which either party to the marriage professes. The parties may observe any ceremonies for the solemnization of their marriage, but certain facilities are prescribed before marriage can be registered under this Act by the Marriage Officers. Provision is also sought to be made for permitting persons who are already married under other forms of marriage to register their marriage under this Act, and thereby avail themselves of the provisions under this Act.

The Indian Christian Marriage Act, 1872, and the Indian Divorce Act, 1869, dealing with the law of marriage and divorce of the Christians is very old. A Bill to amend and codify this law, entitled the Christian Marriage and Matrimonial Causes Bill, was pending before the Parliament in 1962. That Bill lapsed when the particular Session of the Parliament was dissolved. It seems that "the Christian marriage and divorce law appears outdated compared to other matrimonial laws which have been more recently enacted".[31] In order to change the law, the consent and cooperation of the Christian Church and community are needed. The Church is still not inclined to liberalize the law. For instance, in the recently formulated constitution of a Church, it is recorded that "the Church of North India declares its belief that our Lord's principle and standard of marriage is a life-long and indissoluble union for better or for worse of one man with one woman to the exclusion of all others on either side".[32] Therefore, the matter concerning the change of law concerning marriage and divorce pertaining to the Christians is to be dealt with great caution and consideration.

[31]Kumud Desai, *Indiau Law of Marriage and Divorce*, Second Edition, N.M. Tripathi Private Ltd., 1972, p. 157.

[32]*The Marriage Law of the Church*, Chapter VI. The Constitution of the Church of North India, including the Faith and Order of the Church, 1974.

DIVORCE AMONG THE MUSLIMS

Divorce among the Muslims is related to the religion and culture of the Muslims for several centuries.

The form of marriage amonst the Arabs in the days of Mohammed was polygyny. Women captured in warfare were either married or kept as mistresses. In addition, marriage could be contracted by paying *mahr* (bride-price) to the father or kin of a woman. In both methods, the prominent idea was the husband's right in the woman captured or purchased. The idea of property in the wife found expression in the law of divorce and in the privilege exercised by the husband over his wife. There were two forms of divorce, *khola* or divestiture and *talaq*.

Khola was a friendly arrangement between the husband, the wife's father by which the latter repaid the dowry and got back his daughter. This implied that on return of the consideration, the rights that were purchased by the husband came to an end and the woman was set free from his domination. The privileges of the husband over his wife relate to the sharing of his conjugal rights with others, inheritance of his widow by his heir and his absolute discretion to divorce his wife at pleasure. It was customary among the Arabs to lend one's wife to a guest to show one's hospitality. An Arab desiring a noble offspring would ask his wife to live with a great man. When an Arab was away on a journey, he would hand over his wife to a friend during his absence. That the Arab had no regard for the chastity of his wife proceeded naturally from the fact that he regarded her as his property which he was free to enjoy or dispose of in any manner he thought best.

Islam has perpetuated both forms of divorce current in pre-Islamic Arabia, although there is an obvious leaning toward the form known as *talaq*.

One of the grounds for the dissolution of marriage was that the bride, claiming to be a virgin, was found not to be so by the bridegroom. The law of divorce, wherein the marriage obligation is considered and the punishment for its breach meted out to the female alone, is a logical corollary of the principle that a woman can be sexually owned by one man only. This domination of the man over his wife is further asserted by the fact that the man was permitted to divorce his wife at his own pleasure and without justifying his action. And, this is not the whole story. Woman was not free even when *talaq* (divorce) was pronounced. She had to wait for three menstrual periods to pass in order to ascertain whether she was pregnant. During this period of waiting, *iddat*, the husband had the right to resume his marital rights over the divorced wife, and she became his wife once again without any further ceremony to revalidate the marriage. Nor was the consent of the wife necessary for this resumption. This peculiar situation is due to the fact that in the old Arabic law, the husband's right over the woman was not finally lost by repeating a formula for dismissal. It was only when the formula for dismissal was repeated three times or when the period of waiting was allowed to elapse without the husband's revoking his act either by express words or by conduct, that divorce was complete and the woman was freed from her wifehood.

It is possible that Mohammed was not greatly in favour of divorce as he aimed at the stability of the family. Hence, divorce was permitted only if the parties fear that they cannot keep within God's bounds. A tradition is also quoted, that "the thing which is lawful but which is disliked by God is divorce." The prophet also sought to minimize the possibility of divorce by enjoining that a divorced wife could not be taken back, unless she had been married to someone else and divorced by him.

The later jurists in Islam attempted to restrict the frequency of the divorce. According to them, "*talaq*, emanating from the husband was really prohibited, except for necessity, such as the adultery of the wife."

Amer Ali would have us believe that the Prophet gave to the women the right of obtaining a separation on reasonable grounds. The Quranic law of divorce does provide for separation by women but not on terms favourable to them. As the formula for dismissal had to be repeated thrice before the divorce was complete and irrevocable, a woman might be kept in a state of being neither wife nor divorce. In order to save herself from this state of suspense, it was open to her to ransom herself from her husband for a sum agreed upon by both of them, once the husband had pronounced divorce against her. Similarly, when a wife was desirous of divorce, and if her husband agreed to it, she paid back the *mahr* and got herself free. The law of divorce among the Muslims asserted man's domination over his wife, and the status of the woman affected in another way too. A system where the wife has continually hanging over the head, the apprehension of divorce, cannot but prove an abiding source of uneasiness to her. It is stated that "divorce of a wife was possible to the husband at will."[33] Liberty of divorce has been freely exercised by the faithful both in ancient and in modern times.

Marriage, according to the Islamic Law, strictly speaking, is a civil contract. It is a contract made between two persons of opposite sex with the object of intercourse, procreation and the legalising of children. Being a civil contract, no priest or *Qazi* is necessary for its performance.

The word *talaq* is usually rendered as "repudiation"; it comes from a root *tollaqa* which means to release (an animal) from a tether; to repudiate the wife, or free her from the bondage of marriage. So, the expression *talaq* signifies an absolute power which the husband possesses of divorcing his wife at all times.

Muslim Personal Law regulated matters concerning Muslim marriage. But a specific legislation was enacted in 1939, known as "The Dissolution of Muslim Marriages Act VIII of 1939." In order to consolidate and clarify the provisions of Muslim law relating to suits for dissolution of marriages by women married under Muslim law and to remove doubts as to the effect of the renunciation of Islam by a married Muslim woman on her marriage tie."

Under this Act of 1939, a woman married under Muslim Law shall be entitled to obtain a divorce-decree for the dissolution of her marriage on any one or more of the following grounds :

(*i*) that the whereabouts of the husband have not been known for four years;
(*ii*) that the husband has neglected or has failed to provide for her maintenance for a period of two years;
(*iii*) that the husband has been sentenced to imprisonment for a period of seven years or upwards;
(*iv*) that the husband has failed to perform without reasonable cause his marital obligations for a period of three years;
(*v*) that the husband was impotent at the time of marriage, and continues to be so;
(*vi*) that the husband has been insane for a period of two years

[33]James, Hastings, Ed., *Encyclopedia of Religion nnd Ethics*, Vol. VIII, T & T Clark, Edinburgh, 1915, p. 170.

or is suffering from leprosy or a virulent venereal disease ;

(*vii*) that she, having been given in marriage by her father or other guardian before she attained the age of fifteen years, repudiated the marriage before attaining the age of eighteen years; provided that the marriage has not been consummated.

(*viii*) that the husband treats her with cruelty, that is to say:

(*a*) habitually assults her;

(*b*) associates with women of evil repute;

(*c*) attempts to force her to lead an immoral life;

(*d*) disposes of her property or prevents her from exercising legal rights over it;

(*e*) obstructs her in the observance of her religious profession or practice; or

(*f*) if he has more wives than one, does not equitably in accordance with the injunctions of the *Quran*;

(*ix*) on any other ground which is recognised as valid for the dissolution of marriage under the Muslim Law.

It is felt that there is need for change in the Muslim Law concerning marriages in India. This is obvious from the legislations in other Muslim countries. In Pakistan and Bangladesh, a Mohammadan male cannot commit bigamy without the previous permission in writing of the Arbitration Council ; such marriage without the permission of the Arbitration Council being void. In Pakistan, the Muslim Family Laws Ordinance 1961 brought about radical and progressive change in family laws. It made, inter alia, registration of all marriage under Muslim law compulsory by section 5. Further, section 6 of the Pakistan Family Laws Ordinance 1961 provides, "no man during the subsistence of an existing marriage shall, except with the previous permission, in writing of the Arbitration Council, contract another marriage, nor shall any such marriage contracted without such permission be registered under this Ordinance." Under this Ordinance of 1961, any Muslim wife on the ground of her husband's taking an additional wife without the written permission of the Arbitration Council can seek dissolution of her marriage.

There have been Muslim Women's Movements also advocating the cause of change in Muslim Law concerning marriage and divorce.

Muslim women in India are not much in favour of easy divorce.

In a recent study of the status of Muslim women in Indore city, it was found that majority of the Muslim women (90 per cent housewives, 68 per cent teachers, and 52 per cent college students) opined against the desirability of divorce, meaning that they are against divorce, so as to promote stability of marriage and family.[34]

DIVORCE AMONG PARSIS

As far back as 1835, efforts were made by the members of the Parsi community to have laws suitable to their social requirements, but these early efforts proved abortive. Ultimately, in 1855, the Parsi Law Association was established for the purpose of drafting special Bills for law applicable to Parsi community, relating inter alia to the law of marriage and divorce. The Act that was passed as a result of this was the Parsi Marriage and Divorce Act, (Act XV of 1865).

The Parsi Marriage and Divorce Act of 1865 was based on the Matrimonial Causes Act, 1857 of England, and its principal effect was to make Parsi Marriages monogamous. Since then, circumstances changed. However, the Parsi Marriage and Divorce Act of 1865 was itself defective in many respeets. Adultery by itself or adultery coupled with some other offence serve as the only ground for divorce under that Act. On no other ground eould marriage be dissolved by divorce under it. Again, a section of that Act empowered only the wife to ask for judicial separation on the ground of cruelty, or, because, her husband brought a prostitute in his house; the husband had no remedy by way of seeking judicial separation. To remedy these defects and to bring the law of marriage and divorce in conformity with the current conditions and views of the Parsi community, the Parsi Marriage and Divorce Act, 1936, was enacted. The Act seems outdated like the Indian Divorce Act 1869.[35]

On the basis of this legislation of 1936, we may mention that the following are the important features of Marriage and Divorce among the Parsis:

[34]Krishna Rajwade, *Status of Muslim Women in Indore City*—Unpublished Ph. D. Thesis in Sociology, Indore University, 1979.

[35]Kumud Desai, *Indian Law of Marriage and Divorce*, 1972, p. 125.

(*i*) A Parsi is a person who professes the Zoroastrian religion;
(*ii*) In the case of marriage of a Parsi who has not completed the age of 21 years, the previous consent of his or her father or guardian is necessary for a valid marriage;
(*iii*) No bigamy is permitted;
(*iv*) Every marriage will be certified by the officiating priest;
(*v*) In any case where consummation of the marriage is impossible for natural causes, such a marriage may be declared null and void;
(*vi*) Both the husband and wife have the right to apply for divorce under specified grounds.

A word of conclusion regarding divorce in different religious communities. As we have seen above, divorce is permitted in all the religious communities by social legislation enacted by the Government. Except in the case of the Hindus, all other legislations are old. There is a national debate on the need of a uniform social legislation relating to marriage and divorce for all communities in India, instead of separately for Hindus, Muslims, Christians, Parsis and so on. There are difficulties in this connection, yet, there may be several common factors that could be applied to all alike.

DIVORCE AMONG THE TRIBALS

Most of the primitive peoples have allowed dissolution of marriage under certain circumstances, although the mores differ. Among them, there is considerable variation in the degree of marital stability. Some of the simpler hunting peoples, as far instance, the Vedas of Ceylon, do not allow divorce at all. In general, however, marriage is more flexible, and separation and remarriage are permitted. The divorce procedure itself is likely to be very simple. A *Zuni* wife who no longer wishes to keep her husband indicates her decision by placing his personal belongings at the entrance of the house; when he returns from work and sees his things, he takes the hint and returns to his parents' home. In the case of a consanguinous family, like that of the *Zuni*, divorce is not serious in its effects on the children, since the largest family organization remains intact, and the children continue to have the influence and association of the other adult members of the group.

For this reason, and others, divorce is probably more common among preliterates than it is in modern society. While divorce is made easy, it is not encouraged, for, divorce always disturbs some important family functions. The more numerous and significant the social and economic functions of the family, the more serious becomes the disruption of marriage.

Divorce is commonly practised among the Indian tribals also, and may be obtained by one of the parties refusing to continue to live in wedlock by abandoning the spouse. The Khasis permit divorce for reasons of adultery, barrenness and compatibility of temperament, but the separation can take place only after mutual consent. In some cases, the party desiring the dissolution may have to pay compensation to the other party. There is no possibility of remarriage between two such people who have separated by divorce. The divorce has to be a public ceremony. The mother gets the custody of the children.

The Gond allow divorce freely on grounds of marital infidelity, carelessness in household work, barrenness and quarrelsome disposition. Either party can take the initiative in obtaining a dissolution.

Instances of divorce can be cited from other Indian tribes too.

THE RATE OF DIVORCE

Methods of measurement of the rate of divorce. There are several methods of measurement of the rate of divorce. One method is to find out the ratio of divorce to the total populalon, for instance, the number of divorce per 1000 population. Another method is to find out the ratio of divorce in the population of fifteen years old and over. Third method is to find out the ratio of divorce in the married population. The number of divorces each year per 1000 married population would constitute a much more logical measure than either of the above methods, for, it would be less subject to the variables mentioned for the country as a whole. Yet, there is another method, that is, to find out the ratio of divorces to marriages in a given year. This measure is expressed in two ways: the number of divorces granted in a period per 100 marriages contracted in the same year; or the number of marriages to one divorce in the same year. With all the above variables operating, it is apparent why one cannot give an absolutely correct divorce rate[36]. It seems, for many years, the United States of America, had led the world in the divorce race. Between 1867 and 1948 the population in the United States increasedly about 300 per cent, marriages slightly over 400 per cent, and divorces about 4000 per cent.[37]

(*i*) *The rate of divorce in the United States of America.* The rate of divorce in the United States of America from time to time is shown below:

Divorce in the United States

Year	*No. of Divorce*	*Divorce per 100 Population*	*Divorce per 100 Marriages*
1870	10,962	0.3	3.1
1900	55,751	0.7	7.7
1930	195,961	1.6	17.4
1960	393,000	2.2	25.4
1970	715,000	3.5	32.8
1971	761,000	3.7	34.6

Source: US Departments of Health, Education & Welfare—Vital Statistics of the United States.

Despite the difficulties with the various measures of divorce, it is clear that divorce has been increasing in the United States. The estimate that currently about one in every three marriages will end in divorce is more than likely a little low.[38]

In recent years, over 700,000 divorces have been granted annually in the United States. In the last ten years, about six million marriages ended in divorce (during 1963—73).[39]

(*ii*) *Rate of divorce in the United Kingdom.* Not only in the United States, but in countries like England also, the devorce rate has been increasing. In England and Wales, there have been 71,661 divorces in 1970, put in 1973, it was 98,948. The divorce rate per 1000 population in England and Wales in selected years is given on page 53:

[36]R.E. Baber, *Marriage & the Family*, 1953, pp 446-50.

[37]W. Waller, *The Family*, A Dynamic Interpretation, p. 532 quoted by H.M., Johnson, Sociology, 1961, p. 171.

[38]F. William Kenkel, *The Family in Perspective*, 1973, p. 314.

[39]Ibid., p. 310.

Divorce in England

Year	*Rate per 1000 Population*
1911	0.07
1950	1.30
1970	4.70
1973	8.40

This clearly shows that in three years between 1970 and 1973, the divorce rate in England has just doubled.[40]

Some sociologists have held that there is no need for any alarm owing to this high rate of divorce. One of the reasons for the high rate of divorce, according to them, is relatively early marriage. If there is a continuance of a low age at marriage, there may be a relatively high number of divorces. A rising proportion of young married adults may tend to raise the divorce rates for the general population and for married females aged 15 and above.[41]

It may also be mentioned that even though the United States has one of the highest divorce rates in the world, "there is no indication that people are disillusioned with the institution of marriage."[42]

(*iii*) *The rate of divorce in India*. Statistical information on divorce in India is very limited. Therefore it is difficult to work out the rate of divorce in our country. According to the 1971 Census of India, there were 8,707,000 divorced or separated women.[43] Further, with reference to the investigation undertaken by the present writer, it can safely be concluded that the incidence of divorce in India is rapidly increasing, particularly from 1960, and more particularly from 1976. It may be recalled that the Hindu Marriage Act was enacted in 1955 and its major amendment in 1976.

[40]Robert, Chester, *Divorce in Europe*, 1977, p. 77.

[41]Carter & Plateris, *Trends in Divorce and Family Disruption*, quoted by Winch and Goodman, in Selected Studies in Marriage & Family, 1968, pp. 571-72.

[42]Landis Judson, *The Family and Social Change: A Positive View*, The Voice of America, Forum Lectures, *The Family*, 1964, p. 100.

[43]*Census of India*, 1971—Table 4-A—Age & Marital Status in India.

Chapter 3

THE BACKGROUND OF THE SPOUSES IN DIVORCE

INTRODUCTION

INFORMATION concerning the socio-economic and cultural background of the spouses is important in as much as it could be related to their behaviour pertaining to marital dissolution. In identifying the background, the following aspects of the life of the couples are significant :

(*i*) Type of family ;
(*ii*) Level of education of the spouses at the time of marriage;
(*iii*) Caste/Community/Tribe;
(*iv*) Economic class;
(*v*) Occupation at the time of marriage;
(*vi*) Religious training received at home;
(*vii*) Religious inclinations;
(*viii*) General cultural background; and
(*ix*) How their caste/community/tribe is correlated with their economic class and level of education.

TYPE OF FAMILY OF THE COUPLES

In India, we have both nuclear and joint families in most communities, whether rural or urban. The type of family, joint or nuclear, do matter with regard to marital disruptions also.

The family is the focal point for many of the fears, frustrations and resentments of a complex and frustrated society. The members of the family reflect in their personal time many of the social tensions and conflicts. And in this matter, there is difference between the various types of family. Fonseca has pointed out that "the typical kind of joint family or in some cases the extended family has been the cause for a good deal of conflict and has led to dissatisfaction among many modern couples."[1] For more reasons than one, persons prefer to sever from the joint family today. At the same time, there are those who desire the security and the benefit of the joint family status. They are perpetually on the horns of a dilemma, being aware that the needs are met in a better way by the joint family on the one hand, and yet, wanting to be independent on the other.

Vast majority (70 per cent) of the spouses in the present study lived in joint families. The joint families were of different types again. 65.5 per cent of these were of the traditional pattern, meaning that the spouses lived with the husbands' parents, brothers, sisters, etc. 2.5 per cent of joint families were of rather very small size. They included the unitary family and only husband's mother. Though these were originally of the traditional joint family type, other members were lost either through death or through transfer to other places. 2 per cent of the couples lived at the wife's place (husband's in-laws). This was to protect and maintain the wife's family as they had no male member.

Twentysix per cent of the couples lived in single families. The males were already separated from the parental family, because of job and transfers or they have cut off from the joint family after the marriage. In one case, the couple had hardly established a family of their own. The period of cohabitation which was rather short was spent in a hotel. In 4 per cent cases, the question of family did not arise at all, because, they never cohabited. The marital bond was disrupted as soon as it was made.

It is interesting to note that in spite of the greater incidence of joint families, divorce also took place In traditional joint families, conjugal relationships are affected. In most of the joint families even today, free movement of the spouses is not allowed, especially in the presence of the elders. A son is expected to be loyal first towards his parents and then only to his wife. These values are inculcated from childhood and as a result, a young man sees his wife as a person of lesser importance, as compared to his own family members. In joint families, strifes and jealousies are com-

[1]Mabel Fonseca, *op cit.*, 1966, p. 19.

mon. This is more manifest among the women folk. Sometimes, it is found that mothers are so much emotionally attached and dependent upon their sons that they cannot tolerate if they start loving their wives more than the mother. Many mothers knowingly or unknowingly destroy the happiness of their own children, simply because of their egoistic whims. Husband's sisters also can create a lot of mischief. With the coming of a sister-in-law, their importance in the family is considerably diminished, the affection and love they received from their brothers snatched away by a stranger. A strife to win the affection of the same man by his sister and wife simultaneously can create antagonistic attitudes towards each other. More often, a man prefers his wife to his sister, and this it but natural. This creates frustration and jealousy in the sister, and she wants to destroy the happiness of the sister-in-law at any cost.

Also, joint families give more importance to traditions like dowry and other forms of give and take. When the demands and expectations of the in-laws of the husband are not fully met, often a girl is made to undergo all sorts of humiliation or even torture. Modern educated girls find joint families all the more problematic. It curtails their freedom to a great extent, and enforces various types of controls and restrictions on their behaviour. Their ability to subject to humiliation or injustice is comparatively decreased and they retaliate, which creates the situation worse in respect of husband-wife relationships. There is a wide variation between the expectation of a mother-in-law regarding her daughter-in-law and an educated young girl about her status and role as a wife. Often, the gap is so great that conflict between the two becomes unavoidable.

With all these problems, still marital relation in a joint family is considered to be more stable as compared to that in a nuclear family. In a joint family, marriage is never a bond between two individuals; it is a chain which links and binds the two families together. Everyone concerned is interested in maintaining the bond. There is a strong sense of family ego in the joint family. Anything which can undermine the prestige of a joint family is usually avoided by all members. Such are the things which can be said in favour of the joint family.

In the same way, single family has its own advantages and disadvantages. A single family is often termed as a conjugal family which means that it is based on the conjugal bond, or, in other words, conjugal bond is considered to be of foremost importance. Here, the husband and wife move freely with each other and their mutual love and affection are not cut down by any exigent factor. A wife has full freedom to manage her household affairs according to her choice, and she is not under the control of any other female. There is no female competing with her for her husband's affections. In spite of all these, a single family is considered to be relatively unstable. In the modern setup, problems between individuals can crop up at any time. The spouses are not under the watch or control of the elders. Strifes may go on without any effort of reconciliation which finally break up the marital bond irrevocably. In the study of marital disruptions by Fonseca in Bombay city, it was found that over 45 per cent of the sample lived within the joint or extended family environment.[2]

EDUCATION OF THE SPOUSES AT THE TIME OF THEIR MARRIAGE

Education of the husbands and wives is important in the phenomenon of legal divorce. Therefore, the level of education of the couples involved in divorce was inquired into.

The data are shown in the Table 3.1.

TABLE 3.1

S. No.	*Level af education*	*Husband*		*Wife*	
		No.	%	*No.*	%
1.	Postgraduate	45	22.5	22	11.0
2.	Graduate	48	24.00	24	12.00
3.	Undergraduate	38	19	67	33.5
4.	Below higher secondary	24	12	14	7.00
5.	Middle school	27	13.5	28	14.00
6.	Uneducated or below primary	18	9	35	17.5
	Total	200	100	200	100

This table shows that vast majority of the respondents are literate. Further, 46.5 per cent of the husbands and 28 per cent

[2]Mabel, Fonseca 1966, *op cit.*, p. 57.

wives are graduates or postgraduates. The percentage of uneducated women is almost double of that of men. This is mainly because, female children are sent to School in a number of lowercaste communities.

The table also indicates that the males are better-educated than females at the time of marriage. The highest frequency of males falls in the undergraduate group (33.5 per cent). The percentage of male postgraduate (22.5 pet cent) is more than double of that of the female postgraduates (11 per cent)

The type of interaction between the husband and wife when the wife is more educated than the husband has been investigated. One husband said, "I have just completed higher seeondary, and got into business, whereas my wife was a graduate when we got married. I was too busy to pursue my studies. I feel my wife looks down upon me. She thought of me rather uncultured and uncouth, though she never expressed it verbally." This feeling of the husband may be simply due to his own sense of inferiority. Another husband said, "I have done higher secondary, and then got into mechanical training and directly started working. My wife is a graduate and she has taken a course in library science. Due to higher education, she thinks too high of herself, and tries to show off every time. In the presence of my friends, she talks and acts in such a way that I and they feel slighted. I feel very much offended at it, and I tried to explain to her, but then she did not seem to care at all." In two other cases, the opposite reaction appeared. In both the cases, the husband had high school education only, whereas the wives had attended college. The husbands had a sense of inferiority, but they tried to get rid of it through aggressive behaviour. One young wife said, "my husband was only a higher secondary. I did not mind it at all, because he was in a good business, and earned very well. But my husband and his mother were very conscious of it. Every time, they used to taunt me, saying, "In spite of college education, you cannot do such and such thing properly." Another young wife was taunted and subjected to physical assaults, just because of the husband's inferiority complex. But, it should be mentioned here that in the majority of the cases, the higher education of females did not have any adverse effect on the marital relation ship of the couples.

According to Terman, two very important questions arise with regard to the influence of education on a couple.

The first is the relation of happiness to the extent of education that a spouse had, and the second is the difference in educational status between the spouses.[3] Various other authors have considered education as an important criterion in rating marital adjustment, satisfaction and happiness. Some like Merrill and Truxall stress education in role-conflict and role-expectations between couples in marriage. Still, others like Nimkoff and Hamilton discuss the effects of formal education and its bearing on happiness in marriage. Burgess and Cottrell report that with some, increased chances of success in marriage go with a rising level of education. At the same time, among them, Terman, Bernard and Kirkpatric consider it only a negligible correlation. Merrill and Elliott stress divorce in terms of educational roles[4].

The census survey of married couples in the United Statets showed that "although marriage instability exists at all socio-economic levels, the general trend is for marriage breakup to be more profound at the lover status lewels."[5]

Our experience in Madhya Pradesh shows that most of the illiterate and low caste segments of the population do not approach judicial courts for obtaining divorce, although they have much family disorganization; they prefer customary divorce through the agency of village and cast *panchayats*, or by private transactions as bill of divorcement or *farkat nama*. It may be mentioned here that customary divorce prevails generally in the lower strata of society which is very poor, but in my study, it was observed that certain higher castes also took advantage of this. Further, with reference to the present study, it cannot be said with certainty whether education hinders or promotes the incidence of divorce among Hindus. Kapadia has pointed out that "it is not possible to predict whether education exercises any restraining or corrective influence with regard to divorce."[6]

[3]L.M. Terman, *Psychological Factors in Marital Happiness*, McGraw Hill Book Co., New York, 1938, pp. 187-9.

[4]Truxall & Merrill, *Marriage and the Family in American Culture*, Prentice Hall, New York, 1953, pp. 203-4; E.E., Merrill, *Courtship and Marriage*, Henry Holt & Co., Inc. 1959, p. 245.

[5]Kenkel, *op. cit* 1973, p. 316.

[6]K.M. Kapadia, *op. cit.*, p. 298.

CASTE/COMMUNITY/TRIBE OF THE SPOUSES

The present study is concerning divorce among Hindus. However, under the purview of the Hindu Marriage Act, communities like the Sikh and Jain as well as tribals are included. The Act states as follows:

This Act applies :

(*i*) to any person who is Hindu by religion in any of the forms or developments including a Virashaiva, Lingayat or a follower of the Brahmo, Prarthana or Arya Samaj;

(*ii*) to any person who is a Buddhist, Jain or Sikh by religion: and

(*iii*) to any other person domiciled in the territories in which this Act extends, who is not a Muslim, Christian, Parsi or Jew by religion.[7]

Among the Hindus, there are innumerable castes and sub-castes with marital and socio-economic restrictions. According to sociologists, caste is the most frequently mentioned peculiarity of the Indian social structure, and one of the chief characteristics of the caste system is choice of marriage partner within the caste group itself (caste endogamy). Sardar K.M. Panikkar has correctly pointed out that "the three thousand major units of castes enumerated in earlier census returns constitute a factor of the highest sociological importance. These castes are rigidly exclusive and each claims superiority over the other".[8]

There is variation in the phenomenon of divorce in different castes and communities. Table 3.2 indicates the same (see page 61).

It is seen that the highest number of divorces is from *Brahmin* Caste. These *Brahmins* belonged to various Provinces and cultural regions of the country, as shown in Table 3.3.

It may be worthwhile to explain in brief the phenomenon of divorce in each community in our study, so as to comprehend their cultural background *vis-a-vis* divorce.

[7]*The Hindu Marriage Act*, 1955 (Amended upto 1976)—Section 2—Application of Act.

[8]K.M. Panikkar, *Hindu Society at Cross Roads*, Asia Publishing House, Bombay, 1961, Third Edition, p. 36.

TABLE 3.2. Caste/community/tribe of the divorced spouses

S.No.	*Name of the caste/tribe*	*Husband*		*Wife*	
		No.	*Percentage*	*No.*	*Percentage*
1.	Brahmin	83	41.5	81	40.5
2.	Kshatriya	9	4.5	7	3.5
3.	Vaishya (Banka)	30	15	30	15
4.	Kayasth	8	4	8	4
5.	Khatri	3	1.5	4	2
6.	Sonar	3	1.5	4	2
7.	Yadev	3	1.5	3	1.5
8.	Sch. Castes (Harijans)	31	15.5	31	15.5
9.	Tribals	7	3.5	7	3.5
10.	Jain	18	9.00	19	9.5
11.	Sikh	5	2.5	5	2.5
12.	Others	—	—	1	0.5
	Total	200	100	200	100

TABLE 3.3. Classification of Brahmin divorcees on the basis of their Provinces/Cultural regions of origin

S. No.	*Type of Brahmin*	*Husband*		*Wife*	
		No.	*%*	*No.*	*%*
1.	Maharastrian Brahmin	43	52	44	54
2.	Madhya Bharat Brahmin (mostly of Malwa region)	31	37	29	36
3.	Gujrati Brahmin	4	5	4	5
4.	Bengali Brahmin	3	3.6	3	3.6
5.	South Indian Brahmin	2	2.4	1	1.4
	Total	83	100	81	100

1. *Maharashtrian Brahmins.* The Maharashtrian Brahmins (forefathers) may have migrated from various parts of Maharashtra State. Holkar and the Scindia States were ruled by Maratha kings, and, therefore, they must have been encouraged by the then States which have since been merged into the present State of Madhya Pradesh. In so far as the marital ties are concerned, it is seen that the Maharashtrian Brahmin group is less

tradition-bound. Women's education and employment are also much more among them as compared with other Brahmins in our study. Some of the factors that might have facilitated divorce among these Maharashtrian Brahmins are: (*i*) equality of women in the family, (*ii*) high rate of education among women, (*iii*) economic independence of women, (*iv*) absence of dowry as such, and (*v*) modern outlook in life.

Besides these, the stigma of divorce is much less among them. One respondent said, "our community does not look down upon divorces. They recognize that if a marriage is not working, it should be broken, either by man or by woman". Another highly enlightened member of the community (non-divorcee) said, "in our community, we do not treat divorce as anything abnormal or unfortunate. Before twenty years, there was a divorce in my own family. But, even at that time, I remember that was made hardly an issue".

Migration to urban centres and consequent detachment from their own ethnic group also must be an important factor in helping high rate of social mobility among them. Fifty per cent of the divorces among them took place for comparatively minor reasons such as (*i*) inability to adjust, (*ii*) wife's unwillingness to stay with in-laws, (*iii*) suspicion about fidelity, (*iv*) constant quarrels over small matters and so on. What the researcher feels is that had such problems arisen in other Brahmin communities in the study, not even 50 per cent of divorce cases would have taken place. In other Brahmin groups, unlike among the Maharashtrian, divorce is considered to be the last resort, and, people, especially women go for divorce when there is no other alternative. Sixtyfive per cent of the female-divorcees of the Maharashtrian Brahmin community said that they were not at all repentant about the divorce; in fact, they did not do much to prevent divorce as such. One divorced woman said: "When I found that my marriage is not worth-continuing, I stopped bothering about it. Of course, I did not go to the Court for a divorce: it was my husband who went. But I did not go to defend myself either. I wanted my husband to fight out the case".

Another Maharashtrian Brahmin lady, who came away from her husband's place, after a small quarrel said: "Of course, my husband came several times to meet me. He tried through his friends also. But I had decided not to go. Even before the presentation of the petition for divorce, he had come to see me. But I flatly refused to see him. I never attended the court as I did not want to defend myself". A third woman, who married rather late, and who came away from the place of the husband only because she did not like the behaviour of her in-laws, said: "Anyway, all these years, I have lived without a husband. If living with a husband is not a pleasant affair, I would rather live alone or with my parents." These are only a few outstanding examples. There are several others, whose marriage would have worked, had they been tolerant, and willing to give little more time and effort. Maharashtrian Brahmins tend to have quick and easy divorce, with the least efforts for reconciliation or adjustment.

2. *Brahmins of Madhya Bharat origin (mostly of Malwa region).* Out of the 31 cases of these Brahmin-husbands, two had inter-caste marriage. One had a love marriage with a Harijan gril, whom he left later on due to persuasion of the parents and relatives. Another had married a Kayastha girl in a hurry with the help of a newspaper advertisement. Later on, he found out that the girl was a bad character, and had no interest in married life. The remaining 29 were caste-marriages. Except 2 cases, all other spouses have left each other, after facing serious problems for quite some time. Of the two cases, one is a college girl, who was forcibly married by her parents when she was just completing her high school. The girl did not like the atmosphere in the house of the husband. Her husband was rather shy and retreating. The girl went to her parants' place and refused to go back. In her own house, she was given entire freedom even to move around with boys. She joined a women's college. She made friendship with some girls and boys and continued an unfettered life. The husband and his people tried to bring her back, but she refused to come. In the meantime, the husband applied to the court for restitution of conjugal rights. After this there was some type of compromise between the parties and the husband also agreed for divorce. The girl is in love with a Muslim boy whom she wants to marry. Her parents are objecting to this marriage. But the girl confided that any time she got an opportunity she will go away and marry the same boy.

The other Brahman couple came from entirely different backgrounds. The husband hailed from a family where there were several step-brothers and sisters and where father was an eccentric. They never had a congenial atmosphere in the home. Though well-educated and employed, he retains the unfavourable impact of the setbacks he had received from an unhealthy home in childhood. He also has an eccentric personality, and is a difficult person to live with. The wife, on the contrary, came from a sophisticated and cultured family. The differences soon came to the top and the parties could not pull along together.

3. *Gujrat Brahmins.* In these cases also, very little efforts were made by the parties concerned to adjust and nurture the married life. The couples lived together just for a couple of weeks or months and left, although the final separation took place after 1½ year of marriage.

4. *Bengali Brahmins.* In the Bengali Brahmin cases, loose morals of the wife and extreme cruelty on the part of the husband resulted in marital failure and dissolution.

5. *South Indian Brahmin.* There are two South Indian Brahmin divorcee-husbands in the study, whereas South Indian divorcee-wife is only one. The other married a north Indian Christian.

In the table dealing with the caste/community/tribe of the respondents, there are other castes and communities besides and the above, and the same is dealt with hereunder.

1. *Kshatriyas.* Out of the total 9 husbands, 4 are Maratha Kshatriyas and the rest five are Rajputs. The number of wives is only 7. This means, two men had intercaste marriage. A Marathi zamindar's son and a Rajput had love marriages. It was only the Maratha zamindar's son's marriage which lasted for a few years. He fell in love with a Maharashtrian Brahmin girl and married her. In the other case, though the boy was in love with a girl, he did not want to marry her. He was already engaged, and he knew that his father would not allow any other marriage. So, the boy refused to marry. But the girl and her father insisted forcefully to him and the marriage was arranged within a few hours. The couple stayed together for 3 or 4 days. Meanwhile, the date of his marriage to the engaged girl was drawing near. He tried to take the wife to his home. But his parents plainly refused to accept this girl as the daughter-in-law. She was thrown out, and the boy was married with the Rajput girl, with whom he was already engaged.

Amang the Maratha Kshatriyas, women's education and even employment is becoming popular. Out of the total three Maratha Kshatriya wives, two are working. As compared to this, all the four Rajput divorced women were neither employed nor educated.

Rajputs are still very much tradition-bound. Some of the important factors causing low status of women in the Rajput community are (*i*) absence of female education, (*ii*) dowry system, (*iii*) authoritarian joint family pattern, and extreme importance of father figure. Rajputs were erstwhile rules of principalities or villages and they still try to maintain their distinct identity by holding on to the traditional patterns of behaviour. A real resistance to change, especially change in the role and status of females, can be observed in Rajput families. Their women also take great pride in maintaining the old traditions and are unwilling to break them even when circumstances warrant.

2. *Vaishyas* (*Banias*). This is another important community in this region. The social organization of this community is extremely complex and there ate numerous divisions among them. The present researcher did not go into a detailed analysis of the sub-groups among them, but the main groups she came across are shown in Table 3.4.

TABLE 3.4 Subdivisions of the Vaisya (Bania) community

S. No.	*Name of the subgroup*	*Husband*		*Wife*	
		No	*%*	*No*	*%*
1.	Agarwal/Gupta	15	50	14	46.6
2.	Neema	2	6.6	2	6.6
3.	Sindhi	9	30	10	33.4
4.	Gujrati	4	13.4	4	13.4
	Total	30	100	30	100

The Table 3.4 shows that the highest incidence of divorce is among the Agarwals/Guptas. Of course, in the general population of the region too, their number is the largest. Next come the Sindhis. Majority of them are businessmen. All of them belonged to either middle or upper class. Money seems to be a very important factor in causing marital problems among the Sindhis.

In the Gujrati business community, the women were highly educated and were capable of earning their own living. Women also had an important role in decision-making. In all the four cases, the women married after they were fully satisfied about the details of their husbands. The period of engagement was sufficiently long. The couple met each other frequently and went out also. The girls were even allowed to go to their would-be husbands' homes and stay overnight. In all these cases, it is interesting to know that it was the wife who left the husband. In one case, there was no possibility of adjustment, because the husband was a drug-addict, and lost his mental balance. In all the other three cases, the women seem to have left due to their own whims. One wife never cohabited with the husband. Another stayed for 3 or 4 months and then left. A third being the only child of her parents desired to be with them. She left the husband's home after the birth of a child.

3. *Kayasth*. There are 8 husbands and 8 wives (4 per cent each) in this sub-caste. It is believed that in the past, due to their intelligence and quick wit, the kayasths were honoured in the courts of rulers, and they received rewards also. Today also, this community is regarded as a progressive one. All the male respondents belonging to this community are well-educated and well-placed in life. There were two engineers, one businessman, one high-ranking government official, one advocate, one teacher and two officials in semi-government concerns. All the female respondents were also well-educated. Even after their progress in education and material life, this community is conservative in its social outlook.

4. *Khatris*. Khatris in our study originally belonged to Punjab. All the Khatri couples belonged to the upper economic class.

5. *Sonar Caste*. Though originally pursuing the occupation of goldsmith, some of them have left this traditional occupation. In our study, two continue as goldsmiths, whereas one is an engineer.

6. *Yadev*. Yadevs are originally cowherds. None of the respondents in our study followed this occupation at present.

7. *Harijans*. There are sub-groups among them. All of them are still in poor occupations like daily-paid labour, mill-worker, peon, etc. The women are also in similar occupations. There is very little education among them.

8. *Tribals*. They originally belonged to tribes like *Bhil*, *Khol*, *Kamar*, and *Kahar*. Today, they have lost their tribal identity, and are more or less merged with the lower castes of the city population. This process of tribals turning into castes is found elsewhere too in our country, Anthropologists and seciologists have pointed out that from very early times, there has been a gradual and silent

change from tribe to caste. This change has taken place in a number of ways, and, it is believed that most of the lower or exterior castes of today were formerly tribes.

9. Jains and Sikhs. There are 23 husbands and 24 wives belonging to these communities. In fact, the Jains and Sikhs are two different religious groups, different from the Hindu group as such. But in the present study, they are also treated as part of the Hindu community, because, as mentioned earlier, the law governing marriage and family among Hindus governs them also. (See Section 2-Application of Act (1), a, b, c (2) & (3).

Among the Jains in this study, there are two main groups, namely, (*i*) the Jains of Rajasthan who have been permanently settled in Malwa region, and (*ii*) the Jains of Gujrati origin. In social customs, Jains exhibit a close similarity to the Vaishya community of the respective regions. This similarity may be due to the uniformity in their occupations. Both the Jains and Vaishyas are mainly businessmen.

The Sikhs have entirely different social customs and values. Originally belonging to Punjab and Haryana, they have migrated to many other parts of India in pursuit of better opportunities in life. All the Sikhs in the present study belonged to Jat community (Jats are a sub-group of the Sikhs). Though detached from the site of original culture, this community maintains its identity as an entirely distinct group. Even today, they are strictly endogamous. Further, they continue to maintain close ties with the Punjab villages to which they originally belong.

10. Others. In this category, there is only one female respondent, a Christian married to a Hindu, and living with him, following the Hindu way of life. For divorce also, they applied under the Hindu Marriage Act. This was the only case of inter-religious marriage in the whole sample.

There were 8 inter-caste marriages, out of which 4 were love marriages and four arranged ones. In all, there were four Maharashtrian Brahmin female spouses marrying non-Maharashtrian males. One married a Punjabi, another a Bania, third a Maratha Kshatria and fourth a Kayastha. One inter-caste marriage was that of a Sindhi woman and Kayasth man; another between a Sonar girl and Rajput boy; a third between a Gujrati Jain woman and Brahmin man. The last was between a Kayasth girl and a Brahmin boy. Here too, it may be mentioned that out of the total 8 inter-caste marriages, 50 per cent were of Maharashtrian Brahmin women.

ECONOMIC CLASS OF THE COUPLES

The economic class is related to the phenomenon of divorce as has been pointed out by several researchers as a result of their studies. According to the United States Bureau of the Census, people of lower income have more divorce than those of higher income. Therefore, Kenkel remarks, "although marriage instability exists at all socio-economic levels, the general trend is for marriage breakup to be more profound at the lower status level in our country."[9] In India, family disorganization is rampant in the lower stratum of the society. In the slums of Indore, it has been seen that family life is rather loose. Many a time, wives leave their husbands and children without much ceremony and simply start living with other men. The same thing happens with regard to husbands also. In the 1930's it was found in the United States that "more divorces occur in the higher classes."[10] But now it is found that "the higher the socio-economic status of a group, the lower their divorce and separation rates."[11]

The present study revealed that the economic class of the spouses was as under:

TABLE 3.5 Economic class of the couples

S.No.	*Economic class*	*No of couples*	*%*
1.	Upper economic class	15	7.5
2.	Middle class	145	72.5
3.	Lower class	40	20.00
	Total	200	100

[9]Kenkel, *op. cit.*, 1973, p. 316:
US Bureau of the Census Current Population Reports Series 20, 84, Oct. 7, 1971, p. 4.

[10]Terman, M. Landis, *Psychological Factors in Marital Happiness*, Mc-Graw Hill Book Co., New York, 1938, p. 167.

[11]Udry, Richard, *The American Journal of Sociology*, 1966, 72, pp. 203-09 & 1967, pp. 673-74.
quoted by Winch and Goodman, in Selected Studies in Marriage and the Family 1966, p. 572.

The economic class of the couples was determined on the basis of their (*i*) family income, (*ii*) occupation, and (*iii*) the ancestral economic status. It is an established fact that the economic status of a person or family determines their life and social relationships. The way of family living, food habits, recreation, care and upbringing of children, husband-wife relationship, parent-child relationship, etc. are greatly influenced by the economic background. In an upper class family, great stress is laid on the affectional responses recreation and nurture of children, whereas such matters are of secondary importance in a lower class family. Their main concern is to feed the mouths and to meet the other minimum necessities of life. In the middle class family, the life pattern, ambitions aspirations and standards of behaviour are much different from those of the other two classes. Professional ambitions are much more in this class. Stress on the career of women is also found more in this class. Women's education, employment, economic independence, moving along at par with men in all walks of life are apt to produce changes in the values, attitudes, and other views of the members of the middle economic class.

OCCUPATION OF THE HUSBANDS AND WIVES AT THE TIME OF MARRIAGE

There is much relationship between occupation and marital and familial life. The study of occupations today lays so much emphasis on the individual and his personality that it is worthwhile to note its role in marital discord. Burgess & Locke observed that "various studies seem to show that divorce is relatively high among persons engaged in occupations necessitating frequent absence from home, involving intimate contacts with the opposite sex, and controlled relatively little by the community."[12]

Several years ago, a comprehensive study of divorces by the United States Census showed that (*i*) commercial travellers, actors musicians, physicians and stenographers had the highest divorce rates; (*ii*) bankers, plumbers, lawyers, butchers, professors, servants and merchants ranked next, and (*iii*) miners, manufacturers, clergymen, carpenters, and farmers ranked lowest in frequency.

The study by Fonseca in Bombay revealed that although the

[12]Burgess & Locke, *The Family*, 1950, p. 634.

nature of occupation cannot determine for us discord as peculiar to a particular occupation owing to fluctuations in income, it is ineteresting to note that "discord in the clerical and skilled, business, unskilled and unemployed classes appears to outweigh discord in the professional class."[13]

The information concerning the occupation of the couples at the time of marriage is shown in the Table 3.6

TABLE 3.6. Occupation of the spouses at the time of marriage

S. No.	*Type of occupation*	*Husbands*		*Wives*	
		No.	*%*	*No.*	*%*
1.	Central Civil Services	2	1	—	—
2.	Medical doctors	5	2.5	4	2
3.	Engineer	6	3	—	—
4.	Advocate	6	3	—	—
5.	Professor	6	3	1	0.5
6.	Officer	8	4	—	—
7.	Businessmen	26	13	—	—
8.	Office Assistant	4	20	15	7.5
9.	School teacher	12	6	9	4.5
10.	Mily-Service	5	2.5	—	—
11.	Technical worker	6	3	1	0.5
12.	Nurse	—	—	1	0.5
13.	Farmer	4	2	—	—
14.	Goldsmith	2	1	—	—
15.	Tailor	1	0.5	—	—
16.	Driver/conductor	2	1	—	—
17.	Mill-worker	2	1	—	—
18.	Peon	5	2.5	—	—
19.	Labourer	5	2.5	1	0.5
20.	Others	6	3	1	0.5
21.	No regular work (including students)	51	25.5	167	83.5
	Total	200	100	200	100

To explain further, 11.5 per cent of the husbands were engaged in high ranking jobs like officers, engineers, doctors, professors and advocates. Out of the total 26 businessmen, 5 had largescale

[13]Fonseca, *op. cit.*, 1966, pp. 42-46.

business, 10 had medium type business like shopkeepers and the rest 11 were petty traders. Out of the 5 military service men, one was a major, the rest were ordinary soldiers. 31 per cent of the men were engaged in ordinary jobs like school teacher, office assistants, technical jobs like mechanics and so on. Four were farmers. But, only one was a well-to-do farmer. The rest were farmers who had small pieces of land. Four husbands were self-employed, 2 were goldsmiths, one was a tailor, and another auto-rikshaw driver. Eight husbands were engaged in low-grade occupations like mill workers, and peons. There are 5 labourers. None of them was permanently employed anywhere, but used to take up daily-paid jobs. Three per cent husbands were in other occupations like petty contractors, salesmen, etc. 25.5 per cent of the husbands were not employed at the time of their marriage. Out of this, 7 per cent were just students, and 5.5 per cent were too young to be employed. The remaining 13 per cent (26 men) were unemployed at the time of their marriage.

The percentage of women working at the time of marriage was very low. Only 16.5 per cent were employed at the time of marriage. Maximum number of women were engaged as office assistants (7.5 per cent). Next comes school teachers (4.5 per cent). The percentage of doctors (2 per cent) came next. Only one woman each was engaged in professions like college teaching, technical work, nursing and library work. One woman was earning regularly as a daily-paid labourer. Vast majority of the women (83.5 per cent) were not engaged in any remunerative work at the time of their marriage. 22.5 per cent were students. 27 per cent were too young to work. The remaining 34 per cent of women did not have either the inclination or proper environment to earn a living. The most important factor hindering women to seek employment is community customs and traditions. In many of the communities like Banias, Jains, Sikhs, or even smaller sub-castes women's employment is still looked down upon. Parents are most reluctant to send their daughters for jobs outside the home, because it may affect or destroy their matrimonial prospects. In such conservative communities, employed women are taken as women with loose moral character, and many men do not like to marry working girls. As a result, even when the girls are highly educated, and fit for employment, or even after receiving good positions in the University Examinations, girls are made to reject employment opportunities. The parents' view is: "Let her husband decide if she has to work or not. We don't want her to work." The parents also say, "We do not want the money of our daughters." The present researcher has come across several cases of enlightened parents like professors, doctors, engineers, teachers and businessmen expressing such like views. As a result, many girls do not work till they get married, but start working if their husbands and in-laws permit them to do so. Some of the important conclusions that may be arrived at in this connection are :

(*i*) Out of the working groups, the highest incidence of divorce both among husbands (20 per cent) and wives (7.5 per cent) is of office assistants such as clerks, typists, stenographers, and personal secretaries. This conclusion partly agrees with the findings mentioned by Burgess and Locke in the United States and Fonseca in India, referred to above. This is, because, among other things, they come in close contact with people of the opposite sex in their places of work, travel and recreation.

(*ii*) Among those who work, the next highest incidence is that of businessmen in respect of husbands (13 per cent of the couple). About this too, the findings of Burgess and Locke and Fonseca (mentioned above) are relevant, for, they have stated that "commercial travellers" and people in "business" have the highest rate of divorce.

(*iii*) Majority of the wives (83.5 per cent) do not work. In this connection, it may be mentioned that most women in India do not work outside the home, whether educated or not. In our study, 61.5% women have educated beyond Higher Secondary including graduation and postgraduation. They were fit for employment, and yet, they were not working. Certain surveys have indicated that only 10 per cent of the total earners of Bombay city and 5 per cent of the earners of Calcutta city are women, and most of whom work as textile workers, domestic servants, and cooks, clerks and typists, teachers and others. It seems that the "social sentiment appears to be very powerful in determining the proportion of women seeking work in urban areas."[14]

[14]D.R. Gadgil, *Woman in the Working Force in India*, Asia Publishing House, Bombay, 1965, pp. 19-26.

CORRELATION BETWEEN THE CASTE AND ECONOMIC CLASS OF THE SPOUSES

An effort has been made to find out how caste and economic class are correlated in respect of the divorced couples. The result is shown in the Table 3.7.

TABLE 3.7. Correlation between the caste and economic class of spouses

S. No,	*Caste/community/ tribe*	*Upper Class*		*Middle Class*		*Lower Class*		*Total*	
		H %	*W* %	*H* %	*W* %	*H* %	*W* %	*H* %	*W* %
1.	Brahmins	2.5	3	36.5	35	2.5	2.5	41.5	40.5
2.	Kshatriya	1	0.5	3.5	3.0	—	—	4.5	3.5
3.	Vaishya	1	1	13.5	13.5	0.5	0.5	15	15
4.	Kayasth	0.5	0.5	3.5	3.5	—	—	4	4
5.	Khatri	1.5	1.5	—	0.5	—	—	1.5	2
6.	Sonar	—	—	1.5	2	—	—	1.5	2
7.	Yadev	—	—	1.5	1.5	—	—	1.5	1.5
8.	Harijan	—	—	2	2	13.5	13.5	15.5	15.5
9.	Tribals	—	—	0.5	0.5	3	3	3.5	3.5
10.	Jains	0.5	0.5	8	8.5	0.5	0.5	9	9.5
11.	Sikhs	0.5	0.5	2	2	—	—	2.5	2.5
12.	Others	—	—	—	0.5	—	—	—	0.5
	Total	7.5	7.5	72.5	72.5	20	20	100	100

This table makes it clear that the upper class cases are comparatively few in number, and they are distributed among different castes/communities. No spouse from the lower caste (Yadev, Sonar and the tribal communities) was found to be belonging to the upper class. At the same time, very few higher caste/community spouses belonged to lower economic class (3.5 per cent). It may be noted that vast majority of the lower class respondents was of Harijans and tribals (16.5 per cent). According to our study, Khatris are the most prosperous single group. One other conclusion that may be reached from the above analysis is that there is much correlationship between upper caste/middle caste and upper/middle economic class, while there is no correlation between the lower caste and upper economic class or vice versa.

CORRELATION BETWEEN THE CASTE AND EMPLOYMENT OF WOMEN BEFORE MARRIAGE

The correlation between caste and employment of women before marriage was also drawn. As there is considerable variation in respect of employment of women belonging to different castes, this data of correlation reveals interesting findings, as shown in the table at appendix I. The highest incidence of the working women is from the Brahmin caste. Even in that, the Maharashtrian Brahmins are treated separately, because majority of the unmarried working women came from this single group. Several of the Maharashtrian respondents in this study mentioned that men in their community prefer working women. In this community, men are usually engaged in salaried jobs. For a service class man, a working wife is considered to be an asset. In several Maharashtrian homes, women earn as much as or even more than their husbands. In lower castes (Harijans) and certain other communities (Sonar, Yadev and tribal), not even one woman was found working at the time of marriage. In the lower castes, the main reason for this was that the girls were married at a very early age.

CORRELATION BETWEEN CASTE/COMMUNITY/TRIBE OF THE RESPONDENTS AND THEIR LEVEL OF EDUCATION

The correlation between the various castes/communities/tribes of the respondents and their level of education was analysed, and the result is indicated in the table at Appendix II.

The higher castes have better education as compared to the lower castes. No spouse from groups such as Yadev, Harijan and tribal has studied upto post-graduate level. Brahmin men and women are comparatively well-educated. Khatri men are comparatively well-educated, while women are not. All the Rajput women are illiterate. Maratha Kshatriya women have better education. Highest level of education was noticed in Kayasth community, in respect of both men and women. Education of Harijan men and women is poor. The highest rate of illiteracy was found among them. Jains were comparatively well-educated. No illiterate spouse was found among them. Sikh community men are comparatively well-educated, while women are not.

To conclude, the higher castes have better education, both among men and women, as compared with other castes, particularly lower caste.

RELIGIOUS TRAINING RECEIVED BY THE SPOUSES AT HOME BEFORE MARRIAGE

Our investigation revealed the following facts:

(*i*) 9 per cent of the males and 22.5 per cent of the females received intensive religious training in their homes before marriage. Such training included knowledge of religious books, main principles of religion, religious significance of festivals, *sanskaras*, religious observances like puja, fast, and so on. Most of these things were learnt by the younger generation through observation and instruction by older generation. Family worship was also significant in this connection.

(*ii*) 32.5 per cent males and 37.5 per cent females received "good training" at home.

(*iii*) 37.5 per cent males and 22 per cent females expressed the view that they did not receive adequate religious training at home.

Their parents and elders did not teach them much about their religion, while they received some knowledge about their religion from various sources like books, religious society, etc. It was found that religious training was more among Brahmins and Jains than among others. There was very little or no religious training in respect of spouses of lower castes and tribals.

Females received better religious training as compared with males. This may be due to two reasons. First, the female children are more submissive and they try to learn about religion and other traditions more willingly. Second, the males are given greater freedom to act in their own ways, while the females are taught to conform to traditions.

RELIGIOUS INCLINATIONS OF THE SPOUSES

Most religions teach against the dissolution of marital ties. Religious beliefs and practices tend to preserve the stability of marriage and the integration of the family. The integrating influence of religion has been pointed out by Burgess and Locke also in their studies.

All the respondents in our study said that they believed in God. However, the intensity of faith varied. The females were found more religious than the males. The investigator came across several women who have expressed deep faith in God. One young woman, who was abandoned by her husband for the sake of another woman said: "Though my husband left me, I know my God is still with me. I have complete trust and faith in Him. He keeps me happy. Since I have no family of my own, I get plenty of opportunity to help the poor, and the destitute around me. I feel that God is present in them, and by helping them in small ways, I serve God. If God wants, He can bring back my husband to me. Even if he does not come back, I will continue to serve God." Another young woman said: "The time of the breakdown of my marriage and the court proceedings were too much for me. Many a time, I thought of committing suicide. I have deep faith in God, and it only helped me to overcome all these difficulties." Yet, another highly educated young woman, who was abandoned by her husband, soon after the marriage, owing to some misunderstanding, said: "When my husband left me, I thought life had come to an end for me. I was too shocked. But by a strong power, I was drawn towards God. Today, all these past things appear only as a distant nightmare to me. Though I am in a job, most of my free time, I use in the service of God. I have great faith in God, and spend a lot of my spare time in reading and hearing the Holy Scriptures. In the midst of all turmoil, I sense the never-failing power of God. Sooner or later, I may devote my entire life for God's work by taking sanyas."

The above are some of the outstanding examples of the religious inclinations of women. It is observed that when problems arise and failures occur in life, women turn to God and matters concerning religion for comfort, consolation and strength.

Thus, we conclude that most of the male and female respondents had some sort of religious training in their families prior to marriage, most of the respondents have some positive religious inclinations, and women tend to have greater religious training and inclinations. It may be noted here that certain other aspects of the religious life of the spouses are discussed in Chapter 4.

GENERAL CULTURAL BACKGROUND OF THE COUPLES IN DIVORCE

By cultural background is meant here, a background conditioned by the customs, traditions, values and mores of the society. In a traditional and religious country like India, this sort of background is very significant. Of course, this background may also be influenced by the type of family, caste, education and other factors.

By traditional, we mean conforming to the traditions. By modern, we mean relating to the present or recent times. The concept of both traditional and modern are, of course, relative. We know that the processes of modernization in the contemporary society are facilitated by a number of other processes like industrialization, urbanization, democratization, secularization and westernization. The effects of such processes are on the Indian society too, which can be seen from the changes that are taking place in our traditional institutions like the joint family, caste, religion, education and recreation. The concept, aims and philosophy of marriage are also influenced by these processes. In fact, the legislation permitting divorce in the Hindu society itself is an example of change and modernization of the Hindu marriage and family. However, there is also a conflict between the traditional and the modern. According to Rama Mehta, one of the causes of divorce in her study was "conflict of modern and traditional attitudes in both men and women."[15] In the wider sociological perspective, this sort of phenomenon we call cultural lag. The husband, though educated and modern, wants the wife to be traditional, even though she is educated. The women enter marriage with a greater sense of their rights, while the men expect them to play the traditional role. These are mutually conflicting. Generally, the women suffer in this situation.

In our study, it is found that vast majority of the respondents (77 per cent males and 68 per cent females) come from traditional homes. It is also seen that there is not much disparity in the cultural background of the spouses (14 per cent of husbands and 22 per cent wives had semi-modern, and 8 per cent husbands and 10 per cent wives had modern cultural background).

[15]Rama Mehta, 1975, *op. cit.*, pp. 44-45.

It goes without saying that family background affects a person immensely. A boy or girl learn to expect from his/her spouse the pattern of relationship and behaviour he has observed in his home, between his parents, or married, older relatives. This is more true about the girls. In our society, it is the girl who is supposed to make adjustments, as she is the person who leaves her family of orientation and goes to a new home to create a family of procreation. Many a time, a girl may have to face different situations for which she was not trained or prepared at her parental home. Usually, in a new situation, a person calls to memory what her mother would have done at a similar situation, and tries to act accordingly. But, in India, every joint family has a subculture of its own. Thus, even after belonging to the same religion, caste and even sub-caste, family traditions may vary widely. If the differences between the families are too wide, problems of adjustment crop up. Many a time, people overcome them gradually, but some may fail in this aspect, and consequently, even risk the marriage. An outstanding example is of a medico girl from a modern family married to a member of a very traditional joint family. In her family, she has seen that people lead a life of complete freedom, and the married people, whether living with the parents or away, were completely independent. Every married member was earning sufficiently. The father also was in a prestigious job. So, money was never considered as a problem. But, when she came to her husband's home, she found a very different situation. Her husband, being the eldest son of the joint family, and very conscious of his responsibilities, had very different attitudes from hers. His father was nearing retirement. One sister was to be married off. A house of their own was to be constructed. For all these, he wanted to collect some money and hence tried to cut down expenditure as much as possible. This appeared very unjust to the wife. Her husband was asking her to sacrifice all the golden dreams, she had conceived of a marriage. Bitter strifes and quarrels arose between the couples. Both felt that their own viewpoint was the correct and just one, and hence, both were not prepared to make any adjustment. Quarrels grew day by day, and finally, they ended in divorce.

In another case, it was the wife who had come from a very traditional family, and, the husband hailed from a modern family. Though the wife's father was a medical doctor, he brought up his large family strictly in accordance with traditions. The respondent was the youngest child of the family, and, by the time she grew up, her parents were already old, and, became all the more interested in religious life, following strictly all the age-old customs and traditions. She was greatly influenced by her parents and became a close adherent of the old traditions. The husband, on the contrary, came from a very liberal home. His father was a high-ranking Government official. He was accustomed to luxurious life. Complete freedom was given to children in many matters. As a result, the children had developed very independent attitudes. For instance, there was no strict rule about the time one has to reach home. As a result, he was in the habit of going out, and did not return even late at night. The wife wanted that her husband should try to understand her viewpoints and compromise. But the matter ended in the court, and the marriage was dissolved. These cases illustrate the conflict between the traditional and modern in marital and familial situations.

CONCLUSIONS

In this chapter, certain general characteristics of the husbands and wives in divorce are stated. This will also acquaint us with the background of the couples, so as to relate the same with various patterns of their behaviour.

To state succinctly, the following are some of the important findings in this connection:

1. Vast majority (70 per cent) of the spouses lived in joint families, of different types. It is interesting to note, that, in spite of the greater incidence of joint families, divorce took place.

2. Majority of the respondents (91 per cent men and 82.5 women) is educated. 46.5 per cent men and 28 per cent women are graduates or post graduates. Surely, males are better-educated than females.

3. As for the castes/communities/tribes of the divorcees, it is found that the highest number of respondents are from Brahmin caste (41.5 per cent husbands and 40.5 per cent wives) belonging to different regions in India. Maharashtrian Brahmins are more prone to divorce than others.

4. On the basis of economic class, it is found that the highest percentage (72.5 per cent) is from middle class. The chief criteria

for the determination of the economic class were family income, occupation of the respondents, and the ancestral economic status.

5. The spouses in divorce belonged to various occupations like elite services, Doctors, Engineers, Lawyers, Professors, Teachers, Businessmen, Office Assistants, Technical Workers, Nurse, Farmers, Goldsmiths, Tailors, Drivers, Mill workers, and labourers. The percentage of women working at the time of marriage was very low (16.5 per cent). Of all occupations, maximum number (both for men and for women) was from the occupational group, "Office Assistants".

6. Correlation between caste and economic class of the respondents seems to indicate that there is much correlationship between upper caste/middle caste and upper/middle economic class, while there is no correlationship between lower caste and upper economic class or vice-versa.

7. Correlation between caste and employment of the female respondents showed that the tendency for unmarried women to work outside the home is more in castes such as Brahmin, Kayasth, and Vaisya (particularly Sindhi bania), while it is relatively less in caste such as Kshatriya, Sonar and Yadev;

8. Correlation between caste/community/tribe and education of the respondents showed that the higher castes have better education as compared to lower castes, both among men and women.

9. As for religious training at home, it was observed that Brahmins and Jains have more than others. There was very little or no religious training in respect of spouses of lower castes or tribals. Females received better religious training as compared with males.

10. Wives in divorce are more religiously inclined than husbands.

11. The divorced spouses belonged to different types of cultural background. Vast majority of the respondents come from homes where traditions are still in vogue. Conflict between the traditional and the modern cultural right in the family set-up was found to be a significant factor in some cases of marital dissolution.

Thus, it can be said that the socio-economic and cultural backgrounds are important determinants in marital disruptions.

Chapter 4

MARITAL RELATIONS AND ADJUSTMENT BEFORE MARRIAGE

INTRODUCTION

ADJUSTMENT in marriage is a significant phenomenon. Adjustment with the other partner is really vital. The relationship which a man has with a woman in marriage is perhaps the highest form of relationship, because it involves physical, emotional, spiritual and social aspects of life. Marital adjustment is an adjustment of two personalities which had different socio-cultural backgrounds. The success of family life very much depends upon the success in marital adjustment by the husband and wife. Marital maladjustment results in conflicts and tensions and many a time in divorce.

It may be said that perfect adjustment in marriage is hardly achieved, because each individual has his/her own personality. Further, one's own personality is not static; it changes from time to time. These days, however, there are greater problems of marital adjustment, owing to a number of reasons. The growing emphasis on personal freedom and identity in today's society is resulting in a sky-rocketing number of divorces, and a search for alternate life styles to marriage, especially in Western countries, according to a leading expert on marriage counselling, Dr. Laur Singer, one time president of the American Association of Marriage and Family Counsellors.[1]

According to Koos, "adjustment in marriage is the achievement of the expectations the couple have of their marriage.[2]

[1]*Indian Express*, News Report, Marriage now Anachronistic, February 28, 1973.

[2]Earn L. Koos, *Marriage*, Henry Holt & Co., N. York, 1958, p. 156.

According to Burgess and Locke, the basic factors in marital adjustment are personality characteristics, cultural backgrounds, social participation, economic status, response patterns, and sex desires.[3] In her study of the working women, Promilla Kapur defined marital adjustment as "that state of relationship in marriage in which there is an overall feeling in husband and wife of happiness and satisfaction with their marriage and with each other."[4]

In our study, an attempt has been made to study marital adjustment/maladjustment in relation to several factors such as: (*i*) type of marriage and family, (*ii*) premarital contacts/relations, (*iii*) caste/community/tribe, (*iv*) age at marriage, (*v*) expectations in marriage (*vi*) dowry, (*vii*) sexual life, (*viii*) collective participation of husband and wife in different activities like household work, attendance of social functions, (*ix*) economic and religious life, and (*x*) religious inclinations.

TYPE OF MARRIAGE OF THE DIVORCED COUPLES

Vast majority of the couples (91.5 per cent) had arranged marriages. 6.5 per cent of the couples had love marriage. One per cent of the couples had mixed marriage, that is, love-cum-arranged. In the remaining one per cent cases, marriage was arranged by the spouses themselves; they did not have responsible relatives to help them; they were teachers who had crossed middle age.

Arranged marriage is the traditional pattern of marriage in India. But, with the increasing urbanization, women's education and employment, social mobility and contact between sexes, love marriages are gradually increasing in number. In our study, only a few cases (6.5 per cent)had love marriage.

Further investigation in to small number of love marriage (6.5 per cent) revealed that in majority of these cases, the approval of parents was not forthcoming.

As for agencies involved in the arrangement of the marriage it was found that in majority of the cases (66 per cent), intermediaries like relatives and acquaintancss were used. Many a time marriage occurs between people whose family members are known to each

[3]Burgess & Locke, *The Family*, 1950, pp. 464-471.

[4]Promilla, Kapur, *Marriage and The Working Women in India*, 1972, p. 21,

other for a long time. In such cases marriage might occur even when one or both the parties are not very keen. In 5 per cent cases the couples agreed for the marriage only for their parents' sake because, their parents wanted to link up themselves through marriage with their friends' families. Advertisement in newspapers, magazines, etc. seemed to be another popular method for the arrangement of marriage. It is definitely helpful in many ways, and many are the couples happily married with the help of newspaper advertisements. Yet, there are chances of fraud in this method. One remarkable example may be cited here. Miss H is a 35 years old South Indian girl settled at Indore. As it was difficult to find a proper mate for her, and she was advancing in age, her brother advertised in *Sarita*, a popular journal in Hindi. Immediately, they got a response from a well-employed middle-aged gentleman. He came personally saying that he had none to help him in the matter of marital negotiations, and hence could not get married so far. The marriage was arranged soon, and the groom left for his job, after a few days, promising to take the bride as early as possible. After a few months only, it was detected that he was a fraud and had married twice before.

It was inquired if the marriages were arranged in a planned and thought-out manner. More than 50 per cent felt that their marriage was not a well-thought-out or planned one. They confessed that they entered into the matrimony without making sufficient enquiry about the partner and his/her background. A good number (37.5 per cent) of the candidates or parents just liked the boy or girl and arranged the marriage without bothering further.

The researcher is led to conclude that unplanned and unthoughtful marriages have greater chances of disruption as is found in about 40 per cent cases in our study. Duvall and Lewis have pointed out that "hasty, poorly-planned marriages" tend to result in divorce.[5]

PRE-MARITAL RELATIONS/CONTACTS

The pre-marital relations and contacts the spouses had among themselves and other members of the family were looked into. In this

[5]Duvalla, M. Evelyn, & Lewis, S. Dora, *Family Living*, The Macmillan Co., New York, 1950, pp. 233-37.

connection, our findings are mentioned below.

Matching of horoscope is an important precedent for marriage in most of the Hindu communities in India. In our study, except in the cases of lower castes and tribes, and love marriages, in majority of the cases, horoscope-matching was done before marriage was fixed. A good number of respondents felt that the other spouse produced bogus horoscope and that was the main reason for the failure of the marriage. Engagement is supposed to be an essential precedent to a normal marriage. Engagement is a formal announcement that both parties like each other and hence they have decided to get married. In our culture, particular engagement is the final decision to arrange marriage between a girl and a boy. The decision is taken by the parents/elders, with or without the consent of the marrying couple. In former times, it was only a ritual between elders of two families. Even after engagement, things continued as they were. It is only after the actual ceremony of marriage, or, *gauna*, a couple would start knowing each other. Many elders realize the need of young people getting familiar with each other before the marriage. As a result, some amount of freedom is given to the young couple after the engagement ceremony.

The incidence of engagement in our study was found to be as high as 98 per cent. In the remaining 2 per cent cases, marriage was arranged hurriedly and hence there was no time for engagement. In another two per cent cases, the couple had court marriage. They planned to keep their marriage a secret for some time, and therefore, did not want to have any engagement. In three per cent cases, the couples had love marriage unapproved by parents, and, so, there was no engagement.

The interval between engagement and marriage is also important for marital stability. In our study, it was found that in 12 per cent cases, the period was below one month, in 20.5 per cent cases between one and three months, 16 per cent cases between 3 and 6 months, in 22.5 per cent cases between 6 months and one year, and in 22 per cent cases between one and two years or more.

Actual pre-marital relations between the husband and wife was investigated into. It was found that in 45 per cent cases, the partners had just seen each other. "Showing the girl" is a formality in many communities. A boy and girl are allowed to just see each other. In 35 per cent cases, little more free contacts, like going together for movies, shopping, attending functions, etc., were allowed. In 20 per cent cases, no contact existed between the spouses before marriage.

PRE-MERITAL CONTACT IN DIFFERENT COMMUNITIES

Efforts were made to draw the correlation between caste/community/tribe and the type of pre-marital contacts between the spouses. This will reveal a particular community's attitude towards such matters, or, in other words, how far a community has changed from the traditional or conservative pattern.

The Kshatriyas and the tribals were the two communities which kept up the tradition to the greatest extent (57 per cent of these couples did not have any pre-marital contact whatsoever). Among the tribals, early marriages were in large number, and hence, the question of contact between the spouses does not arise. But among the Kshatriyas, though adult marriages were found, any type of contact between the boy and the girl was not permitted. This is more so, among the Rajputs. They observe *purdah* and it is the boy's mother or other female relatives who see the girl. Among the scheduled caste *Harijans* too, early marriages are very common, and so the boys and girls do not get opportunity to have contact with each other. It is found that majority of the people in several castes allowed the boy and girl just to see each other. The percentage of the Sikhs is the maximum under this category. Free contact between the spouses was also found in several communities. The maximum incidence in this respect was of Brahmins (27 per cent). Out of the Brahmins also, the Maharashtrians are more liberal and most of them had free contacts before marriage. Gujrati Brahmins too allow very free contacts between engaged couples.

AGE AT MARRIAGE

The age of the divorced spouses at the time of their marriage is shown in Appendix III.

It is generally agreed that the age at which a person enters into marital relationship definitely affects his/her capacity for marital adjustment. One of the reasons for child marriage in India is that if a girl is sent to her husband's home right from early years, she completely adjusts and identifies with the customs and traditions of her husband's home. This might be true to some extent. But, one should not forget that marriage is a continual process of adjustment which requires a lot of understanding and wilful sacrifice on the part of both the partners. These capabilities develop gradually. We cannot expect mature behaviour from a very young boy or girl. Very late marriages may also create difficulties for adjustment.

Our analysis of the age at marriage showed that the age-group (16-20) had the highest incidence in the case of wives (40 per cent) and the age-group 21-25 had the highest incidence (48 per cent) in the case of husbands. 60 per cent girls got married before they completed the age of 20. 12 per cent of the wives and 4 per cent of the husbands were married before they attained the age of 15 years. It has been calculated that in the present study, the mean age at marriage in the case of husband is 24.83 and that of the wife 19.13.

Differences in the Age between the Spouses

Sociologists and social workers generally regard disparity in the age between the spouses as a causative factor in the creation of family tensions and maladjustments. Speaking about the age differences of mates in the American society, Folsom has pointed out that "there is no moral taboo or legal restriction but marriages of great age difference are regarded as undesirable, especially when the woman is older."[6] In the study of Fonseca, it was found that the median age difference of the couples was seven years.[7]

In our study, 99 per cent cases, the husband was older than the wife. The highest number in any particular age-difference group was of 45 years (20 per cent). The highest age difference observed between the spouses was 17-18 years, and this was found only in one per cent cases. The mean difference in age between the spouses in the study as a whole was found to be 4.47 years, that is, on an average, the husbands are older than wives by say about 5 years. It was inquired from the respondents as to what should be the ideal age-difference between the two spouses, and also, who should be older. All the respondents, males as well as females, opined that ideally, the husband should be older than the wife. Further,

[6]Folsom, K. Joseph, *Family and the Democratic Society*, John Wiley & Sons, Inc,, N. York, Fifth Printing, p. 9.

[7]Fonseca, *op. cit.*, 1966, p. 46,

majority of the respondents (82 per cent) said that the ideal difference in age between the two spouses should be 3-5 years.

Consent of the Spouses for Marriage

Consent of both the bride and the bridegroom is necessary for a proper marriage. If the couples are joined together in marriage without their consultation and consent, it is likely to create difficulties later on. Therefore, this matter was also investigated. In vast majority (72.5 per cent males and 55 per cent females) the spouses were consulted and they gave their consent for the marriage. It, however, was revealed that seeking their consent was meaningless, as the elders decide everything and then only the young people are consulted. One young man said, "My father had already given word to the girl's father before he asked me to see the girl. At the very first sight, I did not like the girl and I informed my father of the same. But my father said he had already given word and therefore I had no choice but to marry." In another case, Mrs S. said "I had no father, and I was the only child of my mother. My mother's friend had a son and he persuaded his mother to ask for my hand in marriage. I knew the boy from childhood, and never liked him. But I was helpless because of my mother had consented for the marriage." 8.5 per cent of the husbands and 14 per cent of the wives were too young to be consulted, at the time of marriage and hence, the question of consultation or consent did not arise. 8 per cent of the males and 18 per cent of the females were not consulted at all, although they could have been. The parents decided the marriage of their accord, and thought it unnecessary to involve the opinion of the youngsters. 2.5 per cent males and 4.5 per cent females were married against their wishes. From the above analysis, we may conclude that even today, a good number of marriages are arranged without ascertaining the wishes of the actual partners involved in marriage, resulting in marital maladjustments and dissolution; women's wishes and choices are more neglected as compared with those of men.

EXPECTATIONS IN MARRIAGE

According to some sociologists, "expectations are approved patterns of behaviour transmitted to the person through communications."[8] The expectations to which a person responds are patterns of behaviour he expects from others and which he may expect from himself. Once a person incorporates these group expectations in himself, he uses them in weighing and criticising his potential future behaviour as well as the behaviour of others.

Society is a bundle of roles and statuses of its members. In these, the mutual expectations are very important, and these expectations are institutionalized, and so, become part of our culture. In the institutions of marriage and family, we have the imaginations of the expectations about different members. For instance, we formulate the image of a husband, wife, father, mother, son, daughter, daughter-in-law, father-in-law, mother-in-law, and others on the basis of role expectations and traits of personality. A man marries a woman, or a woman marries a man, with great expectations, with regard to their roles in future. But if those expectations are not fulfilled, complaints, frustrations, conflicts and tension start, which may even lead to marital disruptions and dissolutions.

In our study, husbands of all economic classes most frequently expected of their wives that they should be good cooks. Food is one of the basic needs of life, and, it is usually observed that men are fond of good food cooked at home. Eating outside the home has not yet become common or popular. So, it is but natural for the men to expect of their wives to cook well.

The second commonest expectation was that a wife should take care of the personal needs of the husband. This meant cooking food of his choice, serving the food, washing and ironing of clothes, mending the cloth, and assisting him as is required under various circumstances. The third important expectation is that a wife should be affectionate. This expectation was much more in the upper and middle classes as compared to lower classes. It is seen that it is the educated and the higher income group people who give importance to the emotional needs. For lower class people, physical needs are of greater importance. The fourth expectation of the husbands about their wives was that they should keep the house well which among other things meant cleaning, sweeping, dusting, washing of utensils, physical arrangement of furniture, etc. In this matter too, the upper and the middle classes give more importance as compared to lower class people. The fifth expecta-

[8]Burgess & Locke, *The Family*, *op. cit.*, p. 277.

tion was that the wife should be submissive to the husband. In other words, the wives should submit to the wishes of their husbands in all matters. This expectation was less frequent in the upper and middle classes. Sixthly, the wife will supplement the family income. However, no upper class man expected his wife to work. While a little more than one-third of the middle class husbands wanted their wives to work and earn, vast majority of the lower class men wanted the same. This is obvious because of the poor economic condition of the lower class people. The seventh important expectation of the husband is in regard to the adjustment with their parents and relatives. By adjustment is meant paying the parents and relatives of the husband due respect and consideration, serving them and helping them. Majority of the upper class, about one-third of the middle class and a few of the lower class husbands expressed this expectation.

To conclude, it may be mentioned that most of the husbands. had high expectations about their wives. Most of these expectations are traditional ones. In other words, despite the fact that most of the husbands are educated and are engaged in urban pursuits, they retained the traditional expectations. Elsewhere, we mentioned of cultural lag as one of the causes of marital conflicts, tensions and disruptions. This is true in the case of the expectations of the husbands about their wives.

The wives also had great expectations about their husbands. Women of all economic classes expected that their husbands should love them and provide for their physical needs. The psychological aspects of love and fulfilment of physical needs were mentioned together by the wives. Several of them considered the latter as the natural outcome of the former. Even the working women felt that their husbands should provide for their needs and should not depend on the wife's salary.

The second expectation expressed by the wives is taking them out for cinema, picnic, etc. Girls in urban areas needed protection and they were escorted by parents or other relatives till the time of their marriage. As a result, women develop a dependent type of personality. After marriage, this dependence is transferred to the husband. Moreover, most of the wives are economically dependent upon their husbands, and, hence, they cannot look after thmeselves in any matter in which money is involved.

The third expectation was that their husbands should care for them more than the husband's parents and relatives. The frequency of this expectation is comparatively less in the lower classes. Some of the wives felt that their husbands continued to love and take care of their parents and relatives more than their wives.

The fourth expectation expressed by the wives is that the husbands should help them in times of troubles and problems. One of the important problems is adjustment with the in-laws.

To be treated as equal partners was the fifth expectation of the wives about their husbands. Two-thirds of the upper class women expressed this view. Also, one third of the middle class and a small number of lower class women.

The sixth expectation was relating to the bringing of gifts for the wives by the husbands. In this case also, the number of upper class women was two-third, while that of the middle class was less than one-third. In lower classes, this expectation appeared rare.

To conclude, it may be said that women of all the economic classes wanted their husbands to love them and take care of their physical needs. Expectations of being treated as an equal partner and bring gifts was observed mostly in upper class cases.

Correlation between the Educational Standard of the Women and their Expectation

An attempt to correlate the educational standard of the women and their expectations in married life was made. It revealed that (*i*) the expectation of love, especially, care of physical needs, was more found in the less-educated sections. As the education of women increased, their expectation that the husband should provide for the physical needs gradually decreased; (*ii*) the desire to be taken out for cinema, outing, etc. was more expressed by the relatively less educated women. This may also be due to the fact that many of the well-educated women were in employment, and hence, less dependent; (*iii*) the desire to be cared for more than the husband's relatives was comparatively more in the well-educated groups, that is, those who are educated above high school standard; (*iv*) the desire for equality and educational level of the female respondents showed a definite correlation. No women below the undergraduate level said that they desired equality with men. Among the under-graduates too, the incidence was comparatively low. It was highest in women of graduate and post-graduate level. Similarly, the desire for special symbols of affection like gifts was also found in the higher educated groups. These go to prove that higher the education, greater the demand by women for equality, identity, and demands for expression of love and affection.

DOWRY AND DIVORCE

Dowry is "a payment made to the groom on the occasion of a marriage by the father or kinsmen of the bride, or the property brought by the latter into marriage."[9]

According to the Dowry Prohibition Act, "dowry means any property or valuable security given or agreed to be given either directly or indirectly (*i*) by one pary to marriage to the other party to the marriage, or (*ii*) by the parents of either party to a marriage or by any other person, to either party to the marriage or to any other person; at or before or after the marriage, as consideration for the marriage."[10]

Dowry is related to divorce inasmuch as the giving or taking of dowry creates conflicts and tensions in some families which may ultimately result in divorce too. In the study of marital disruptions in Bombay city by Fonseca, it was found that dowry was also a cause for marital discord, disorganization and desertion.[11] In the study of Rama Mehta also, it was found that dowry was an important issue, the women were married with dowry and that was one of the main considerations in the final settlement of the marriage negotiations.[12]

In our study, dowry was paid in over ninety per cent (91.5 per cent) cases. However, there was variation in the kind and amount of dowry in different castes/communities/tribes. The demand for dowry was highest among the Banias, Jain and Kayasth communities. Here, the boy's party put their demand before marriage. Cash payments, furniture, radio, mixer, refrigerator, almirah, cot, and even motor-car were included. Dowry is found among Sikhs, Sonars, Yadavs and Khatris also. In the scheduled castes, dowry in the form of cash was not paid. Utensils, silver ornaments, and small items of gold and silver were things usually given as dowry

[9]H.P., *Fairchild Dictionary of Sociology*, 1944, p. 99.
[10]*The Dowry Prohibition Act*, 1961 (No. 28 of 1961) Secs. 1 & 2.
[11]Fonseca, *op. cit.*, p. 82.
[12]Rama Mehta, *op. cit.*, p. 40.

among them. Demand of dowry by the boy's party was not found among them. The girl's party gave whatever they could afford. Among the spouses of tribal origin also, dowry was not demanded. Parents gave to their girls gifts out of free will. Among the Gujratis also, huge dowry was not found. In fact, it was observed that the groom's party gave to the bride's party valuable gifts in the form of clothes and ornaments. Among Maharashtrian Brahmins also, dowry was not demanded usually. In 8.5 per cent cases where no dowry was involved, it was found that there was love/self-arranged marriages.

Dowry as a Problem in Marriage

There is much publicity about dowry as a serious problem in urban India today. Our data shows that only in 18 per cent cases of our study, dowry appeared as an acute problem. In these 18 per cent cases, dowry became a major hindrance in marital happiness. Even after the couple started living together, the husbands, or more often, the in-laws, troubled the wives in many ways. Taunting, slighting in the presence of others, criticising, not providing food and other physical provisions, beating and tormenting were some of the ways in which the girls were harassed. In some cases, the quarrels arose because the girls' parents could not give the full dowry promised at the time of marriage. In several other cases, though the girls' parents have paid the full amount of the dowry, the husband and/or the in-laws became greedy and demanded more and more money. One highly-educated and well-employed lady said, "I was paid a considerable amount of money, ornaments, clothes and utensils as well as other household articles as dowry. Just, after the marriage, my mother-in-law and husband demanded most of these things including my saris. They said, a sister-in-law was to be married off immediately, and she was to be given these as dowry. I gave away the things willingly. I thought, after all, I and my husband are earning well and we can buy things gradually. After six months of marriage, my husband asked for a sum of twenty thousand rupees. My parents are not very well-to-do. Still they managed this amount for my sake. My husband had said that this is a loan, and it will be returned later. After a few months, he started asking for more money. This time, I got wild and said I will die rather than asking for more money from my parents. My husband said plainly that he married me only for the sake of money, and he has no interest, if I could not pay the money. I tried my best to make him understand but he remained adamant. I was giving him all the money I was receiving in the form of salary; yet, he was not satisfied. Finally, we had to part for good." Another woman and her infant son were locked and made to starve for two days, just because the wife's parents could not make payment of a part of the dowry promised to be paid at the time of marriage. Another girl said tearfully, "the whole problem started at the time of marriage. My mother-in-law was given a sari by my parents, according to the custom. She did not like the colour of the sari. Later, my parents promised to replace it by a better one. But, she and my husband were very much annoyed. They said by giving such a sari, we have insulted them. Troubles started right from that point. They began criticizing about all other things received as dowry. I was never given any peace of mind." Another young girl was driven out of the house just after two months of marriage, because her parents could not meet the demand of more dowry. Yet, another young girl was often beaten by her husband and in-laws because she failed to bring more dowry. In another interesting case, the woman said, "my husband and I were not allowed any privacy, because my in-laws were not satisfied with the dowry. My mother-in-law and brother-in-law used to sleep in the same room where I and my husband slept."

The above are some of the typical examples of the miserable tales of dowry victims.

Dowry as a custom or practice is different from the dowry-problem as such, for, although dowry was found in 91.5 per cent cases of our study, only in 18 per cent cases, dowry emerged as a problem as such. The dowry problem was most intense in the Jain community. The next major group in which dowry problem was acute is the Vaishyas.

SPOUSES AND THEIR EARLY DAYS OF MARRIAGE

Early days of married life are very important in relation to marital adjustment. It is during this period, the spouses enter into close physical and emotional relationship in their marital life. It is in this period that they get to know each other intimately. In Western culture, soon after the wedding, the couple go for honeymoon. The honeymoon period is "a short holiday period after marriage, which is spent by a newly-wedded pair in travelling or otherwise, before settling down to their new life together."[13] In Indian society also, some educated couples go for honeymoon or a post-marital outing. Some go to health resorts like Kashmir, or places of pilgrimage like Ujjain and Onkareshwar near Indore, or Banaras in Uttar Pradesh. This depends upon their economic condition also. Some others visit relatives and friends and some others go for movies. Thus, although we do not have honeymoon as it may be practised in the west, yet the early period of married life is spent by the couple by remaining together for intimate relationships. Several matters concerning adjustment/maladjustment in life may be found right in this period. These may, later on, determine the chances of stability or instability in marriage. Efforts for adjustment are very much required. It is because of these that some sociologists have held that "in general, the divorce frequency is highest in the early period of married life."[14]

In our study, by "early days" is meant, upto a few weeks or three months after marriage. An analysis of the type of husband-wife relationship in the early days of marriage shows that 75 per cent of the couples "liked" each other, or "loved" or "loved very much" during the period. In the case of 25 per cent couples, in some (11 per cent) they "did not like" each other, in some (3 per cent), they "hated" each other, and in the remaining (11 per cent), they had "no relationship" whatsoever. In these 11 per cent cases, the husband-wife relationship right from the very beginning was in trouble. Either they separated immediately after marriage or they were married in such an age that they did not understand the real meaning of conjugal happiness.

It seems that the level of education of the couples played an important role in the husband-wife relationship in the early days of marriage, more so, the education of the female spouses. The female spouse is the one who has to join her spouse, and not *vice versa.* Most of the adjustments are to be made by her. Also, education of the female spouse affects the family life much more than the education of the male, because it is the female who manages the home. Thirdly, the status of the male in the family is not much

[13]H.P. Fairchild, *Dictionary of Sociology*, ibid, p. 143.

[14]P. Robert, Winch, & Robert, McGinnis, *The Family*. Henry Holt and Company, New York, 1959, p. 522.

affected, whether he is educated or not. Our study showed that the female graduates had closest love relationship with their husbands during the early days of marriage. The lesser-educated group did not say that they had very close relationship with their husbands. Not only emotional, but also other socio-economic factors (such as child marriage, facilities for privacy, family traditions, etc.) must have affected the relationship between the spouses in the lesser-educated groups. Most of them belonged to the lower, or lower-middle class, where they lived in over-crowded houses which do not provide any privacy for free husband-wife relationship.

SEXUAL LIFE OF THE DIVORCED SPOUSES

Satisfactory sexual life is an essential factor for a happy married life. This is the bond which unites the two partners. Sex is a strong biological urge in any mature being. This instinct is essential for the perpetuation of the species. Unlike in animal society, in human society, sexual instinct is controlled and regulated by social customs, values and norms. Marriage is the only socially approved institution through which sex instinct can be satisfied and children born. In human beings, sex is not merely a biological need ; it is closely interwoven with the emotional life. Sex is a natural outcome of a deep affectional bond between the husband and wife. If a person does not enter into sexual life with this attitude, it becomes an almost superficial and meaningless act. Baber has stated that "in any tentative list of the basic causes of marital unhappiness, there is general agreement that sex incompatibility with its myriad contacts with other aspects of marriage should rank high."[15] According to Sait, "there is general agreement that sexual maladjustment is an underlying cause in most cases of marital friction."[16] But, it is important to realize that it is the sex relationship in its emotional as well as physical aspects that plays a major part in married life. Sexual maladjustment in most cases is not primarily a physical matter but due to psychological causes.

The sexual satisfaction in the life of the spouses was investigated in our study. It was found that majority (71.5 per cent) of the res-

[15]R.E. Baber, *op. cit.*, p. 238.

[16]Sait, Una Bernard, *New Horizones for the Family*, The Macmillan Company, New York, Third Printing, pp. 584-85.

pondents were satisfied in sexual life. In the remaining cases, the respondent were either partially satisfied or not satisfied at all. In a good number of cases (16.5 per cent), it was found that the sexual dissatisfaction was not due to sexual incapacity of either spouse, but mainly due to emotional problems. One young wife said, "we had satisfying relationship with each other in the beginning. I have two children also. But once my husband started indulging in bad habits, I started hating him, I had developed an aversion towards him, and I hated to have sex with him. For some time, I put up with him, but later, I could not." Mrs N., a young medical graduate said, "it is not that my husband is unattractive. In the beginning, I enjoyed my relationship with him. But, as I came to know about his relationship with some other women, I could not persuade myself to have sex with him any more." Mrs V., a very young pretty girl, said, "I could not enjoy sexual relationship with my husband, because he had some sort of venereal disease. In my mind I always felt an aversion towards him when he tried to have relationship with me." Another young divorcee, Mrs U., said," Once, my in-laws tried to trap me to have sexual relationship with some other man for the sake of money. My husband was not present at that time. When he came back, I told him about this incident. He did not show any reaction and I started hating my husband from that moment, and never had sexual relationship with him any longer."

Somewhat similar instances were narrated by male respondents too. Mr B. said: "I married a lady of my own caste, who was introduced by some acquaintance. Just after a few weeks, I came to know that she was a woman of bad character, and, that she had relations with serveral men before. I stopped all sorts of contact with her." Another male respondent, Mr G., said, "I had a child marriage, and for several years, I had not even seen my wife. All of a sudden, *gauna* was done, and my wife was brought. We had lived just for a few days, when I started realizing that my wife was pregnant. I told my elder sister-in-law about my doubt, When enquiry was made, my wife accepted her guilt."

Many a time physical or mental incapacity of one of the spouses also may be the cause for dissatisfaction in sexual life. One young wife, Mrs A. said, "I lived at my husband's place for more than two years. I never had a satisfying sexual relation with my husband. He was partially impotent."

Another very young female divorcee, Mrs S. said: "It is true that I lived with my husband for a few months, and even have a daughter. But I never had a satisfying relationship with him. He was a drug-addict, and was always in a state of intoxication. I don't think that he ever knew what he was doing." Yet another woman said, "My husband was mad. Right from the time of marriage, his behaviour was always abnormal. Though I lived with him for some time, and have a daughter, I never had a satisfying sexual relationship with him. I was afraid to be alone with him especially at night. In the middle of the night, he will get up and try to throttle me or abuse me." A young educated (postgraduate) man said: "I never had any satisfactory relationship with my wife. Right from the time of marriage, my wife's behaviour was abnormal, and I used to feel uneasy. After a few weeks of marriage, she became pregnant. From that time onwards, her behaviour became all the more abnormal. Only later, I came to know that she was a mental patient, even before the marriage."

Impotency of the husband accounted for 3.5 per cent cases where sexual relationship could not be established between the husband and wife. Impotency can be temporary or permanent as revealed in the present study. Some husbands who could not perform their sexual duties due to physical incapacity in the first marriage, could do so in the second marriage, and have children too. It is possible that with one woman a man is not able to establish sexual relation, while with another woman, this may be possible.

Physical incapacity of the wife was responsible for unsuccessful sexual life in some cases. In all the cases malformation of the female genitalia was the cause. In one case under study, a girl had no vagina, and this was detected after the marriage. She was operated upon, and a vagina was made artificially. But even then, she could not perform sexual intercouse, and so, divorce was granted on this ground.

In some cases, husbands did not take any initiative for the sexual act. One highly-educated lady, Mrs N. said, "I lived with my husband for quite some time, but he never showed any interest in me. He was in love with somebody else, and wanted to marry her. His parents did not allow that marriage, and got me married with him. He was an extremely sensitive person, and could not forget the other person. Because of this, he could not have any relationship with me." Another young wife said: "Right after the time I reached my husband's house after marriage, I found that my husband was surrounded by a number of girls. He introduced them as his 'sisters.' But, even after late night, these 'sisters' were not going away, and were moving with my husband with unusual freedom. He was more interested in them and did not seem to take note of me. We slept too late after all his friends departed, and by that time, he was too sleepy. Just after a few days, he had to leave for a new place. Though I went once, I was asked to return."

Some husbands did not show interest in their wives, because of their love affairs elsewhere. Some husbands had strong suspicion about their wives and hence did not want to have relationship with them. One young husband said: "The moment I saw my wife I knew that she was a girl of bad character. The marriage was arranged by my parents, and I had not seen the girl before marriage. Right on the first night, I said to the girl that she is a person of loose morals. The girl accepted her fault and promised to be better in future. But I had decided not to have anything with her. The very next morning, I informed my relatives about my decision. They tried to persuade me to accept her, but I plainly refused. I left the house, and returned only after she was taken away by her parents."

In certain cases in our study, the women were not interested to establish sexual relation, as they had love affairs elsewhere and they gave in for the present marriage only because of the pressure of parents. In some cases, the spouses did not get time and facility to establish sexual contact immediately after marriage. Sickness, death in the family, and lack of leave, etc., were some of the reasons. By the time these hindrances were removed, the other spouses had decided to quit. Thus, the marriage finished before it ever started. Our main conclusions, therefore, in this section are:

(*i*) Although in majority of the cases in the present study, sex dissatisfaction was not the only cause, in about 30 per cent cases, it was.

(*ii*) Sex-satisfaction is a very complex phenomenon; it has not only physiological reference, but also psychological, and social, as pointed out by sociologists like Sait mentioned above. William Ogburn, another sociologist, who had extensive research on family sociology, has pointed out that "if there is the sex aspect of marriage, this failure may be due to psychological and cultural factors that impinge on sex and disturb its operation."[17]

(*iii*) Sex is an important aspect of marital life, and its non-fulfilment will cause serious repercussions in marital adjustment. Each case of this type is to be viewed in its own perspective.

PRIVACY IN THE LIFE OF SPOUSES IN DIVORCE

Time and sufficient privacy to be together especially during the newly-wed period is absolutely necessary. This is the time when a couple has strong emotional and physical attraction towards each other. In a traditional society like India, the emotional and physical needs of the young couple are many a time neglected. In Joint families, where several nuclear families live together, to get any sort of privacy during day time is rather very difficult, if not impossible. Many urban families have inadequate residential accommodation, and they live in over-crowded and congested areas of the city. Hence, to have privacy during nights is also difficult in many cases.

This aspect of the marital life of the spouses in divorce was investigated in the present study. It was found that 42 per cent of the respondents did not have any privacy or had insufficient privacy. The problem of privacy was more acute in the lower classes where several family members used to live in a single hutment or in one or two rooms. The problem of privacy was noticed in the middle class families also. It was revealed that this problem (absence of privacy) along with other factors resulted in marital maladjustment and dissolution.

DIVORCED SPOUSES AND THE EATING PATTERNS

Cooking and eating of food is a very significant aspect of family living. The participation of various members of family in the preparation and eating of food is also important, because it manifests the inter-action and integration of the family.

[17]William F. Ogburn & F. Mayer, Nimkoff, *Sociology*, Eur-Asia Publishing House, New Delhi, Second Indian Reprint, 1972, p. 510.

Data collected in the present study show that in a majority cases (71 per cent), the members of the family did not eat together. This may have contributed towards marital disharmony at least to certain extent directly or indirectly. The main reasons for not eating together were unfavourable family traditions, inconvenient working hours of the husband, and the dislike of the husband in this matter.

ATTENDANCE OF SOCIAL FUNCTIONS BY THE SPOUSES DURING MARRIED LIFE

Social functions included marriage parties, religious functions, cultural functions, picnics, excursions and clubs. In our study, it was found that only in 28 per cent cases, the couples attended such functions together. This is indicative of the absence of unity in the family of the couples in divorce, which may have been responsible, at least to a certain extent, for their marital disruptions.

It was also found that the incidence of the husband and wife attending the social functions together was maximum in the case of upper class, less in the middle class, and the least in the lower class.

OCCUPATION OF THE SPOUSES AT THE TIME OF DIVORCE

The occupation of the respondents at the time of marriage has already been mentioned in Chapter 3, 'The Background of the Spouses in Divorce'. (Occupation of the husbands and wives at the time of marriage). But here, we are dealing with the occupation of the respondents at the time of their divorce. Our data in this connection is shown in the table at Appendix IV.

It is found that 92 per cent of the men had regular employment. A small number of men (8 per cent) could not secure any gainful employment even after marriage. In such cases, unemployment of the husband and consequent economic hardship were major causes for cutting short their marriages.

Only 34.5 per cent of the women-respondents were employed outside the home just before divorce. Earlier (Chapter 3—The Background of the Spouses in Divorce) we have seen that only 16.5 per cent of the women were employed at the time of marriage. This shows that 18 per cent of women took up employment after marriage. This was to meet the situation arising out of divorce. Even when the divorce proceedings were in progress, these women had to take up employment. Mrs R. a young woman employed as an office assistant said, "I belong to a well-to-do family. None of my sisters work. When I found that my husband does not stick to any job and his income is very insufficient and irregular, I decided to take up a job." An upper class woman said: "When I got married, my husband was a prosperous business man. But gradually, he lost his business and it became difficult for us to feed our three children. I decided to take up a job. Luckily, because of my good academic record, I was able to secure a good job without any difficulty."

As for the men, there is some change in the employment position before the marriage and after the marriage. Before marriage, 25.5 per cent were unemployed, whereas after marriage, only 8 per cent were unemployed. This is because, some were just students at that time as mentioned in the previous chapter (Chapter 3). These newly-employed men became businessmen, office assistants, technical workers, and labourers.

Before we close this section it may be stated that,

(*i*) although the number of men employed has increased after marriage (that is, by the time of divorce), as compared with the time of marriage, it did not necessarily mean that the economic condition of the family improved. This is because of the negligence and unhealthy personality traits of the husbands.

(*ii*) The number of women-workers has definitely increased after marriage. Most of the new entrants started working because of the indifference of their husbands or their inadequate income. After marriage, children were born, who were also to be supported.

(*iii*) Economic problems do contribute towards marital disruptions.

Satisfaction of the Wives with the Occupation of their Husbands

In our society, even today, the husband is considered as the bread-winner. Even when a woman is working, her earning is considered just as a supplementary source of income, and not the main one.

In our study, only 46.5 per cent women are satisfied with the occupation and income of their husbands. It is found that most of the women who expressed dis-satisfaction are working-women.

Working Hours of the Husband

Working hours of the husband, who is also the head of the family, is very important, because it influences the interaction between the spouses, and also between the parents and the children. When people have a fixed working time, they tend to form a definite routine for the day-to-day life. In this routine, a definite time is made available to be spent with members of the family. This is of great value for marital adjustment and familial solidarity.

In our study, it is seen that 45 per cent husbands had regular working hours. 30 per cent men had irregular working hours. These included civil services, touring jobs, doctors, technical hands, private businessmen, transport workers, and others. In these occupations, people do not get sufficient time to be with their family. This, in turn, creates dissatisfaction in women. They would seek emotional, or even physical relationship elsewhere. The problem of time was maximum in the case of businessmen. Mr M., an upper-class businessmen, said: "My working hours are so long and irregular that I could not be sure when I will reach home. Often, I would reach home only late at night. My wife, an educated and active young woman, got tired of this routine. Soon after sending the children to school, she also started going out. In the beginning, it was only to while away time, and to kill boredom. But later, she developed certain undesirable relationship." Another husband who had to be away several days and nights every month on account of his job-tour said, "In my absence, my wife started illicit relations with other men. Through one of them, she had a child also. I took divorce only on this account." A sales representative, who had to be out of home for twenty days a month disclosed: "Ours was a love marriage and I was very fond of my wife. We both were quite young, and my wife was still a student. When I used to be on tour, she used to go to club, with her male friends. In the beginning, I did not know about it. By the time I came to know the full details, it was too late. She lost all interest in me."

Twelve per cent of the spouses were staying apart on account of their occupations. Those who were in military service could not take their wives along.

Some men were in such jobs where frequent transfers were involved. Hence, it was very inconvenient to have the family along with them.

In some cases, the wives were employed in their own home-towns or states and they were forced to go back on duty, just after marriage.

Working Hours of the Wives

Vast majority (65.5 per cent) of the women had no work at all, outside the home, and they were fulltime house-wives. Even when women were working, they preferred jobs which have regular hours of work. Further, their employment did not affect the management of the home. Either they finished the household work themselves, and then went to work, or, they have done part of the work and for the remaining, took help of maid-servants. All the working females felt that their employment or working hours did not adversely affect their family life.

Therefore, with reference to the data concerning our study, we are led to conclude that women's working outside the home need not be a detrimental factor to marital and familial welfare, harmony and cohesion. Most of the working women in the study preferred such jobs as they could look after the family and do the jobs simultaneously.

Of course, in a few cases, the wives left the husband's home soon after the marriage on the pretext of joining duty and later refused to return. In all these cases, however, it was not the employment as such which caused the separation; the wives either had emotional attachments elsewhere, or did not like the home environment of the husband, and, therefore, did not want to go back. There are a few cases in which the wives took up employment against the wishes of their husbands. In all these cases, it was seen that the women went to work not because they were career-conscious, or they wanted to shirk the marital/familial obligations, but because their husbands were not supporting them well. In her study of the working women, Promilla Kapur found that "wife's employment as such does not affect marital adjustment favourably or adversely."[18] She has further held that the fact of wife's having to be in job out of economic necessity as such did not much affect her marital adjustment adversely. Locke has also concluded that "gainful employment of the wife outside the home is not associated with marital adjustment or maladjustment."[19]

MATTERS CONCERNING MONEY AND THE SPOUSES IN DIVORCE

Economic condition of the family is very important in marital adjustment. In our study, it was investigated as to (*i*) who, in the family of the divorced couples, controlled the family purse, (*ii*) how was the agreement between the spouses regarding the spending of money, and (*iii*) the general economic condition of the family with reference to debt/saving.

Who, in the Family of the Divorced Couples, Controlled the Family Purse

In maximum number of cases (40.5 per cent), the parents of the husbands controlled the family purse. In the joint family pattern, the parents continue to exercise control over money and other important family affairs even after they have stopped earning. In 21.5 per cent cases, the husband himself kept the money. The incidence of wives managing the money was very low (5 per cent). This shows that in most of the families, even today, the position of the wife is inferior, and she is either not trusted, or not treated as equal partner in money matters. In 5 per cent cases, the purse was open to both the husband and wife. They both spent as and when need arose. In 3.5 per cent cases, the husband kept his, and the wife kept her money separately. Needless to say that this happened in those families where the wife was also working and earning.

To conclude, (*i*) the traditional joint family pattern of the *karta* or the head of the family keeping the purse is followed, to a great extent, in the families in our study, and (*ii*) wives as such do not have much control over the purse even now.

[18]Promilla, Kapur, *Marriage and the Working Women in India*, 1972, p. 558.

[19]Locke, J. Harvey, *Adjustment in Marriage*: *A Comparison of a Divorced and Happily Married Group*, N.Y., 1951, pp. 358-60, quoted by F. Robert, Winch, & Robert McGinnis, *The Family*, 1959, p. 487.

Agreement of the Spouses Regarding Spending of Money

It was seen that 47 per cent of the couples had no disagreement in the way in which the money was spent. 32 per cent disagreed with each other in matters regarding money. This happened mainly when one of the spouses was extravagant and/or had bad habits like drinking. More often, women were exploited economically. When they were not earning, their physical needs were not adequately met. When they were earning, several men tried to snatch away their meagre earnings to spend for their own personal matters. 2 per cent women stated that they were exploited by their husbands. Mrs B. revealed; "When I found that my husband is earning too little most of his income he spent on account of bad habits like drinking and gambling, I was forced to look for a job. I established myself in a job and started earning very well. Soon after, my husband left his job and became a parasite on me. He started demanding money every day, and, if I did not give him, he would go to my friends and take money from them. I was fed, up, and was forced to break away from him at last." A highly-educated young wife, pointed out; "I was brought up in a liberal family, where money was never an issue. All the people who earned enjoyed complete freedom to spend their money. But when I came to my husand's house, I found an entirely different setup. Here, all the money was pooled by the elders, and even for minor personal expenses, one was not left with a penny. Every time I needed the smallest item, I had to beg someone, though I was earning as much as my husband. This situation was very much frustrating to me."

The General Economic Condition of the Family with Reference to Debt Saving

Savings and debt are indicators of the economic condition of a household. Economic wellbeing or problem do count in marital adjustment. Burgess and Locke have held that "economic items such as moderate income, savings, occupations characterized by stability and social control, regularity and continuity of employment, may all be indicating a stabilized and socialized personality which readily adjusts to the situation of marriage."[20]

The incidence of saving and debt in the families where divorce

[20]Burgess & Locke, *op. cit.*, pp. 468-69.

took place was studied, and it was found out that in 39 per cent cases, there was saving, 12.5 per cent debt, and in 27.5 per cent there was neither saving nor debt. As for the remaining 21per cent, the data is inapplicable.

All the 12.5 per cent indebted families belonged to the low income group. While the earning was meagre, expenses for non-essential and wasteful items like drinking, smoking, eating outside the home, etc., were high, with the result that many a time, women were forced to borrow money in order to meet the basic needs of the family. Majority of those who had neither saving nor debt belonged to the middle class.

We conclude that the general economic condition of the families in divorce was not very satisfactory, as majority did not have any saving. This may have been one of the causes directly or indirectly leading to divorce. Kenkel has pointed out that "low income would seem to have a great potential for producing problems and conflicts of family living. If about nothing else, the low income husband and wife could always argue about improved bills."[21] Several years ago, Mowrer found that financial tension was the major situation in from 30 per cent to 40 per cent divorces he investigated. These findings are all the more important in India also, because, we do not have so far social security provisions such as unemployment, allowance, old age pension, etc., as may be found in the economically developed countries like the United States, England and Germany.

PARTICIPATION OF THE HUSBAND IN THE HOUSEHOLD WORK

A house can be managed well only when both the husband and wife understand each other and try to assist each other. In our country, somehow or other, it is found that home management is considered to be the responsibilty of women alone. Men do not extend any assistance. In the traditional joint families, where there are a number of women, and all the women are full time house-wives, husbands need not have worried about the management of homes. But, in modern times, especially when the role of women has sufficiently changed, and the joint families have

[21]**Kenkel, 1973, *op. cit.*, pp. 317-18.**

given way to single families men's duty to assist in management of home has definitely increased. However, most of the indian males seem to be unaware of these changes as revealed in our study. In majority of households (53 per cent) in the present study, the husbands left the entire responsibility on their wives. Only in a small percentage of cases (26 per cent), the husbands extended some sort of assistance to their wives. This state of affairs can create tensions and discord in the family. If a wife is earning and providing for the maintenance of the family, she has every right to expect full cooperation and assistance from her husband. Even a non-working wife needs a lot of support from her husband as the help she traditionally received from her elder female relatives and neighbours are becoming fewer day-by-day. Some wives were rather bitter at the lack of sympathy and understanding shown by their husbands. As one working wife, Mrs L., has put it, "I go to work in the morning after finishing all household work, and getting my both children ready for school. I come in the evening dead tired. I have to go and get provision and again start cooking, help the children with their lessons, wash clothes and press the clothes for the next day and so on. My husband has no worries. He goes off early in the morning, and returns late in the night. He hardly cares for anything, neither does he help in any of the household matters." Another working wife said: "My office hours and that of my husband are identical. I had to get up early in the morning and cook not only for ourselves, but also for his grand-parents, alongwith whom we were living, get the children ready, do cleaning and washing and a thousand other things. All that my husband had to do was to get himself ready, and even for that, many a time, he expected my help. We were bringing in equal salaries. Then, why could he not share the household duties equally?"

In conclusion, we can say that most of the husbands still do not take sufficient interest in household matters, and leave the entire responsibility of home management to their wives. This was a great burden for those women who were working outside the home, and in those families, there were many other members than those of the nuclear family. These did, therefore, create problems of marital adjustment.

SUPPORT OF OTHER MEMBERS OF THE FAMILY BY THE SPOUSES

In the discusssion about the types of family of the respondents (Chapter 3—The Background of the Spouses in Divorce), we have pointed out that 70 per cent were joint family. In these joint families, the parents and relatives (mostly, siblings of the husband) lived. The spouses had to support them. Whether the matter of supporting the parents and other members of the family in these cases was agreed to by both the spouses was investigated. It was found that in 20.5 per cent cases, there was discord in this regard. In former times a Hindu wife was trained to put up with such situations, but in modern times, educated wives are not prepared to make sacrifice for the sake of others, and thus, marital discord occurs, which eventually leads to the dissolution of marriage. To cite an example, Mrs L. stated, "I got married rather late. I was in a job for a number of years, and was earning well. When I got married, my in-laws started demanding my entire salary. Later, I discovered that my father-in-law was a chronic alcoholic and all my hard-earned money is squandered by him. Thence, I refused to give him any money. My husband got very annoyed, and due to this particular problem, we separated."

RELIGIOUS LIFE OF THE SPOUSES

The present study did not reveal many cases of marital discord on account of religious beliefs and practices of the spouses. There was only one per cent inter-religious marriages. One was that of a Hindu (Brahmin) marrying a Christian girl, and the other a Brahmin marrying a Jain girl. In both these cases, religion as such was not a cause for friction. There was only one case where religious belief and practice became a major hindrance to marital adjustment. In this case, both the spouses belonged to the same community (Maharashtrian Brahmin). The husband hailed from an educated and enlightened family, whereas wife from an orthodox one. Due to her poor education, and lack of contact with enlightened people, she was extremely superstitious, right from the beginning. After marriage, her behaviour took an abnormal turn (worship of some evil spirits). Therefore, she was left at her parents' place. Eventually, the husband severed all connections with the wife, resulting in divorce too.

HOBBIES OF THE SPOUSES IN DIVORCE

The spouses in our study had various types of hobbies such as: (*i*) reading, (*ii*) games, (*iii*) picnics, (*iv*) knitting, (*v*) internal decoration, (*vi*) modelling, (*vii*) poetry, (*viii*) acting, (*ix*) music, (*x*) dancing, (*xii*) gardening, and (*xiii*) hunting. The more frequent ones being reading, game, picnics and tours, knitting and guardening. A small percentage of men and women did not have any hobbies.

Hobbies were the main cause of friction in 8 per cent cases in our study. One young wife said, "My husband is so fond of roaming and card-playing that I never get any time with him. Even in the honeymoon days, he would come from the office and will either go off with his friends and return by midnight or will sit and play cards for hours and hours. I will finish all household work and wait and wait for him in vain." Another woman said: "Right from the beginning, I was interested in games, dramas writing and other hobbies. My husband and his parents did not like any of these. The major trouble between us started after I had acted in a drama." One husband said, "My wife was very fond of roaming about. I was too busy in my own work, and did not get time to check her hobbies. When I came to know of her wayward behaviour, I warned her but she did not listen."

Thus, it was found that in some cases, hobbies of husbands and wives stood in the way of marital harmony of the couples. These cases were found in the middle and upper classes only.

FRIENDS OF THE SPOUSES IN DIVORCE

It was investigated as to how far the friendship and associations of the husbands/wives contributed to marital discord. It was found that 11 per cent men and 7.5 per cent women had undesirable and questionable type of friends/associations. All the undesirable friendship/association of the women were with the members of the opposite sex. Some of the unhealthy friendship of the men was also with members of the opposite sex, including women of questionable character.

Thus unhealty friendship/association was responsible for marital problems and dissolution at least in certain cases.

HOUSING CONDITIONS OF THE COUPLES IN DIVORCE

Housing is a major problem in Indian cities. It is estimated that at least 25 per cent of our city-dwellers live in slums. There seems to be some correlation between housing conditions and marital happiness.

In our study, only 28 per cent couples had 'good' or 'very good' housing accommodation. In 31 per cent cases, the couples had just 'ordinary' accommodation. In 41 per cent cases, the housing accommodation was 'very poor' or 'poor'. These indicate that the housing facilities of the couples on the whole was not satisfactory. Many lived in one room or two room houses which was neither sufficient nor healthy for the spouses,

A husband and wife need sufficient privacy to lead a healthy family life, including that of sex. In an over crowded home, "everyone is in everyone else's way. This causes tension which may be one of the reasons for marital discord. Children are very much affected due to slum living in Indian cities."[22]

CONCLUSIONS

In this rather lengthy chapter, we have dealt with various matters concerning the life of the divorced couples such as type of marriage of the divorced couples, premarital relations/contacts, age at marriage, consent of the spouses for marriage, expectations in marriage, dowry and marriage, spouses and their early days of marriage, sexual life of the spouses, privacy in the life of the spouses, eating patterns of spouses, attendance of social functions by the spouses, occupation of the spouses at the time of divorce, working hours of the husbands and wives, matters concerning money and the spouses, general economic conditions of the family of the spouses, participation of the husband in the household work, support of other members of the family by the spouses, religious life of the spouses, hobbies, friends and housing conditions of the spouses.

All these were probed into, in order to assess how far these promote or hinder the marital relations and adjustments in the life of the divorced spouses. It was found that in some cases these do

[22]S.D. Singh & K.P. Othen, *Slum Children of India*, Deep Publications, 1982.

contribute marital maladjustment, and in some others, these do not. For instance, joint family living was found to cause use marital maladjustment where the wife's identity and freedom were not permitted, and where the wives were expected to serve the in-laws and other relatives. In majority of the cases, on of the causes of marital discord was that the marriage was not entered into after sufficient thought and preparation. Premarital contacts between the spouses were rather superficial. As for the age at marriage, 60 per cent of the girls got married before they reached the age of 20. The mean age at the marriage of the husband is 24.83 and that of the wife 19.13. Some couples had child marriage, while others had late marriage. Both were detrimental to marital adjustment to a great extent. The median age difference between the spouses is 4.47. It however, ranged from 0 to 18 years in individual cases. Majority of the respondents opined that the ideal pattern should be that the age difference be 3-5 years, the husband always to be older than the wife.

Although the consent of majority of the respondents was taken before marriage, in many cases, it was just a formality. The parents had already decided upon the matter. Expectations in marriage by both the husbands and wives seemed to havs a significant role in the matter of marital adjustment. Non-fulfilment of expectations created marital discord. To be good cooks, take care of the personal needs of the husband, to be affectionate, be submissive to the husband, etc., were some of the important expectations of the husbands, while love, fulfilment of physical needs, taking them out for cinema, picnic, etc., were some of the main expectations of the wives. It was discovered that there is variation in the expectations of the husbands/wives on the basis of their economic class. Payment of dowry (cash or kind) was almost common. Demands for dowry both at the time of wedding, and later on, did create problems for marital harmony. There is considerable variation in dowry with respect to different communities. The early days of marriage are important in marital adjustment. In 25 per cent cases, the spouses did not like each other. Sex satisfaction is related to several psychological and socio-cultural factors. In about 30 per cent cases, there was no sex satisfaction. In several cases, it was found that non-attendance of social functions by the couples together was a symptom of marital discord. Husbands had greater desire to live in joint family than wives because to the former, it was more advantages, but to the latter, it was not. There were about 25 types of occupations in which the spouses were engaged at the time of discord. It was discovered that considerable number of husbands were employed in business, and clerical jobs, while in respect of wives, teaching was the most popular occupation. Majority of the wives (65.5 per cent) were unemployed. There was slight difference in the occupation of the husbands before marriage and after marriage. Some were students at the time of marriage, while they were found working at the time of divorce. The number of woman workers increased after marriage. Most of the new female-entrants started working due to the indifferent attitude and inadequate income of their husbands. However, women's working was not found detrimental to marital harmony in the present study. The working hours of some husbands (30 per cent) were not helpful in marital harmony as they had irregular and long working hours, especially those who have private business, touring jobs and as medical doctors. Money matters in most cases were dealt with by husbands or heads of joint families. Even working women had not much say in the matter. This did cause marital discord. Some families suffered from financial debt.

This affected marital adjustment. Supporting other members of the family (besides the nuclear family of the couple, consisting of the spouses and their children) was very common in the present study, because of the incidence of joint family in large number. In most cases, husbands' relatives were supported. This was a matter of disagreement between the spouses in about 21 per cent cases. As for the religious life of the spouses, it was found that there was no serious problem of marital adjustment on this score. This makes us to think that although the religious beliefs, practices and attitudes of the urban Hindu men and women did not change substantially, they have no taboo to go in for divorce.

The spouses had a large number and variety of hobbies. In a few cases (8 per cent) it caused marital discord. In a small number of causes, unhealthy friendship/association of the husband/wife led to marital maladjustment. In a large number cases (41 per cent) poor housing conditions existed. Overcrowded houses prevented healthy atmosphere and privacy for the spouses, which in turn, facilitate marital discord. At the end, it may be mentioned that when several factors work together simultaneously, maladjustment occurs. Thus, if some or several of the factors such as joint family living, poor economic condition, absence of freedom, demands of dowry, disparity in expectations and fulfilments and disagreement in the matter of supporting other members of the family, work together, there may be marital and familial maladjustment and divorce.

Chapter 5

CAUSES OF DIVORCE

INTRODUCTION

IN this chapter, we deal with the causes of divorce. But these causes are discussed in three sections, namely, causes of divorce as given by various sociologists/social scientists; grounds for divorce according to the Hindu Marriage Act; and the cases of divorce as found in the present study.

As legal dissolution of marriage, divorce is primarily a legal phenomenon. But this complex phenomenon is to be viewed from various angles such as physical, mental, social and cultural. The law for divorce has been made keeping in view all, or most of these aspects. Most countries of the world have made law for divorce, in which grounds are stipulated under which divorce may be availed of. These legal grounds are not just isolated legal causes, but they do signify the socio-cultural view point also. Therefore, when we deal with the causes of divorce, we have to keep in mind the legal and sociological viewpoints.

There are certain basic causes of divorce related to the bio-psychological and marital/familial aspects of the life of the spouses. These my be applicable to almost all societies. But, then, there are certain causes which are relevant to the modern society. Therefore, a good number of sociologists have pointed out the causes for the increasing rate of divorce in modern times.

CAUSES OF DIVORCE ACCORDING TO VARIOUS SOCIOLOGISTS/SOCIAL SCIENTISTS

Johnson has stated that certain aspects of culture and social structure are likely to be associated with a high divorce rate. He has listed the following "causes" for a high divorce rate:

(*i*) Religious tolerance of divorce;
(*ii*) Legal tolerance of divorce;
(*iii*) Increased industrialization;
(*iv*) Urbanization;
(*v*) Birth control;
(*vi*) Greater geographical mobility;
(*vii*) High vertical social mobility;
(*viii*) Heterogeneity of population; and
(*ix*) High demands on the intimate affectional side of marriage.[1]

All these factors are inter-dependent also. Kephart has correctly pointed out that "from the sociological perspective, causes are generally thought of as inter-related links in a sequential chain of events rather than as single factors."[2]

Elliott and Merrill have held that "the real reasons for divorce are obviously those tensions and irritations which make it impossible for a man and woman to "get along" within the bonds of matrimony."[3]

According to Green, "the proximate reason for the high divorce rate is the prevalence of extravangant expectations in marriage, but the ultimate explanation is to be found in the social forces which undermined the traditional family's structure."[4]

To Sweedlun and others, in modern times, the increase in divorce may be attributed to such reasons as (*i*) change in the attitude of the people (less stigma attached to divorce); (*ii*) faulty education about marriage and family, (*iii*) lack of family unity, (*iv*) urbanization. (*v*) small-sized family and childless marriage, and (*vi*) more legal provision in favour of women for securing divorce.[5]

According to Baber, the real causes of divorce involve the same

[1]H.M., Johnson, *Sociology*: *A Systematic Introduction*, Routledge & Kegad Paul, Ltd., London, 1961, pp. 171-174.

[2]William, M., Kephart, *The Family, Society, and the Individual*, Fourth Edition, Houghton Miffln. Co., Boston, 1977, p. 517.

[3]M.A., Elliott, F.E., Merrill, *Social Disorganization*, 1950, p. 433.

[4]Aronold, W., Green, *Sociology*, Fourth Ed , 1964, p. 437.

[5]Sweedlum, Verne, & Others, *Man in Society*, Vol. I, 1956, pp. 99-102.

factors that cause marital unhappiness in general such as unfaithfulness, jealousy, insanity, feeble mindedness, poverty, laziness, quarrels over the family purse strings, relatives, impotence, frigidity, excessive sex passion, drunkenness, nagging, religious differences, female independence, temper, disease, and a host of others infinitum.[6]

According to Bertrand Russell, where family feeling is strong, for example, in France, divorce will be comparatively rare, even if it is equally easy. Divorce is a symptom of deeper social trends, which have undermined the moral and economic basis of the monogamous family. It is possible that the lessening of the social taboos and the general easing up of conventions have given many couples the courage to come out into the open and end their incompatibility by legal divorce. Growth of industry and the increase in wealth, strong feeling of individualism, feminist movements, and a host of other things may have also facilitated divorce.

According to Carter and Plateris, "a majority of divorces are obtained on grounds least unpleasant to advance under existing State law and easiest to establish in a legal proceeding."[7]

Goode has summarized a number of variables related to divorce proneness, such as urban background, marriage at very young age, short acquaintance before marriage, unhappy marriage of parents of the couples, non-attendance at church or mixed faith, disapproval of the marriage by kin and friends, general dissimilarity in background, and variation in mutual role obligations of husband and wife.[8]

In her study, Fonseca found that the major factors for marital discord were ill-treatment by husband, interference and ill-treatment by in-laws and family members, infidelity, financial difficulties, personal defects, vices, incompatibility, sex difficulties, health, living conditions and several other minor factors.[9]

Dominance on the part of the in-laws, dominance of the husbands, by their parents, desire on the part of the in-laws to secure

[6]R.E., Baber, 1953, *op. cit.*, pp. 490-491.

[7]Carter & Plateris, quoted by Winch and Goodman, in, *Selected Studies in Marriage and the Family*, 1968, p. 564.

[8]William, J., Goode, *Family Disorganization in Contemporary Social Problems*, Ed., Merton & Nisbert, London, 1963, p. 425.

[9]Fonseca, 1966, *op. cit.*, p. 65.

jobs for the wives outside the home, physical defects of women, and disparity between the husband and wife with regard to their social outlook were some of the important causes for divorce revealed in the study of Rama Mehta.

In our country, the institutions of marriage and family are in transition. Consequently, decline in the understanding between the spouses, decline in the sacramental nature of marriage, development of unrealistic marriage expectations, breakdown of communications between the spouses and economic problems, etc., are important factors for divorce.

GROUNDS FOR DIVORCE ACCORDING TO THE MARRIAGE ACT

Our work is on Divorce among Urban Hindus. Divorce among Hindus is governed by the various provisions of the Hindu Marriage Act, passed in 1955, and, thereafter amended from time to time especially in May, 1976.

Section 13 of the Hindu Marriage Act lays down various grounds of divorce such as the following (applicable to both the spouses):

(*i*) Voluntary sexual intercourse with any person other than his or her spouse;
(*ii*) Cruel treatment;
(*iii*) Desertion for two years;
(*iv*) Ceasing to be a Hindu by conversion to another religion;
(*v*) Of incurably unsound mind/mental disorder;
(*vi*) Suffering from a virulent and incurable form of leprosy;
(*vii*) Suffering from veneral disease in a communicable form;
(*viii*) Renouncing the world by entering any religious order;
(*ix*) Has not been heard of as being alive for a period of seven years or more;
(*x*) No resumption of cohabitation as between the parties to the marriage for a period of one year or upwards after the passing of a decree for judicial separation;
(*xi*) No restitution of conjugal rights as between the parties to the marriage for a period of one year or upwards after the passing of a decree for restitution of conjugal rights;
(*xii*) Mutual consent, on the ground that they have been living

separately for a period of one years or moıe, that they have not been able to live together, and that they have mutually agreed that the marriage should be dissolved, on the motion of both the parties made ı.ot earlier than six months after the date of the presentation of the petition, and not later than 18 months after the said date.

What acts would constitute cruelty depends upon the circumstances of each case. Several factors like environment, status in society, education, cultural development, local custom, social condition, physical and mental condition of the parties are to be considered when deciding the question of cruelty. Serious charges of unchastity and unfaithfulness made by a spouse against the other constitute mental cruelty falling within the ambit of legal cruelty.

Under section 19 (1) of the Indian Divorce Act, and section 12 (i) (a) of the Hindu Marriage Act, impotence of the respondents is a ground for annulment of marriage. If impotence ceases and marriage is consummated any time before the institution of the proceedings for divorce, the ground is no more available. Sometimes, impotency may be mental or moral, which means the person is capable of intercourse, but is incapable of having it with a particular person.

The respondent's wilful refusal to consummate the marriage is a ground for voiding the marriage. Virginity tests (under medical examination) are useful in establishing that the woman is still a virgin, that is, she did not have intercourse with her husband. The court cannot compel a person to undergo medical examination, but by refusal to do so, the court can only draw an adverse inference.

Under section 12 (i) (c) of the Hindu Marriage Act, a marriage can be declared void if the consent of the petitioner or guardian was obtained by force or fraud. The fraud must not have been known to the petitioner before the marriage, the proceedings must be instituted within one year from the date of marriage, and the fraud has not been condoned by intercourse subsequent to the discovery of the fraud.

Under section 13 (i) (iii) of the Hindu Marriage Act, unsoundness of mind is a ground for judicial separation and divorce. Marriage Laws (Amendment) Act lays down that the term mental disorder means mental illness, arrested or incomplete development of mind, psychopathetic disorder, or any other disorder or disability of mind and includes schizophrenia.

Section 13 (1) (ii) of the Hindu Marriage Act specifies that if a person has ceased to be a Hindu by conversion to another religion, this may act as a ground for dissolution of marriage. The act does not forbid the continuation of a marriage between parties one of whom has ceased to be a Hindu. That is, conversion of one party to another religion does not make the marriage dissolved; it only affords a ground to the other spouse to claim divorce. The right to get a divorce under this law is given to the party who continues to be a Hindu.

Under section 13 (1) (A) (i) as it stood prior to amendment, either party to the marriage may present a petition for divorce on the ground of non-resumption of cohabitation between the spouses for a period of two years upwards after passing the decree of judicial separation. After the amendment in 1976, the minimum period is fixed as one year. Resumption of cohabitation means voluntary cohabitation. For the decree of restitution of conjugal rights also, the same time limit is applicable.

Divorce by mutual consent has been provided in section 13 (B) of the Hindu Marriage Act (amended upto 1976). According to this provision, both parties may jointly petition for a decree of divorce on three grounds:

(*i*) They have been living separately for one year or more;
(*ii*) They have not been able to live together; and
(*iii*) They have mutually agreed that the marriage should be dissolved.

Such a petition is liable to be kept in abeyance for at least one year in respect of Special Marriage Act, and six months in the case of the Hindu Marriage Act. The parties may move the petition after six months, and the court may pass a decree for dissolving the marriage. For the purpose of divorce by mutual consent, the parties need not prove anything other than that is laid down in Section 13 (B) as mentioned above.

There are certain additional grounds for a wife to present a petition for divorce when (*a*) her husband is guilty of rape, sodomy or bestiality, (*b*) the husband has married again, and (*c*) her marriage (whether consummated or not) was solemnized before she attained the age of 15 years and she has repudiated the marriage before attaining the age of eighteen years.

Bigamy is an important ground for divorce. To bring home a charge of bigamy, it must be established that the alleged marriage had been solemnized after due observance of rites and ceremonies. Cohabitation with a woman for some time may not be taken as marriage, but continuous cohabitation for a number of years may raise the presumption of marriage. A marriage cannot be proved merely by statements which relate to the existence of any relationship or by admission made by the parties to the marriage who may at times be actuated by ulterior motives. But, in addition to these, if parents of the parties concerned give evidence of any ceremony in connection with solemnization of marriage, the marriage will be affirmed. In case of second marriage also, the essential ceremonies will be constituting the marriage must be proved. Admission of allegation by the accused is not a sufficient proof. In a case of bigamy, the following things are to be proved:

(*a*) That the complainant had been validly married to the accused;
(*b*) That the accused contracted a second marriage during the subsistence of the first; and
(*c*) Both marriages were valid and strictly according to law governing the parties.

When the prosecution relies upon customary rites and ceremonies, then, such ceremony which validates and completes such marriage must be proved.

CAUSES OF DIVORCE AS FOUND IN THE PRESENT STUDY

The causes of divorce found in the present study are shown in three sections.

Factors Responsible for Starting Serious Conflicts between the Husbands and Wives (Data Collected through Interview)

During the course of the interview with the divorced-respondents they were asked to state what were the first serious causes (starting point) for divorces that occurred in their married life. The replies received are shown in the table at Appendix V.

It will be seen that in all, there were as many as 26 factors responsible for starting serious conflicts between the husbands and wives. The most frequent causes are cruelty (11.5 per cent), husbands' interest in other women (11 per cent), husbands having no regular job and substantial source of income (9.5 per cent) and interference of in-laws/relatives (8 per cent).

After spending a few days/weeks/months/years of married life, these factors came to the scene, to create conflicts between the spouses. Later on, the conflicts grew, worsenened and/or other factors came to light. Thus, these factors are not unrelated to the complaints made by the husbands and wives later on.

Complaints of Husbands and Wives against each other (Data Collected through Interview)

Complaints are a part of conflicts in family life. Conflicts and tensions in family start with different types of complaints. According to Burgess and Locke, "some conflict is inevitable and normal in the family, as it is in every area of human life."[10] Conflicts, many a time, lead to tension also. A conflict is a fight of any sort, ranging from a slight difference of opinion to uncompromising warfare. Conflicts arise and and are solved, with little or no rift in the basic unity of the family. A tension is an unsolved conflict. Tensions are the result of conflict situations in which certain basic frustrations are not resolved. When impulses, habits, wishes and expectations are blocked, the person is restless and attempts in one way or another to find its expression.

The prevalence of conflicts in marriage is indicated by Terman's findings upon the number of complaints reported by husbands and wives as occurring in their marriages. Some of the complaints are concrete manifestations of deeper conflicts and tensions. These conflicts and tensions later on, many a time, result in marital dissolution also.

In the present study, attempt was made to record the complaints of husbands and wives and examine them, in almost the same fashion as was done by Burgess & Locke.[11]

The table prepared in the present study is given in the table at Appendix VI.

It is seen that from out of the complaints of husbands against

[10]Borgess & Locke, *op. cit.*

[11]*Cf.* Burgess & Locke, *op. cit.*, p. 564—Table 23—Complaints of Husbands and Wives listed in order of their Frequency.

their wives, "poor management of home and income" was the complaint of the highest frequency (90—or say, rank 1). As for the complaint of the wife against the husband, "cruelty" was of the highest frequency (99—rank 1). The second complaint in order of frequency was "insufficient income." This was second for both husbands and wives. "Wife non-adjusting" was the third most important complaint by the husbands, while "interference of in-laws" was the third highest complaint by wives. Other complaints of husbands in order of frequency were interference by in-laws, wife quarrelsome, interested in other men, incompatible nature, not affectionate, etc. While that of the wives were husband quarrelsome, squanders money, husband not affectionate, vices (smoking, drinking, etc.), interested in other women, demand for dowry, etc. Some complaints of low frequency in respect of hubands were barrenness, physical defects, wife alcoholic, and wife tried to murder husband. Similarly, the complaints of wives low frequency were husband mentally unfit, considerably older, tried to kill the wife, thereatens to commit suicide and poor health.

Legal Grounds on the Basis of which the Decree of Divorce was Granted by the Judge (in the basis of Judicial Court Record)

Judicial Decree for divorce is granted in individual cases by the court concerned on the basis of certain specific grounds provided in the law. The various grounds for divorce under the Hindu Marriage Act, 1955, have already been discussed in the beginning of this chapter. A survey of the grounds mentioned in the cases under study showed the following data (see table on page 123).

It may be pointed out that divorce cases were very hard and few in number before the year 1976, when substantial amendments were carried out in the Hindu Marriage Act. Therefore, it may be logical to put two periods for divorce cases, namely, one before 1976, and the second after 1976. There is also variation in the grounds of divorce pertaining to both these periods. For instance, mutual consent as a ground was never allowed before 1976. 26.5 per cent our cases were of mutual consent and all these were after decreed the Amendment of 1976.

In the United States of America, desertion, cruelty, and adultery are the three commonest grounds on which divorces are granted.[12]

[12]R.E., Baber, *Marriage and the Family*, 1953, pp. 450-58.

Economic Class and Divorce

Ground	*Percentage*
	26.5
...nd later decree of divorce	
	23.5
	14.00
...on for many years	12.5
... decree of restitution of	
...nd later divorce	6.5
...summated	3.5
...sband or wife	3.5
	3.00
...ships	2.5
	2.00
...e, later confirmed by the	
	1.5
	0.5
	0.5
Total	100 per cent

As mentioned earlier, it should be reiterated that the legal grounds for divorce are not necessarily the real reasons for obtaining a final decree. A majority of divorces are obtained on grounds least unpleasent to advance under existing law and easiest to establish in a legal proceeding.

Detailed Integrated Analysis of Various Causes by the Researcher

After taking into consideration, (*i*) the factors responsible for starting serious conflicts between the husbands and wives, (*ii*) the complaints of the husbands and wives against each other, and (*iii*) the legal grounds on the basis of which the decree of divorce was granted by the judicial court, the researcher has attempted at an integrated, detailed analysis of the various causes of divorce as found in the present inquiry. Each cause is considered separately.

Cruelty. In several cases, the wives complained that they were treated with cruelty either by husband or the in-laws, or both. Cruelty was also the most important factor responsible for starting serious conflicts between the husband and wife, as shown in Appendix V relating to this chapter. Cruelty was again the complaint with highest frequency in Appendix VI.

The complaint of cruelty was maximum in the lower class

than in the middle class, and then in the upper class. Physical cruelty like assaulting and not giving food was more common in the lower classes, but was present in considerable number in the middle class also. Cruelty was mainly found in joint families, and many a time, the in-laws were directly or indirectly responsible for cruelty. For instance, in all the cases where the women complained that they were not given enough to eat, it was by the mother-in law. Several women revealed that cruelty of their husbands resulted from the complaints and allegations the in-laws (mother-in-law, sister-in-law, brother-in-law, etc) made. In some cases, the in-laws also actually participated in the cruel behaviour. For example, one wife was often beaten by her husband, mother-in-law, father-in-law and brother-in-law. In two other cases, the wives reported that they were locked up in rooms and not given food or even water. In another case, a graduate wife reported that her husband often assaulted her at the instigation of her mother-in-law and sister-in-law. In two cases, the husband together with his parents, plotted to kill the wife. In several cases, the cruelty extended to children as well.

The cruel treatment was in nuclear families also in considerable number. For instance, a couple was living away from their parents and the husband was not earning anything. Whenever the wife told him to do some work and earn, she was beaten up mercilessly. In another case, it was reported that a wife was subjected to extreme physical torture. Here again, the husband was not earning. The husband forced the wife to practise prostitution and whenever she objected, she was beaten. Moreover, the husband used to tie her up and make her to have relationship with many men. Due to this the young women started having severe bleeding. The husband planned to sell her to a man for Rs 4,000. Luckely, the girl was rescued by some other relatives. Both these were cases in the lower economic class and Harijan caste.

Cruelty as such was not reported by men, though some men mentioned that their wives' behaviour caused them a lot of mental torture and affliction. In two cases, the husbands alleged that the wives attempted on their lives by poisoing them. In one case, the wife hereself confessed that she had tried such a step out of extreme frustration.

Thus, cruelty, in one form or another was a serious cause of divorce in our study. It is held that cruelty in matrimonial law may be of infinite variety, it can be subtle or brutal. It may be physical or mental; it may be by words, gesture or by mere silence.

Legally, cruelty must be of the type to satisfy the conscience of the court that the relationship between the parties had deteriorated to such an extent due to the conduct of the other spouse that it has become impossible for them to live together without mental agony.[13]

Interference by in-laws An important problem of the married Hindu woman is adjustment with the in-laws, more so, in large joint families. In Indian families, a son's loyalty is divided among his parents and his spouse and in the authoritarian joint family, the greater share of his loyalty goes to his kin and not the spouse. The female spouse finds herself in the midst of strangers, many of whom are hostile, without anybody from whom she can expect sympathy and understanding. The mother-in-law is the commonest person with whom a bride finds problems. A mother-in-law has authority and control in the family, but, at the same time, she finds an opponent and a rival in the new daughter-in-law. The next relative who usually causes troubles for the bride is husband's sister. If the husband has an unmarried sister, who stays with him, the chances of quarrels between the wife and the sister are very high. Like the mother, the sister also starts seeing the new bride as an enemy who snatches all the affections of her brother. A brother who was very doting until now, may neglect the sister totally because of his engrossment with the new bride. This can create feelings of bitter jealousy in a sister. Even otherwise, jealousy between two females of the same age is nothing uncommon.

Husband's elder brother's wife is another person with whom a young wife has to face problems. Being the elder daughter-in-law of the house, she has higher authority and status in the family.

There are other relatives like father-in-law, brother-in-law, uncle or aunt-in-law, grand-in-laws and so on

In our study, 41.5 per cent of the female spouses reported that they had problems with their in-laws. The various kinds of problems they have faced are shown on next page.

[13]A.N., Saha, *Marriage and Divorce*, 1981, pp. 119-124.

S. No.	*Complaints of wives against in-laws*	*Frequency*
1.	Exploitation by making to work too hard	47
2.	Not providing physical comforts	45
3.	Instigating husband against her	45
4.	Physical cruelty	42
5.	Mental torture	25
6.	Insult	21
7.	Interference in privacy	15
8.	Persuading husband to leave her	9
9.	Enforcing strict purdah	7
10.	Forcing her to have immoral sex relation	5

A few typical examples of interference by the in-laws which eventually led to marital dissolution are given below:

One young divorcee said, "I belong to a rather rich family, and I had never faced any hardship in my life, till I reached my husband's house. Just after a week of marriage, my mother-in-law started treating me with extreme cruelty. She will make me to do all the household work and will give me only two dry chapatis to eat. Often, I have wished to steal some chapatis and eat, but was terrified. So, day and night, I remained almost hungry."

Mrs D. said, "My husband was a businessman. He used to leave home by 8 in the morning and return only after 9 at night. As soon as he comes back, my mother-in-law and elder sister-in-law would start telling him all sorts of things against me. They made him very suspicious about me, especially my character. I was always in the house, and never went out alone; still they made him believe that I had affairs with another man. I tried to explain to him. But his mind was greatly poisoned and he started treating me without any affection or love. Every night, he used to quarrel with me and threat to commit suicide, because of my alleged bad character. I tolerated it for some time, but when it became beyond endurance, I left his house."

Mrs E., an upper class middle-aged lady said, "The mental agony I have undergone while I lived with my husband and in-laws is unexplainable, My husband was inhuman, but my father-in-law also added fuel to the fire. He derived special pleasure from doing so."

Mrs H., yet another woman, said, "My husband was highly educated and was employed in America. My sister-in-law had better education than me. Though I belonged to a very rich family, they all thought of me much inferior, and expressed it whenever they could."

Mrs K., a lower economic class divorcee said: "I was always ill-treated by my in-laws. My husband had great love for me. But my in-laws taught him that he could get a better wife if he left me."

Privacy is an essential need for a married couple. Many husbands and wives do not get enough privacy because of lack of proper accommodation. But in some cases, husband's relatives purposely interfered in the privacy of the couple. This happened due to various reasons. In a few, the elder sister-in-law of the male spouses were in love with them. They were jealous of the wives, and did not want them to have close relation with their husbands. They interfered in the couples privacy whenever possible. One uneducated wife, Mrs. S. said, "My husband was living with his so called brother. He had, in fact, no brother. I soon noticed that my husband was more interested in the sister-in-law than in me. He used to give all the money to her. Whenever he came home, he used to talk to her only. My sister-in-law also saw to it that I get as less time with my husband as possible." Another young wife, Mrs D. said, "My husband was working in a foreign country. There, he stayed with his elder brother's family. After marriage, when he was preparing to go back, I asked him to take me along. He was very reluctant. Later, due to great persuasion from my parents and brothers, he took me along. But, when I reached his place, I found that he had no interest in me. Whenever I asked him to take me out, he used to persuade his sister-in-law also to go along. His sister-in-law was also very jealous of me. Whenever, the two of them were together, they made it very clear that they did not want my intrusion."

Sometimes, an over-interfering parent, especially mother, also may come in the way of a husband and wife. This happens more when husband is the only son of the mother, and more so, if the mother is a widow and she has no other attachment. Under these circumstances, the mother and the son may be so much attached to each other that they forget the presence of the spouse, and sometimes avoid her purposely. Mrs K. a bank clerk, has put it this way: "My husband was the only son of my mother-in-law. They were so much attached to each other that there was no place for me. Even when we went on a short honeymoon trip, she accompanied us and spoiled all the fun. She behaved as if she was his wife, and not I." Mrs P., a young teacher, revealed: "My husband was the only son of my mother-in-law, and she was a widow for many years. The mother and son tried to be together always so that I never got any privacy with my husband." In some cases, the in-laws deliberately interfere with the privacy of the couple. A female divorcee said, "My mother-in-law and brother-in-law used to sleep in the same room with me and my husband. They did not want to give us any privacy, even during night.

7.5 per cent of the divorcee-wives said that their in-laws interfered with their freedom. They were not allowed to go out even with their husbands. A few were not allowed to meet their own relatives. Mrs A., a young girl said "my mother-in-law watched me day and night. My uncle stayed just opposite to our house. But my mother-in-law never allowed me to go there. Once or twice, I went there, because, my father had come, but my mother-in-law went with me and remained there all the while, and took me back, alongwith her." Mrs K. said, "After marriage, I went to my husband's place and stayed there for $1\frac{1}{2}$ years. During this period, I was never allowed either to go out alone or to meet anybody. I asked permission just to see my parents, but was never allowed. Once, I saw my parents in a marriage party, but was not allowed to talk to them." It looks rather strange and inhuman indeed.

4.5 per cent of the divorcee-wives felt that they were abandoned by their husbands mainly because of the in-laws persuasion. Some of these marriages were against the wishes of the parents. Mrs K. a lower class divorcee-wife said, "I was always illtreated by my in-laws. Not that my husband had great love for me, but my in-laws taught him that he could get a better wife if he left me." A graduate divorcee, Mrs M. said, "There was some misunderstanding between my parents and in-laws after our marriage. I came away due to this. My in-laws persuaded my husband not to take me back."

Purdah system is still widely prevalent in the Hindu society, though the strictness with which this custom is observed varies from family to family. Many of these divorcees had observed *purdah* in the presence of various relatives. But, majority of them did not mind it, as they have accepted as a norm of their society. At the same time, a small percentage (3.5 per cent) of women did not like the severity of *purdah* system that existed in their in-laws families. This happened where they were allowed freedom in their own homes and the in-laws families were conservative. A scheduled caste divorcee. Mrs K. who had child marriage and who later refused to go to her husband said, "In my home, there was no *purdah* and I was always allowed to move out with my brothers. But in my husband's family, I had to cover my entire face and grope for the way. I went there a couple of times after I grew up. I knew I could not adjust there and hence refused to go back." Mrs M., a young Jain divorcee said, "My mother is a very liberal person. She never allowed my sister-in-law to keep *purdah*. But when I went to my husband's home, I was made to cover more than half of my face. I used to feel suffocated as I was not at all used to it.

2.5 per cent of the wives complained that they were forced to enterinto illicit sex relation by their in-laws. In one case, a young girl was trapped in the house with a stranger, so that he may take advantage of her. The in-laws expected monetary benefit from this. In all the other cases, some male relatives of the husbands tried to have sexual relation with them. One of them, Mrs D., a low caste divorcee said, "when we got married, my husband was not earning. We were put upwith an uncle of his. Soon, the uncle started making evil approaches towards me. When I said this to my husband, he did not seem to mind. Another scheduled caste girl, Mrs K. said, "Once when my husband was away, in the middle of the night, my brother-in-law came to my room. He approached my cot and tried to touch me. I got up and threatened to shout, and then only, he left the room.

2.5 per cent female divorcees complained that their in-laws made their husbands marry another girl even before they were divorced. One young low-caste divorcee said, "My mother-in-law did not like me and always used to quarrel with me. I was thrown out of the house by my husband and mother-in-law. As soon as I got out, she looked for another girl, and got my husband married."

2.5 per cent working women said that all their earnings were snatched by their in-laws. One working wife, Mrs L. said, "First of all, my in-laws wanted me to leave my job and sit at home. But when I refused to do it, they started taking all my salary. A teacher, Mrs P. said, "As soon as I got my salary, my mother-in-law used to take the whole amount. I was not allowed to keep even a *penny*."

2 per cent divorcees alleged that their in-laws, together with their husbands, tried to murder them. One Sikh divorcee said: "I came

to know of a plot, that my in-laws were planning to kill me. They had a relative who was a nurse. They wrote a letter to her, asking her to come, so that she might inject some poison in me, and I may be killed. I saw this letter by chance. As soon as I saw it, I escaped from my husband's house."

In a few cases, the in-laws did not allow the wives to go to their husband's house as the in-laws did not like the marriage. In some cases, the children were snatched by their mother-in-laws, and thus, they were subjected to much mental torture.

Thus, there are different types of interference by the in-laws which cause the break of marital bonds. The incidence and severity was highest in the lower class, then in the middle and the least in the upper class. The personal illustrations make the matter very clear, but space does not permit us to give such illustrations in greater detail and number.

25 per cent of the husbands felt that their in-laws were interfering in their marital life directly or indirectly. As such, the wife's parents get very few opportunities to interfere directly in the marital life of couples as it is seldom that a couple lives with the wife's parents. But the in-laws can create a lot of nuisance by influencing their daughters. This is what some of the husbands felt. In all the three economic classes, the husbands complained of in-laws interference, but it was highest in the middle class. In 2 per cent cases where the husbands lived with the wife's people, at their place, their interference was felt very acutely. If the wife was the only child, only female child, or an over-fondled daughter of the parents, their over-anxiety for the daughter resulted in unneccessary interference. Some of the parents sheltered their daughters so much that the moment they faced any problem at their husbands' place, they would seek the protection of their parents. The father, mother, brother, or any other relative of the wife would reach the husband's place as soon as they hear of any trifling problem. This was very much resented by the husbands. Some of them felt that the parents are mostly responsible for the breakdown of their daughter's marriage. One of the husbands said, "Today's parents are commiting a great mistake. They are giving modern education to their girls. But they are not teaching their girls to adjust in their husbands' families." A lawyer husband said, "Now a days, parents are not worried if their daughters live at their husbands' houses or not. They know, that the girls can earn their own

living and hence won't be a source of economic burden on them. Hence, they do not try to send back their daughters, in case they come away." The husbands are of the opinion that by not trying to send the girls to their husbands' place, these parents are destroying their marital life. Some of the husbands complained that their in-laws took a positively strong step to prevent their daughters from going back to in-laws. Some of them even alleged that the parents were desirous of keeping the girls with themselves because the girls also added to their family income. By marrying girls, the parents escaped from the possible criticism of the caste and community. If the girl does not go back, they can always say that "the girls are not willing, what can we do? Or, the girls are ill-treated at the husbands' place. Hence, we are not sending them." It may be possible that in several cases, the parents of the girls interfered only when their girls were facing serious problems. But the husbands felt the other way.

There are cases of son-in-law and father-in-law conflicts also. In Hindu homes, a son-in-law is usually treated with great regard and respect. He is an honoured guest on all important family occasions. Parents of the wife do their utmost to please the son-in-law, because, they are well aware that the happiness of their daughters depends upon the son-in-laws. Even when there are quarrels or misunderstanding between parents of the spouses, the girls parents are very particular to win the favour of the son-in-law. In our study, it has been found that in 19 per cent cases, open quarrels occurred between the relatives of the husbands and wives. Such quarrels were always consequences of severe marital problems faced by the female spouses. In 4 per cent cases, the quarrels between these two parties became so severe that the same resulted in physical assault on each other. It is not necessary that only uneducated or poor people indulge in such behaviour; it happens among the upper class people as well. In a typical case, the wife went off to her parents after having bitter quarrels with her husband for some time. The husband was called to the wife's house on the pretext of trying for reconciliation. But, when he reached there, he faced a different situation. The wife's parents had arranged some *goondas* to beat up the son-in-law. He was manhandled badly. A court case followed. In several other cases also, when a wife was severely beaten up by a husband or his people, wife's parents, brothers, and others retaliated by trying to assault the son-in-law.

It may thus be concluded that severe conflicts between the husband and his in-laws do occur as a consequence of very unhappy married life. So long as there is a chance of saving the marriage, such untoward incidents are avoided by the wife's party. They try for vengeance only after they are convinced that the marriage of their daughters will not survive.

Extra-marital relations. Extra-marital relation of either spouse has been found to be a serious threat to marital stability. This undermines the very foundation of mutual love, respect and trust on which a marriage rests. Our study showed that several men and women indulged in extra-marital relationships, and this destroyed their marriage for ever. This factor is particularly relevant in our Indian context, because, sufficient distance between the two sexes was always observed, and even today a casual friendship between a married man and woman outside the wedlock is viewed with great suspicion.

Among the factors responsible for starting serious conflicts between the spouses (mentioned elsewhere) involving as many as more than 25 per cent of the cases, under different heads such as:

(*i*) Husband interested in other woman,
(*ii*) wife interested in other man,
(*iii*) husband suspicious, and
(*iv*) wife is a bad character.

Among the legal grounds of divorce revealed in our study, 14 per cent cases pertain to 'adultery'. Some of them are actually of this category "extra-marital relations.'

Some (2.5 per cent) upper class husbands complained that their wives had relationship/interest in other men. In two cases, the women had some extramarital relationship with other man while they were living with their husbands. In another case, the wife left the husbands after bitter quarrel. She started living at the place of a low caste married worker, and gradually started having illicit relationship with him. In other two cases, the husbands came to know of the premarital affairs of the wives and this annoyed them intensely.

16.5 per cent middle class husbands stated, that their wives had extramarital relation. There were women who eloped with other men.

These women were engaged in prostitution at least on a part-time basis, who were trying to continue relationship with their former lovers, were of lax sex morals and did not mind the attention of other men and so on. But, at the same time, there were a few cases of false complaint also. For instance, when Mrs V.J. left her husband's home, with her two very young children, due to the cruelty of Mr V.J. and his mother, Mr V.J. started alleging that his wife was a bad character, and that was the reason why she did not want to stay in the husband's house. He alleged such things in the judicial court also, and went to the extent of saying that he had strong doubts about the paternity of the children. Mr V.J.'s relatives confided that the girl was very simple, and straight-forward and she was persecuted by the husband and mother-in-law for the sake of more dowry and due to this reason, she was forced to leave.

Seven husbands from lower economic class also had strong suspicion about the character of their wives. Among the lower classes, more particularly. those belonging to lower castes, sex morality was found to be very lax. Minor lapses are often condoned by both the spouses, though a jealous spouse might object to it strongly. In such cases, the family was observed to be a relatively less stable unit. A typical example may be cited. Mr and Mrs R.N. were staying in a slum area. Mr R.N. was a labourer. One day, when he returned from work, he found that the house was locked. He was rather surprised, more so, because, just before a month, his wife had given birth to a female child, and she was confined to his house as the child was just an infant. After some inquiries, Mr R.N. found that his wife went to live with one of his friends. Mr R.N. did not bother much. According to Mr R.N., he approached the court not to get back his wife, but to get rid of her permanently. He made it more clear by saying that if the marriage was not finished off, legally, the wife might try to come back again, when the other man kicks her out. Incidents like this are not rare among the lower classes. Only when some grave problems are involved, the judicial court is approached. Otherwise, these matters are regularized between the parties concerned, or, through *panchayat*.

Women almost in equal number, complained about the behaviour of their husbands. Five upper class women said that their marriages broke because of the husband's interest in other women.

In one case, a husband from a very rich family, fell in love with a foreign visitor who had happened to stay with the family for some time and went away with her, leaving behind the wife and three young children. In all the other four cases, the wives complained that the husbands had loose morals and their excessive involvement with the opposite sex made life with them impossible. A graduate married to a medical doctor said, "When I reached my husband's home, I found a peculiar situation. My husband had kept three women of ill-repute permanently, and he liked to spend his nights with them. I was married only for the sake of presenting to the society as a legal wife. His real relations were with those women. When I complained to the in-laws, they did not bother. Theirs is a very rich family, and such things went on without any one bothering much about them." Two other young wives (both medical graduates) found similar situations. Both of them had love marriage. After, the first year of marriage, both of them felt that their husbands' interest in them was waning away, and they were easily attracted towards other women. One finished off the marriage in three years, and the other struggled along for six years.

Some middle class women (14.5 per cent) complained that their husbands had extra-marital relations. In most of these cases, the allegations were found to be true. For instance, Mr U. after eight years of married life, and having 3 children, fell in love with his assistant in the office. Mr B. a medical doctor, had extra-marital relations with a nurse. Mr G. had illicit relation with his brother's wife, before marriage, and this continued even after marriage.

Pregnancy through some one other than the spouse is a recognized ground for divorce in the court of law. In our study, five husbands complained that their wives were pregnant through someone else. But, only in two cases they were able to prove it. In both proved cases, divorce was granted on this grounds.

Thus, it may be concluded that extra-marital relation of either spouse is a major eause for marital disruption in all the economic classes.

Mental problems: Modern life is a life of stress and strain. Reimer has pointed out that "neurotic as well as psychotic ailments have been attributed to stresses inherent in the urban way of life."[14]

[14]Riemer, Svend, *The Modern City*, Prentice Hall Inc,, New York, 1955, p. 224 (Insanity in the City-Urban Stress).

Various pressures, namely, economic, familial, social and cultural, act directly or indirectly on the minds of people. Many a time, a person is not able to endure these. With reference to changing societies like India, cultural lag and cultural conflict (e.g., modern educated men/women and traditional family religion in India) are really important in the creation of mental problems. In the present study, mental breakdown was a cause of marital breakdown in some cases. Both men and women had suffered from this problem, though women suffered more than men. All the respondents, in our study, male and female, having mental problems belonged to the middle class.

Among the factors responsible for starting serious conflicts between the husband and wife, mental problem was found in respect of 5 per cent cases. Further, husbands complained that their wives were "mentally unfit." At the same time, divorce was obtained on the legal ground of "unsound mind" in 6 cases, and "epilepsy" in 1 case. "Unsound mind" is a recognized ground for divorce, according to the Hindu Marriage Act, 1955. Mental disorders of any type are of very serious nature, and result in major problems of adjustment. One highly educated husband related his experience as follows: "My wife was a mental patient even before marriage, but this fact was concealed by her parents and relatives. Right from the beginning, I observed that she was not very normal in her behaviour and responses. Within a month, she became pregnant, and, thereafter, the abnormality increased. Her parents said that was due to pregnancy. She was taken away by her parents. After the birth of the child, she was again brought back by me. Right from the day she came back, life became intolerable. She had no sleep. Day and night, she talked and talked often loudly, inviting the attention of all the neighbours and passers by. She was often abusing me and my parents. It was impossible for me to remain in the house because my presence irritated her all the more." Some what similar stories were narrated by several other respondents. Mr S., a Ph.D. holder from a foreign country, faced a similar problem. He was extremely fond of his beautiful young wife. When she showed signs of mental breakdown, it was an agonizing experience for him. He tried his utmost to get her treated even in foreign country. For years, he continued in this state of agony. Finally, he decided to take divorce when he found that no improvement could be possible in the case of his wife. Though remarried, heis still unhappy about the painful past and the fate of his beloved former wife.

Unplanned and unathought of marriage. Unplanned and unthought of marriages may be either arranged ones or love marriages. In either case, the marital relationship is established without giving sufficient forethought. In case of arranged marriages, many people do not care to make rational enquries about the other party. Most information may be only to impress the person at first sight, and unless carefully scrutinized, there can be a lot of discrepancies between the real conditions and the information given. This type of hurried marriages were arranged more in the case of girls than boys. But such hasty marriages can lead to unpleasant or even shocking discoveries later on which will shatter the chances of happiness in marriage.

It may be stated here that out of the 9 "variables relating to to divorce proneness" put forward by Goode, two are" short acquaintance before marriage" and "short engagement or none."[15] According to Duvell and Lewis, one of the causes of divorce in modern society is "hasty, poorly planned marriages."[16] Landis and Landis have also pointed out that "lack of preparation for marriage is a cause of divorce."[17]

Economic hardship. Economic hardship and problems affect family life adversely; familial and economic phenomena are interdependent. With the increasing cost of living, economic problems are soaring high. Economic problems are experienced more when the husband is partially or fully unemployed, or, when he wastes his earnings for non-essential or harmful items like alcohol. In that case, food, clothing, housing and education of the members of the family, particularly children are adversely affected. In such a situation, frustrations arise, creating conflicts and tensions in the family. Such state of affairs will result also in desertion and divorce. Since majority of the married women is not working, they cannot supplement the family income, or substitute the income of the father, as is found in the present study.

Among the complaints of the husbands and wives mentioned in this chapter, "insufficient income" is one of the highest frequency as

[15]William, J., Goode, 1963, *op. cit.*, p. 425.

[16]Duvall, Evelyn Millis and Lewis, Dora, S., *Family Living*, 1950, p. 233.

[17]Judson, T., Landis, and Mary G., Landis, *Personal Adjustment, Marriage and Family Living*, Prentice Hall Inc., New York, 1950, p. 288.

about 46 per cent of the wives and 35 per cent of the husbands expressed it. This goes to prove that economic insufficiency is really an important cause in divorce. Added to these may be considered the complaints (45 per cent) that the wives havs not been able to manage the home and income well, thereby worsening the economic problem.

In respect of management of the family, all the household matters like cooking, cleaning, washing, housekeeping, running the home within the income, care of children or old people, proper management of time, consideration for the likes and dislikes of family members, etc., were involved. According to the information given by the husbands in the present study, some women were lazy, some do not finish the work in time, do not bother about the likes and dislikes of other family members, do not look after children, do not run the home within the limits of the income, and some were not neat and clean and so on. Some such complaints were maximum in lower class, then in middle class and least in the upper class. It is worth-mentioning that many cases of so called poor management of income were not poor management as such. The income was so insufficient as compared to the needs of the family that many women could not manage the home satisfactorily.

Several wives of the lower class complained that their husbands, after finishing their own wages, tried to snatch the wife's earning also, thus, leaving the families literally to starve.

Other sociologists have also observed that economic factor is very important in marital adjustment. Terman has given a list of complaints of husbands and wives. Insufficient income was the complaint with highest frequency [18] Burgess and Cottrell found, that specific economic items such as moderate income, savings, occupations characterized by stability and social control, and regularity and continuity of employment were individually correlated with happiness scores.[19]

Tensions and conflicts may arise if both spouses have different attitudes towards spending. When one wants to save each *penny* and the other is in the habit of spending lavishly, conflicts are unavoidable. If one spouse tries to spend more on one's own personal needs and neglects the needs of the other members of the family,

[18]Burgess & Locke, *op. cit.*, p. 564.
[19]Burgess & Locke, *op. cit.*, p. 569.

resentment is apt to follow. In the present study, about 35 per cent of the women complained that their husbands squandered money either on certain items like gambling, going to houses of illrepute, or on personal items like cigarettes, movies, eating in hotels, aimless wandering entertainment of friends and so on. About 17 per cent of the husbands complained that their wives were extravagant. They were also interested in dress, make up, movies, shopping, etc. Due to such habits of the wives, the economic life of the family was considerably affected.

Some wives (about 13 per cent) said that their husbands were stingy with money. A modern wife feels that she is entitled to spend a certain amount of money on herself, even if she is not earn ing. Decent dress, make-up, outing, movies, entertaining of friends, etc., have become just a normal part of modern life. All these need money, and when a wife is not earning, she has to depend entirely on her husband. Many husbands are not prepared to allow such demands of wives. Let alone their demands, many people are not prepared to spend on the minimum necessary facilities like a maid-servant, an electric or mechanical appliance, etc., which make household work less cumbersome. Some spend money with great difficulty and every time remind the wife of the expenditure she is making. It is but natural for a woman to be frustrated under these circumstances.

Education and economic independence of women. Education along with the advantages it offered has created its own problems in Indian situation. This has particularly reduced the tolerance of women for which Indian woman was well-reputed all over the world. The male authors had successfully kept the women under complete subjugation in all sorts of circumstances through their clever writings. Ignorant, illiterate and tradition-bound women accepted these as God's ordinance for them, and suffered every cruelty, ill-treatment, humiliation, and even atrocity against them. But, today's educated Hindu woman is unwilling to accept the traditional status and role ascribed to them. They are conscious of their rights as wives and this new awareness has created a readiness in them to fight out their causes. Traditional joint family has not changed substantially especially in so far as the status and role of the woman is concerned. At the same time there are educated women in some of these joint families. Where an educated daughter in-law and an uneducated mother-in-law coexist, conflicts in values, expectations and obligations are inevitable, leading to marital disruptions and dissolutions.

In the complaints listed in *Appendix VI* (Complaints of husbands and wives against each other in order of their frequency) complaints of wives such as interference of in-laws (83), demand for dowry (36) and lack of freedom (22) indicate the traditional family atmosphere in the homes of the respondents. These cannot be tolerated by educated and working women.

Emancipation of women and economic independence of women have been important causes of rapid rise in divorce rate throughout the world. It is held that "by placing economic independence within the reach of women, they have with the aid of ideals of democracy and liberty hastened the decline of patriarchal institutions and enabled women successfully to assert their claim to equal political, civic and marital rights."[20]

Fonseca's study showed that "women today no longer occupy a subordinate position in the family."[21] Studies of Hate and Desai have shown that women are inclined to take advantage of the legal provisions of divorce wherever needed.[22] These studies were two decades ago, and by this time, the education and enlightenment of Indian women have further enhanced. Therefore, we can safely conclude that education, employment, emancipation and enlightenment of the Hindu women are causing more and more divorce.

Conservative attitude of the males and in-laws towards female spouse. In spite of increasing incidence of higher education both among the males and females, the attitude towards women is not greatly changed. A sort of double standard is maintained with regard to men and women. Many liberties which the men take are strictly forbidden for women. The comparatively less educated or illiterate in-laws have old values regarding the status and role of daughter-in-law. The husband, even though, he may be well-educated, is influenced by the *patriarchal* form of family, to which he may be accustomed. In most cases, it is found that sentiments like equality of sexes, freedom for women, women's rights, etc., do

[20]Seligman and Johnson, (Ed) *Encyclopaedia of the Social Sciences*, Vol. V, New York, 1948, p. 184.

[21]Fonseca, 1966, *op. cit.*, p. 16.

[22]*Cf.* K.M., Kapadia, 1959, *op. cit.*, pp. 180-81.

not actually penetrate into the hearts and minds of men; most of them are unwilling to accept such modern values too. Women, on the other hand, with the advent of higher education, have started realizing their advantages in the new system and are making efforts to achieve it. Thus, there is a conflict of interests and attitudes between the males and females. This is responsible for a good number of marital disruptions and dissolutions. This aspect has been stressed by Rama Mehta also in her study: "The logic of modern ideas was selectively accepted by men to the detriment of women. The women on the other hand were being educated, earning, and at the same time, their environment was getting less traditional; they, therefore, were entering marriage with a greater sense of their rights. This came in conflict with the male attitude on the wives' role and their own standards of feminine behaviour."[23]

Sexual maladjustment. Sexual relationship is considered to be basis of any marriage, more so, in the initial stages. Whenever the spouses are unable to establish satisfying sexual relationship to both the spouses, marriage is in danger. Physical causes like the impotency of the male and structural malformation of the female sexual organs may incapacitate the couple to enter into healthy sexual relationships. Even when such absolute conditions do not exist, many couples complain that they are not satisfied with their sexual life. Sexual relationship in human beings (unlike among the animals) is not a mere physical activity. Several, physical, psychological and emotional aspects come into play in sexual life. When condusive circumstances do not prevail, in all these fields, sexual activities of a couple may be hampered. Sexual maladjustments do cause divorce. In our study, among the factors responsible for starting serious conflicts between the spouses, on important factor was sexual maladjustment.

Child marriage. Child marriage is a custom in many communities, especially, the lower castes and classes even today, although legislation against it exist for quite some time now (starting from the Sharda Act, 1929). Unfortunately, in traditional countries like ours, custom is still important, and even the law does not come in the way of the custom. Many a time, such marriages pose problems. Children are married before they understand the meaning of

[23]Rama, Mehta, 1975, *op. cit.*, pp. 168-69.

marriage. A young child has no definite sense, ideal, values, purpose or interest in marriage. As he/she grows up, these things become clear to him/her, and then, they develop a personality and identify of their own. One spouse chosen in childhood may be unsuitable and irrelevant, if the other spouse has much disparity in education, training, enlightenment and employment. Such disparity will create maladjustment. Further, in child marriage the boy and the girl do not stay together until *gauna* is performed. In this long gap of separation, one spouse may develop interest and attachment to some other person. Thus, these two factors cause divorce among couples who had child marriage. There are other factors also. This is a peculiar problem in India.

Marriage against the wishes of the spouses. In the present study, there have been cases where the spouses were almost forced to marry the other spouse. Parents still do not approve of the love-marriage idea. Eved when the boy/girl has someone else in view because of his/her liking facilitated by co-education, co-working, etc., the parents ignore such things and ask the boy/girl to marry someone arranged according to their choice. Thus, we see that 91.5 per cent of the marriages in our present study were arranged marriages. Here, we may say that some of these were irrationally arranged, as the spouses were given no sufficient time or opportunity to see and express their views. Proper consent was not obtained from the spouses concerned. Some such cases, naturally, ended in divorce in due course of time.

Incompatibility of the spouses Incompatibility (including temperamental defects) of the spouses has been an important cause of divorce in the present study. 39 husbands complained about the incompatibility of wives, and 32 wives about the same of husbands. Further, 52 husbands have complained that their wives are "non-adjusting." These indicate that there is considerable number of cases of incompatibility. Such cases may have ended in divorce. Burgess and Locke have stated that "there seems to be no doubt that compatibility in temperamental and personality traits is highly important for marital adjustment."[24]

It may be mentioned here that compatibility in a marriage may be gradually achieved. Spouses of different temperament learn to adjust to each other day-by-day. But, in some cases, the opposite

[24]Burgess & Locke, *op. cit.*, p. 466.

might happen. The differences of temperament become obvious day-by-day and with each new revelation, the couple drifts away from each other. Temperament differs from person to person. Various temperamental defects like pessimism, moodiness, hot temper, irritability, aloofness, suspicious nature, secretiveness, etc., are harmful for marital adjustment. If either of the spouses exhibit one or more of these symptoms, problems in marital adjustment may arise. Harmony within a family depends upon deep affectional responses between the spouses. This deep and meaningful relationship never develops even after the spouses living together for many years unless they adjust to each others habits and temperament. In some cases, the temperamental incompatibility is so acute that the couple may be forced to separate from each other immediately.

Quarrelsome disposition of the spouses. Quarrelsome nature of the spouses was another common complaint of men and women of all economic classes. 81 women and 50 men accused their spouses for being ill-tempered or quarrelsome. In many cases, the allegation was both-ways, that is, the wife said that the husband was quarrelsome, whereas the husband said the wife was quarrelsome. It is not surprising that both the spouses thought that the other to be quarrelsome, because, whenever a quarrel occurred, both the spouses participated with equal vigor. Still, it is worth-mentioning that some people are easily irritated and emotional outbursts can occur for trifling reasons. Such was the case of Mr B. According to Mrs M., Mr B., was always irritated and angry, and an outburst of temper and cruelty could occur for the smallest reasons like a missing button on the shirt or the chair is not properly dusted. Similarly, in another case, Mr V.M. said, "you can't imagine what type of a lady my ex-wife is! She can quarrel for days together for a minor reason like that I forgot to bring some small thing she had ordered for."

Wife non-adjusting was the second most frequent complaint of the husbands against their wives, 68 husbands complained that their wives lacked the ability to adapt to the situation in their homes. In our society, it is the woman who has to make all the adjustments, because, it is she who has to leave her own house and go and stay at her husband's place. Unlike the Western cultures, where both the spouses have to make adjustments and go half way on the process, in Indian and other traditional cultures, the wife has to bear the entire burden of adjustment. It is not only with the husband she has to adjust, but to a number of his relatives of all ages and both sexes, who can differ widely in their attitudes, values, habits and interests. The husband himself is often a total stranger. It is possible that the wife has not even seen him before marriage, or even when seen, only for a fleeting moment. As soon as a daughter-in-law comes to the house, the mother-in-law's status is elevated, and the routine household work is regarded by her as below her dignity. A daughter-in-law is expected to know every household work. It is often forgotten that till the previous day she was just a daughter of another household. In many homes, the daughters are not given much responsibilities in household work, because, mothers themselves manage it. These days, girls are also given higher education, and a girl may be spending most of her time in studies, and, therefore, may not have got time and opportunity to be trained in the art of housekeeping. This is particularly true in the case of women pursuing professional qualifications. But with a mother-in-law usually, none of these matters.

When a husband complains that the wife is not adjusting type, that is, she does not adapt herself to the new environment, all these matters must be taken into consideration. A wife's inability to adapt may be an indication of the couple's inability to establish harmonious relationship between themselves. A wife who receives love and affection from her husband will make greater efforts to adapt herself to his home environment. The age at which a girl is married is also an important matter. The attitude of the in-laws towards her is another factor. If they are always critical, inconsiderate and over-exicting, a woman may face difficulties in adjusting with the family situation. If there is close similarity in the habits, values, traditions and patterns of relationships, of the two families, girls make easy adjustments. Her ability to adapt also depends upon the amount and type of training she has received in her own home. It can also depend at least indirectly on the type of marital and familial adjustment her mother has made, because, girls tend to imitate mothers in many matters.

In spite of favourable circumstances at husband's place, a wife may be negligent and may not make efforts to adjust. A remarkable example is, the case of Mr & Mrs G. Mr G. is a high ranking military official and was staying at the place of his work. He is a cheerful person and tries to adjust with people. When Mrs G. reached the place after marriage, Mr G. naturally expected some sort of help from her in household matters. But she never took any interest and Mr G. was often required to look after the household management also in addition to his strenuous work even though Mrs G. was a fulltime housewife.

It is also possible that even after making extraordinary efforts and sacrifices, a wife may be called non-adjusting. Such a case also can be quoted. Mr & Mrs D. was an upper-class couple. Mrs D. was rather young when she got married. She hailed from a sophisticated and loving family. The environment at Mr D's home was very different. It was a joint family, but only Mr D's parents were present in the home. Mr D. had only one sister who was married off early. Mr D's parents had a miserable marital life due to the eccentric and cruel nature of his father. The old man was still active and governed the house. Mrs D. when came to the home, was too young and inexperienced. She was criticised and rebuked at every moment, especially by the father-in-law. Her husband also joined in harassing her. Mrs D. made incessant efforts to learn all the household work. The more she tried, greater demands were made. especially by her father-in-law. Every day, he will insist on new varieties of food specially made for him. Though she used to make them with great care, she would be criticized as an undutiful daughter-in-law. She was insulted in public, and was severely criticized by the husband as well as father-in-law. Three children were born to her. Even in the matter of bringing up children, the father-in-law always got the upper hand. He misguided the children, and tried to bias their young minds against their mother. The broken-hearted Mrs D. endured all this torture for several years, but was forced to quit in the end.

Unhealthy habits like alcoholism, gambling and immorality (vices). It will be seen that among the complaints listed by the wives against their husbands, the following were also found:

Squanders money	— 67 Nos
Vices (smoking, drinking, gambling)	— 45 ,,
Objectionable friendship	— 22 ,,

These substantiate the unhealthy habits of the men. Some men had veneral diseases also. Such habits create constant conflicts and tension in marital life which eventually end in divorce.

Immorality among women is also not uncommon. In the list of complaints by husbands against wives, the following were also found:

Wife interested in other men	— 45 Nos.
Wife pregnant through someone else	— 5 ,,

Similarly, among the factors responsible for starting serious conflicts between the husband and wife alcoholism/drug addiction was reported in 7 cases.

Among the various vices, alcoholism was the chief. As for the causation of alcoholism, two sociologists have stated that "a complex society produces tensions, inhibitions, anxieties and aggressions in the individual which may be temporarily depressed by the use of alcohol.[25] Drinking is both a symptom and cause of personal disorganization. Alcohol can cause serious health problems. In a family where the earning is not much, it creates serious economic problems also. A person can behave abnormally under the influence of alcohol. His relationship with his wife and children is also considerably affected. Many husbands, especially lower class ones, resort to abusing and cruelty towards wife and children, after drinking.

A gambler is also usually disorganized. A lot of money is wasted in gambling. Many people develop an obsession towards gambling and they go on with the game even after losing time after again. Usually a gambler cannot be a regular worker.

Criminal behaviour is absolutely detrimental to society. A criminal's family also suffers a lot. The stigma of arrest, conviction and imprisonment is faced more by the family than the person himself. When the bread-winner is imprisoned, the family faces serious economic hardship too.

Immorality is a wide term including various types of anti-social behaviour. But, in the present context, it only means very lax sex morals. In ten cases, the husbands said that their wives were immoral and indulged in illicit sex very often and with a number of persons. In a striking case, the husband said that he had to change residence very often because as soon as the neighbours

[25] Elliott & Merrill, *op. cit.*, p. 182.

became familiar, his wife used to try to have illicit relations with the men around. Yet, in another case, the husband said that his wife had become a prostitute and indulged in entertaining men for the sake of money.

Desertion. Desertion is another significant cause for divorce. Both husbands and wives of all economic classes had this complaint against their spouses, though the reasons for desertion are variant. In an upper or upper middle class family, a wife may desert a husband for a mere whim of ego, whereas in lower class, it is mainly due to the cruel treatment of husband and in-laws or economic hardships. Desertions observed in our study were of mainly two types—permanent and temporary. In cases of temporary desertions, the husbands used to drive away the wives occasionally and bring them back after an interval of a few weeks or even months. In the same way, a wife may leave the husband and go away after a quarrel, and resume cohabitation after some time. In cases of permanent desertion, the spouses left each other with the intention of ending cohabitation. Both these types of desertions were extremely inconvenient and problematic for the spouses. In the case of women, desertion resulted in serious economic problems; the daily subsistence of the women, as well as their children, if present, created much hardship. In the case of men too, desertion resulted in grave problems, especially, if they were not living in joint families. Cleaning, washing, cooking and a thousand other little things connected with household management made the life of men really miserable. If they living in joint families, these things would not have posed much problem as other female relatives would have helped them.

In cases where children were involved, serious problems arose, both in the cases of men deserting their wives and women deserting their husbands. The children were taken by mother usually, but in a small number of cases, the children were left behind by the mothers. In some of these cases, female relatives of the husband like mother, sister or sister-in-law helped the husband to take care of the children. Even then, the husbands faced considerable problems.

17.5 per cent wives revealed that their husbands had deserted them. Similarly, 13.5 husbands pointed out desertion by their wives. Sociologists have defined desertion as "the irresponsible departure from the home on the part of either husband or wife, leaving the family to find for itself."[26] Some of the consequences of desertion are a humiliating feeling of rejection, uncertainty, economic hardship, lack of care and supervision of children, and anxiety both in the children as well as in the deserted parents. The same sociologists have mentioned that desertion is "the poor man's divorce, signifying that desertion is more commonly adopted by the lower economic classes. In our study also, it is seen that the incidence of desertion is much more in the lower classes than in the middle or upper classes.

Dissimilarity education, intelligence and social status. Some upper class (2.5 per cent) and middle class (8 per cent) men had felt that their wives have either very poor education or were ill-mannered. Great difference between the educational achievement of husband and wife can create several types of adjustment problems. Education widens a person's outlook, it changes his behaviour with in the family and outside also; it improve the understanding and reasoning power of an individual; it changes his interests, attitudes values and beliefs. When one spouse lags much behind the other in schooling, a vast gap in their thinking, behaviour, interests, attitudes and values may occur. A middle-school educated wife may be interested in comics and cheap popular books, while her highly-educated husband might feel an abhorrence towards these. Much difference in education between husbands and wives was noticed in the course of the study. For a glaring instance, a post-graduate husband had an absolutely illiterate wife. In such a situation, the couple faced adjustment problems.

By 'poor manners', the respondents meant inability to behave well in public, with each other, and with other people in the home. Manners are learnt in childhood from parents, elders, friends and associates. Once learnt, they are not easily changeable too.

Two per cent upper class and 8 per cent middle class wives felt that their husbands were inferior to them either in intelligence, education, or social status. Higher education in women has resulted in their thinking and evaluating in terms of realities and they do not follow the traditional patterns of behaviour. A poorly-educated husband may still be tradition-bound and his expectation regarding his wife can be according to the old traditions. Consequently, conflicts between the two are unavoidable. If the wife comes from a better-placed home than that of the husband, her

[26]Elliott & Merrill, *op. cit.*, p. 411.

respect for the husband and his family can be considerably less, and this, in turn, can create an inferiority complex or aggressive behaviour in the husband.

7.5 per cent wives (2 per cent upper and 5.6 per cent middle class) complained that their husbands are either ill-mannered or reserved and withdrawn. One case is particularly interesting, where a husband refused to have any relationship with the wife on the plea that he wants to lead a lonely life. In another case, Mrs B., a beautiful wife, was so annoyed with her husband's poor manners in public, that she refused to go out with him any longer.

Too much interest in career/work. This was the complaint of 9 per cent husbands in the present study. They felt that their wives' over-enthusiasm in their own jobs has ruined their marital life. Usually, in our country, a man expects his wife should leave her work and join him at his place after marriage. But several working women were not prepared to do so. Mr CD a Gujrati Brahmin, divorcee said: "My wife had a good job. But my condition before marriage was that she should leave it and join me. After the marriage, she went off, on the pretext that she would finish all the formalities regarding tendering resignation and would come back soon. But even after three months, she did not return. When I enquired again, she said that she had no intention of leaving the job. I tried to persuade her. But she was too adamant." Mr P., another husband said: "My wife had a good job. She was staying away from her parents because of the job. She had a very free life there. As soon as she reached my place, she found that there were several people at home and she would not be able to be free as she used to be. She left saying that she would be coming back soon, but never returned.

A woman's excessive interest in career may be detrimental to her marital adjustment. House-wife's job is also a full-time job, and if she spends her entire time and energy elsewhere, it is but natural that she cannot give time and attention for her domestic responsibilities. The family naturally feels discontented and neglected. Domestic tensions increase. But it may be possible the other way round also. A woman who is unable to find fulfilment in marriage and family turns to job with ardour which takes her further away from the family.

Interference in hobbies. Hobbies are spare time activities and are helpful in the development of the personality as well as in the fruitful utilization of free time. It is refreshing to the mind and often to the body. People may make economic or other personal gains by developing their hobbies. With the development of modern amenities, a person, especially a house-wife can get plenty of spare time. In the tense life of contemporary world, hobbies play an important role in releasing tensions also.

But in a tradition-bound society like ours, the significance of hobbies either in the development of personality, or as a spare time activity is not well-recognized. Hobbies are often considered as deviant behaviour and some hobbies are considered to be harmful. This sentiment is more strongly expressed when a woman tries to develop a hobby of her own. The husband, family and the entire community may criticize the woman's actions severely.

A detailed analysis of hobbies of the respondents and how hobbies interfered in marital adjustment of the spouses is given in the chapter "Marital Adjustment Prior to Divorce."

Barrenness. Barrenness is considered as a curse especially in Indian society. With the great importance of male progeny, from the social, religious and familial points of view, barren women have to face a lot of problems. The Hindu authors have even allowed a man to re-marry if he has no male child through the first wife. Even today, a barren wife may face this danger any time. In village communities, this is an accepted pattern and often, the wives themselves ask their husbands to marry so that they may have children in the home. But the idea of a co-wife is most anoxious to any modern girl. She takes it as a personal insult. Her own excessive desire to be a mother, coupled with the anxious enquiries and often tauntings of her in-laws or other relatives, the disappointment shown by the husband, etc., together create a very critical situation for the wife. In India, ideas of rebirth are still in vogue. A person's sufferings and problems in this world are attributed to her misdeeds in the previous birth.

In the present study, there are examples of extra-ordinary hardship due to barrenness. Mrs A.K., a beautiful Medical Graduate, had a love marriage with Mr A.K. There was great difference between the backgrounds of the husband and wife. The couple was living in the joint family. Mr A.K.'s parents were very unsympathetic or even cruel towards Mrs A.K. Mrs A.K. was the thoroughly disillusioned within two years of marriage. Meanwhile, whispers and taunts started because Mrs A.K. could not conceive till then. Mrs A.K. herself was desirous of having a child. Barrenness, coupled with the ill-treatment of her in-laws and neglect and lack of understanding exhibited by the husband, broke the marriage completely.

Poor looks. Some men (5.5 per cent) felt that their wives were not attractive. Some wives (4.5 per cent) complained that their husbands were poor in appearance.

Physical built, complexion, facial features, etc., are extremely important in determining the appearance of a person. A good-looking man or woman has a great advantage over their aveiage or poor looking counterparts. The first thing which attracts our attention in any person is his/her appearance. Good looks are particularly important in marital relationship. Every man or woman, even a bad-looking one, wants to get a beautiful spouse. Disappointments to some extent are unavoidable, because, really beautiful people are rare and average people have to be satisfied with average partners. When a man/woman is bad-looking, to get married is a great problem. Even after marriage, women are subjected to humiliations at various stages. The in-laws may taunt them directly, husbands may not take interest, and they may be neglected. Rama Mehta also in the course of her study observed that bad-looking wives faced serious problems right from the time of their marriage.[27]

Husband considerably older. As mentioned in the chapter of Marital Adjustment, the husbands were, on an average, 4.5 years elder to the wives. The difference up to 10 years is also accepted as normal by several spouses. But, when wider discrepancy in age exists between the husband and wife, problems may arise. Age determines, to a great extent, the attitudes, interests and mental as well as emotional maturity of an individual. When two individuals differ greatly in age, differences in all these areas can occur, which, in turn, may lead to conflicts. Koos has observed that adjustment can be more difficult if the couple is of markedly different ages.[28] Baber also has said that except under special circumstances, and for certain temperaments, a very large age differential should constitute an extra-marital hazard. A great difference in age sooner or later would lead to a difference in interests and

[27]Rama Mehta, *op. cit.*, pp. 28-31.
[28]Koos, Earl Loman, *Marriage*, Henry Holt & Co., 1958, p. 161.

activities.[29] At the same time, studies conducted by Terman, Burgess, Cottrell, etc., showed that couples with extreme difference in age also were some of the happiest couples.[30] In the present study, a few wives (2 per cent) said that their husbands were considerably older than them, though none of them mentioned this as the most important cause of marital problems. In all these cases, the husbands were older by 15 years or more. All of them confessed that they were rather ashamed to go out with their husbands, because, they appeared as their fathers rather than husbands. Yet, other factors like cruelty, non-support, interference of in-laws, etc., constituted the main reasons for break in their marriages.

Forced to lead imoral life. A few wives (3.5 per cent) said that their husbands forced them to lead immoral life in order that they may earn money. All these women belonged to the middle and lower classes. The husbands were either lazy or out of job. Mrs L. related her experience this way: "My husband had sold almost every household item we had. He had no job. I was trying to earn a little by doing menial work as a household helper. But the earning was so poor that my husband, I and our two children could not have even one full meal a day. Then, I noticed my husband bringing some strange men to the house. First, I thought they came in just as friends. But gradually, the started behaving with me in a curious way. I noticed that they started coming in when my husband was absent. When I talked to my husband, he was very offended and started calling me names. Later, he made it clear that I should have relationship with them, so that our economic problems would be solved. Of course, I refused his suggestion. But, then onwards, he started treating me with extreme cruelty." A lower class woman said her husband used to tie her hands and legs and then make her do prostitution with other men. From each man, he used to take hundred rupees. The woman developed serious bleeding problem due to this. In one case, the parents-in-law tried to trap a young wife with an an old man out of money motive.

Husband had a living spouse. Some wives (2.5 per cent) said that their husbands already had living spouses at the time of their marriage. In some cases, the fact was hidden completely, and in one when it was revealed, it was assured that the husband had deserted the wife for good. In another case, the wife knew that the husband had a

[29] R.E., Baber, *op. cit.*, p. 113.
[30] R.E., Baber, *op. cit.*, p. 113.

wife and children, but still managed to marry him secretly, because, she fell in love with him. The husband vowed to keep her as a lawfully-wedded wife and his affection would remain with her more than with the first wife. In reality, however, the husband's interest in her was only temporary, and for mere satisfaction of sex. He never treated her as a wife, though cohabited with her for several years.

Making false impression at the time of marriage. Many parents, eager to get their children married off well, give wrong information at the time of marriage. Such false information relates to age, education, job, salary, health, etc., of the boy or girl. Most parents do not consider it, unethical or harmful to give such false information. But the fruits of their action is reaped by their sons and daughters later on. Many a time, a husband or wife may feel that they were completely cheated. Hiding of physical defects is commonly found, in case of girls. However, when the husband discovers such physical defects or informations later on, it is but natural for him to be annoyed. Some accept their fate readily, and others relent.

In the present study, 16 wives and 3 husbands said that they were furnished with false information at the time of marriage. One upper-class husband, who is employed abroad said, "My in-laws said that the girl was a graduate and could speak English fluently. These were the two minimum conditions that I had kept for the marriage. But after marriage, I discovered that she had only done first year in the college, and could'nt speak a word of English. I refused to take her abroad alongwith me, because, I knew taking her along would create problems of adjustment there."

A middle-aged wife, Mrs S. said: "When my people went to see the husband's house in a small township, he showed several nearby houses and said that all those belonged to them and the houses were rented out to other people. When I reached his place after marriage, I found out that my husband had no property, and all that he owned was the small broken house in which he and his parents were living." In another case, an undergraduate wife said, "I agreed to the marriage on the basis of the knowledge that my husband had also passed higher secondary. He had no job at the time of marriage. After a few days of marriage, I asked him to give me his certificate, so that my father could try for a job for him, he confessed that he had no certificate, because, he could not pass higher secondary. But, later enquiry proved that he had just completed primary class and could only read and write. This annoyed me intensely and I refused to live with him any more."

Physical defects. Many a time, in our society, there is a tendency to hide physical defects, especially when matrimonial affiliations are to be established. The reason for this is the fear that if physical defects are disclosed, marriage, especially of the girl, may be very difficult.

In the present study, some husbands complained that their wives physical defects were not disclosed before marriage. Two were cases of partial deafness and the third one a case of one extra finger in both hands and legs. In the case of deafness, the parents said that they considered it as a minor problem, because, after all, the girls could hear when loudly espoken to, and the husbands would gradually adjust with this small difficulty. In one of the cases, the parents said, "We had no intention of hiding the thing as such, but our society is such that if even a minor defect is present in the girl, no one is prepared to marry her. My elder girl had a problem of small white patch on her leg. I disclosed it to any boy who would come to see her. But the result was very disappointing. Instead of appreciating the frankness on our part, they spread a rumour in the whole community that such and such a girl had leucoderma and hence not fit for marriage. I got her married with great difficulty. That is the reason why I decided not to disclose the hearing problem my girl had." In the third case, the girl's argument is that, a small extra finger is a very minor problem, it did not affect her life in any way, and it could be removed any time she wanted, through a very small operation; hence, she or her parents did not consider it worthy of mention. She feels the actual problem was the husband's desire for more dowry. Her physical defect was made only a cover.

One wife said that her husband was a crippled person, and this fact was not known to her before marriage. This fact was known to the parents, but they did not disclose it to the girl. The girl had no chance to see the boy before marriage. The parents were interested in the marriage, because, the boy belonged to a well-to-do family, and, they themselves were poor. But, after marriage, when the pretty young girl found out that her husband was a crippled person, she was totally frustrated. Still, she continued to live with him but separated later due to some other family problems.

Dowry. Dowry has become an inseparable part of marriage in India. Parents themselves are eager to give good amounts as dowry to their daughters. The husband or his parents would like to extract as much dowry as possible. Arguments regarding dowry or arrangements for *barat* (marriage party), and other types of give and take are very common at the time of marriage. In several cases, the troubles persist even after years of marriage. In our study, though there were arguments regarding dowry in several cases. it became a mojor threat to marriage only in 18 per cent cases. Though to some extent the problem existed in several communities, it was acutely felt in the trading communities like the Jains and the Banias. Women were harassed in several ways to extract more dowry from their parents. A detailed discussion of the problem can be found in Chapter 4—Marital Adjustment before Divorce.

Nagging/Criticism. Nagging is considered to be a serious feminine fault by Western authors. In Terman's study, the husbands have said nagging as the most serious grievance they had against their wives.[31] In the present study, as many as 15 per cent husbands mentioned that their wives nagged them. Some of them pointed it out as a grave problem and a source of incessant irritation, Mr V.M., a middle class husband said, "My wife used to nag me so much that my life became a continuous misery. Often, her mother joined her and them, it became intolerable.

Nagging and criticism by the husbands was a complaint of wives too, though in fewer number. One wife said, "My husband used to criticise my every move. All my efforts to improve, he labelled as tardiness or uncomeliness. He made me very nervous and I started loosing my selfconfidence. Had I continued longer under such circumstances, I would have gone mad."

Selfish and Inconsiderate. Some wives (10.5 per cent) complained that their husbands were very selfish and inconsiderate. They cared only for their own comforts and pleasures and did not care at all for the welfare of the family. There were some men who were very fond of good food. They could not afford to eat good food every time at home, So, these men went to restaurants and ate there often. This meant a big hole in the family budget but they did not

[31]*Cf.* R.E., Baber, *op. cit.*, p. 184.

care at all. One young wife, a mother of three children, said "I was married at the age of 15 and before I completed the age of 20, I had three children. My husband was extremely cruel and inconsiderate. He was working as a clerk in a government office, and was earning somewhat alright. If he was careful, we could have pulled on without much problems. But he was very fond of eating out, night clubs and friendship with women of low character. He spent most of his earnings on his wanton habits and I and the three children were literally made to starve. Whenever I complained, he beat me up. When the starvation became intolerable, I informed my father. He brought me and children to my parental home. Ever since, I am there." Another woman said with tears flowing down her cheeks, "You won't believe the way my husband and in-laws had treated me. They made me do all the work and hardly gave me anything to eat. I suffered all that. But when my children were born, it became intolerable, I used to beg for small amounts to buy milk for the small children, but both my husband and mother-in-law always refused. The children used to cry and cry and then go off to sleep. My husband did not bother about them. When I saw that my children may die of starvation at my husband's place. I stealthily left my husband's place and came to my parents. Which woman would like to leave her husband's house if she gets the love and care she deserves."

Spouse not affectionate. A large number of husbands (19.5 per cent) complained that their wives were not affectionate. Similarly, a larger number of wives (27 per cent) said their husbands were not affectionate. However, it should be mentioned here that this aspect was not mentioned by the husbands and wives belonging to the lower economic strata. In other words, only upper class and middle class husbands and wives attributed the cause of absence of affection for divorce.

The desire for love and affection is strong in any human being. Blood bonds provide natural affection between parents and children, brothers and sisters, etc. Conjugal love is considered to be the closest relationship of human beings. In traditional consanguinous families, conjugal bond was treated less important. But with the development of modern urban life, impact of Western culture, modern education, changing values and ideals, increasing importance of sex life, etc., affectional relationship between the husband and wife is assigned considerable importance. This is gaining more and more importance in the modern competitive impersonal society. In small communities, neighbours and large family and kinship groups provided a sense of belonging to men and women which has totally disappeared in the industrialized society. Consequently, for the fulfilment of the basic psychological needs of love, affection, sympathy, etc., a person is entirely dependent upon his own family. Even in a large joint family, relationship between the members, that is, between parents and children, or between brothers or cousins are becoming limited and formal. In other words, the intimate nuclear family is the only area where a person can expect affectional responses. If it is not fulfilled within the family, it is, therefore, but natural for a person to be dissatisfied.

Stressing the importance of mutual affection, Burgess & Locke have said that "if a husband or wife desires and receives from the other, the satisfaction of a psychological need such as demonstration of affection, encouragement or sympathetic understanding, the solidarity of the relationship is thereby increased."[32]

Elsewhere, these sociologists have stated that "the mutual need for sympathetic understanding is one of the strongest bonds in family life."[33] MacIver has also pointed out that "in contrast with the *patriarchal* family, the modern family is built on a more intimate sense of personal relationship."[34] When the economic bonds of the family were weakened under the onset of industrialism, the demand that it should satisfy the personal life of the partners grew stronger.

Misbehaviour/insult. 12.5 per cent wives complained that their husbands used to misbehave with them or insult them. By misbeha viour, it was meant, abusing, taunting in public, trying to irritate purposely, speaking ill of them, making wrong allegations, magnifying weak points, speaking ill of her parents, relatives, etc. Many women are very sensitive to this psychological warfare and they do not want to tolerate it. One young wife said, "Whenever I went wrong in any matter, my parents used to be abused. I did not like this at all, and said to my husband plainly that he should not speak ill of my parents in front of me." Another highly educated wife

[32]Burgess & Locke, *op. cit.*, 1954, p. 339.
[33]Burgess & Locke, *op. cit.*, p. 341.
[34]MacIver & Page, *op. cit.*, 1955, pp. 205-6.

said, "My husband is a highly-educated and refined person. But he can't remain without speaking evil of me to everyone around him."

Some upper class husbands and middle class husbands also had such complaints against their wives. Husbands were more sensitive when the wife did not give due respect to their parents and other relatives. One highly-educated Sikh husband's main complaint against his wife was that she does not respect his parents or obey them. Another middle class husband said that just because his wife was a graduate and his mother illiterate, the mother was not shown due respect. Another graduate husband said about his graduate wife, "My wife often used to misbehave with me. That I tolerated. But the disregard she showed to my parents and elder brother was intolerable. Once my father reached our place at the middle of the night after a long travel. My wife did not even get up from the bed. Another time when my mother was staying with me, she fell ill seriously. My wife did not take care of her at all. The burden of looking after her was entirely on me. Another time, my elder brother's small child was left with me for a few months because my sister-in-law was seriously ill. All her work, including making her hair, getting her ready for the school, preparing her tiffin, etc., I had to do. This gross indifference and neglect of duty in my wife was intolerable."

No interest in home. 13.5 per cent wives complained that their husbands did not show any interest in the homes. All these were cases of middle and lower classes. The highest incidence, however, was in the lower class. Some men were entangled with other women, and so they did not show adequate interest in the spouses or children. Some were too involved with the friends of their own sex and group-activities, that they found little interest in home. In certain cases, too fervent pursuits of hobbies took men away from their homes. Some were in the habit of wandering right from early youth and could not leave this habit even after marriage.

Marital unhappiness of parents and other siblings. The type of adjustment, parents have made in their own marriage, has a definite bearing on the adjustment, the children will be capable of making. In the same manner, if the sibblings are happily married, then, the preparedness of the spouses to take divorce is much less. On the other hand, if there are single men/women of advanced age in the family, or there is a divorcee in the family, then, the spouse exhibits a psychological readiness to go for divorce. In this study, it has been found that 12.5 per cent of the husbands and 8.5 per cent of the wives hailed from unhappy or broken homes. A few husbands and wives had a brother/sister who was either a divorcee or separated from his/her spouse or never attempted to enter marital life. Baber has stated that "superior happiness of parents rates very high in predicting value being more important than the combined influence of several such factors as age at marriage, age difference, education, and income."[35]

Lonely sibling position. It is found in our study that the lonely child of the family (only one child, boy or girl) especially female child, faces very hard problem in adjusting to the family of the husband. Similary, in the case of the husband, being the only child, especially if the father is dead, adjustment is difficult. Very strong attachment exists between the widowed mother and the only son and such husbands find it hard to adjust to their spouses. In the case of the only child, their attachment and loyalty towards the parents come in the way of their attachment towards the spouse. The person is torn between the two loyalties, and often, it is the blood bond which dominates the conjugal bond. The parents of such spouses also create problems due to their over-attachment and dependence on the children.

In our study, 8 per cent of the female spouses were the only daughters of the parental families, the rest being sons. When there is only one daughter in a family, she is often shown special love and consideration. 4.5 per cent husbands were also the only sons of their respective families. In a typical case, a mother had two sons but lost one just after the marriage of the spouse under study. So, the divorcee-husband was the only living son of the family. In another case, though a mother had other children, she was probably attached to divorcee-spouse, because, she had lost her husband when this boy was a child, and for many years, mother and son were the only members of the family, the other children being married earlier. Some husbands belonged to families where there were only sons.

[35]R.E., Baber, *op. cit.*, 1953, p. 225.

CONCLUSIONS

Our analysis of the causes of divorce leads us to the following general conclusions:

1. There are innumerable causes of divorce; there are major and minor causes; several causes work together leading to divorce. It may not be an exaggeration to say that there are as many causes as are the number of cases.

2. There are biological, psychological and environmental (familial, economic, social, etc.) causes of divorce. These work in combination, and not in isolation.

3. Several causes are reflected in the complaints expressed by the husbands and wives against each other. The judicial decrees also indicate certain causes.

4. It should be born in mind that the causes indicated in this chapter are the most conspicuous ones revealed in the present study. Other factors apart, it should be emphasized that since marriage is basically an interaction between two personalities (husband and wife), their backgrounds, socialization, goals, attitudes and several other aspects of personality development are responsible for the phenomenon of divorce. We are inclined to agree with Goode that certain background characteristics associated with greater or lesser proneness to divorce, such as the following are important:

(*a*) Urban/rural background;
(*b*) Marriage at a very young age/other age;
(*c*) Short engagement/six months or more;
(*d*) Parents with unhappy marriage/parents with happy marriage;
(*e*) Dis-similarity/similarity of background; and
(*f*) Different definitions of husband and wife as to their mutual role obligations/Agreement or wife and husband as to the role obligations.[36]

[36]William, Goode, In *Contemporary Social Problems*, edited by Robert K. Merton, R.A., Nisbet, Rupert Hart-Daviss, Sono Square, London, 1963, pp. 424-25.

Chapter 6

PROCESS AND PROCEDURE OF DIVORCE

LEGAL PROCEDURE FOR DIVORCE AND OTHER MATRIMONIAL RELIEFS AS LAID DOWN BY THE HINDU MARRIAGE LAW

BEFORE discussing the actual procedure followed by the respondents in the present study, it is worthwhile to mention the actual procedure laid down by law. For obtaining various matrimonial reliefs, the following sections of the Hindu Marriage Act are prescribed:

(*i*) Suit for Restitution of Conjugal Rights	—Section 9
(*ii*) Suit for Judicial Separation	—Section 10
(*iii*) Suit for Annulment	—Section 12
(*iv*) Suit for Divorce	—Section 13
(*v*) Suit for Divorce by Mutual Consent	—Section 13—B
(*vi*) Petition for Maintenance and Expenses	—Section 24
(*vii*) Petition for Permanent Alimony	—Section 25
(*viii*) Custody of Children	—Section 26

Every petition under the Hindu Marriage Act is to be presented to the District Court within the local limits of whose original jurisdiction,

(*i*) the marriage was solemnized, or
(*ii*) the respondent at the time of the presentation of the petition resides, or
(*iii*) the parties to the marriage last resided together, or
(*iv*) the petitioner is residing at the time of presentation of

the petition, in a case where the respondent is at that time, residing outside the territories to which the Act extends, or has not been heard of as being alive for a period of seven years.

Every petition presented under the Hindu Marriage Act shall state as distinctly as possible the facts on which the petitioner's claim for relief is grounded. Such petitions are required to be verified by the petitioner or by some other person competent to do so, as required by the law and such petitions can be referred to as evidence.

Before proceeding to grant any relief, it is the duty of the Court in every case where it is possible, to make every effort to bring about reconciliation between the parties. Efforts are to be made even when the estrangement appears acute. Reconciliation efforts are to be made right at the start of the proceeding and not after hearing. Efforts cannot be given up simply because the counsels inform that reconciliation is not possible. Reconciliation is to be tried even when the petition is fixed for a serious charge like the wife is pregnant through someone else. However, attempt for reconciliation need not be made when a petition for divorce under the Hindu Marriage Act is grounded on either of the following grounds namely:

(*a*) the respondent has ceased to be a Hindu,
(*b*) the respondent is of unsound mind,
(*c*) leprosy of the respondent,
(*d*) veneral disease of the respondent,
(*e*) the respondent has renounced the world by entering into a religious order,
(*f*) the respondent has not been heard of as being alive for the past seven years.

Marriage Law Amendment Act, 1976, has authorized the Court to delegate the task of effecting reconciliation to a third party, named by the parties or if the parties fail to name any, to any person nominated by the Court. For this purpose, the Court can adjourn the proceeding for a period not exceeding 15 days at a time. The Court is to act on the report of such third party arbitrator, if he reports that reconciliation has been effected.

The Court has to take into consideration the conduct of the parties during reconciliation efforts. For example, if a wife agrees to go back to her husband without any pre-condition but the husband does not take her, it shows that the husband has no intention of keeping her. The Court may proceed thereon. The proceedings under the Hindu Marriage Act are to be held in camera, if the parties desire so, or the Court thinks it fit.

In any proceeding under the Hindu Marriage Act, whether defended or not, if the Court is satisfied on the following matters, relief may be decreed accordingly:

(*i*) Any of the grounds for granting relief exists.

(*ii*) When the petition is based on adultery, the petitioner has not in any manner been accessory to, or connived it, or condoned the act, or where the ground is cruelty, the petitioner has not condoned the cruelty.

(*iii*) When the divorce is sought on mutual consent, the consent has not been obtained by force, fraud or undue influence.

(*iv*) The petition is not presented or prosecuted in collusion with the respondent.

(*v*) There has not been any unnecessary or improper delay in instituting the proceeding.

(*vi*) There is no other legal ground why the relief should not be granted.

In every case where a marriage is dissolved by a decree of divorce, the Court shall give a copy of the decree to the parties free of cost.

The respondent in a proceeding of judicial separation, restitution of conjugal rights or divorce can oppose the relief sought for, if the petitioner is guilty of adultery, cruelty or desertion. The respondent also has the right to make a counter-claim for any relief under the Act on that ground, and if the petitioner's adultery, cruelty or desertion is proved, the Court may give to the respondent any relief under this Act to which he/she would have been entitled, had he/she presented the petition.

Alimony Pendente Lite

In any proceeding under the Hindu Marriage Act, if it appears to the Court that the wife has no independent income sufficient for her support and the necessary expenses of the proceeding, it may, on the application of the wife, order the husband to pay to her the expenses of the proceeding and a sum for monthly or weekly maintenance also, having regard to the husband's income.

Permanent Alimony and Maintenances

Any Court passing a decree, either at the time of passing it, or subsequently, on application made by the wife, may order the husband to pay her maintenance. This can be done either in the form of a gross sum or in the form of monthly or periodical payment, for a term not exceeding her life having regard to her own property, her husband's property and conduct of the parties.

Later, if the Court is satisfied that there is a change in the circumstances of either party, at the instance of either party, the court may vary, modify or rescind the order as it may deem just. In the same way, if the court is satisfied that a wife, in whose favour the order has been passed, has either remarried or is not leading a chaste life, it can vary, modify or rescind the order, at the instance of the husband.

Custody of Children

In any proceeding under the Hindu Marriage Act, the court may, from time to time, pass such interim orders and make such provisions in the decree as it may deem to it just and proper with respect to the custody, maintenance and education of minor children, consistent with their wishes whenever possible, and, may, after the decree, upon application by the petitioner, for the purpose, make, revoke, suspend or vary from time to time all such orders and provisions with respect to the custody, maintenance and education of children.

All decrees made by court under the act are appealable to the next higher court, and the appeal shall be preferred within a period of thirty days from the date of the decree.

If both parties present petitions separately either in the same court or in different courts, the petitions shall be tried and heard together.

According to the Marriage Laws Amendment Act, 1976, it is further provided that:

(*i*) This trial of a petition, as far as practicable, consistently with the interests of justice in respect of the trial, be continued from day to day until its conclusion, unless the court finds the adjournment of the trial necessary.

(*ii*) Every petition under this Act may be tried as expeditiously as possible and effort shall be made to conclude the trial within six months from the date of service notice of the petition on the respondent.

(*iii*) Every appeal under this Act shall be heard as expeditiously as possible, and effort shall be made to conclude the hearing within three months from the date of service of notice of appeal on the respondent.

Earlier in the same chapter, we have mentioned that in a matrimonial proceeding, the court may grant the relief prayed for, even in the absence of one party. Such a decree is called ex-parte decree. But if a party approaches the court with a prayer that the ex-parte decree passed against the party should be set aside, the court should readily accept the prayer. In matrimonial disputes, no spouse can be allowed to have a snap judgment against the other. The case may be reopened, tried and final decree granted, provided no reconciliation was effected between the parties.

Analysis of the cases in the present study showed that the following procedure was generally followed in order to obtain a decree from the judicial court:

(*i*) Filing of the petition by the applicant (petitioner).

(*ii*) Issue of notice to the respondent (the other spouse). A notice is sent by post to the respondent. If he/she does not respond to the postal notice, it is advertised in the newspaper. If the husband is the respondent, the notice is stuck outside his door, in case it could not be handed over to him personally.

(*iii*) Reconciliation efforts by the court.

(*iv*) Written statement of the respondent in reply to the notice.

(*v*) Issues for consideration determined by the court.

(*vi*) Recording of the evidence of the petitioner, respondent and witnesses.

(*vii*) Drawing of a decree.

Most of the cases were heard in camera, although some were

heard in open.

If the respondent did not appear even after repeated notices, ex-parte decrees were granted to the petitioners.

An applicant had to appear in the court at least once personally, and, later on, as and when occasions demanded. Many a time, after putting in the personal appearance, he/she was represented by a lawyer for further hearings. A decree is not granted to a petitioner who fails to appear in the court at least once.

In case of joint application, or application of mutual consent, a different procedure is followed. After the parties put in the joint application, the Judge tried for reconciliation. The parties were granted a period of six months to think over the matter. At the end of six months, if the parties again expressed the desire for divorce, decree is granted.

WHO FILED THE PETITION FOR DIVORCE (HUSBAND OR WIFE)?

The present study indicated that the number of husbands and wives going to the court first time for divorce is almost equal. In 15.5 per cent cases, the husband and wife together put in the petition. Before 1976, an application could not be submitted jointly. In several cases, one spouse went to the court first, and later, the other spouse also agreed for divorce and thus, the divorce was granted on mutual consent.

Many a time, a spouse goes to the court just because he or she wants to harass or pressurise the partner. One such husband said, "My wife left with the children, of course, due to some economic problems. Her parents and relatives were better off, and I thought that they would look after her and the kids till the bad time is over. But, even after improving my financial position, I could not get back my wife and children. She was well-settled by this time elsewhere, and had no intention of coming back to me. I had gone to the Court desperately in order to put pressure on her and her people, but then, the opposite thing happened. She refused to attend the court or try to defend herself. She simply did not want to come back. I got a decree of judicial separation and later on divorce in my favour, but this was quite different from what I really wanted."

Another young woman said, "When I came to know that my

husband started living with another woman, I was really desperate. I wanted to get him back at any cost by any means. In a frenzy, I approached the Court just in the hope of nullifying the second marriage, and thus getting him back. But what I actually got was a decree of divorce on the basis of adultery by my husband. Now, what have I achieved with the court fight? My husband got what he actually wanted without any trouble on his part, and I am the miserable loser."

From the fact that the number of petitions is almost equal from both men and women, we may conclude that the Urban Hindu women are conscious of their rights and privileges, and desire to take advantage of the legal provisions in matters marital. Further, women feel aggrieved because of the delinquent behaviour of their husbands.

In the United States of America, "husbands are less apt to file suit for divorce than are wives. Approximately, two-thirds of the decrees are granted to the wives. In most instances, the mother is awarded custody of the children."[1]

DURATION OF THE TIME THE COUPLE LIVED TOGETHER HAPPILY

The first one or two years of marriage are extremely important in the life of any couple. This is the period when a couple learns to know each other. The period immediately after marriage often termed as the honeymoon period (early days of marriage—see type of relationship between the husband and wife during early days of marriage, Chapter 4—Marital Relation and Adjustment before Divorce) is an important phase of marriage. Though we do not have an institutionalized pattern for honeymooning, the significance of the phase cannot be underestimated.

The data collected in this regard showed that

(*i*) in 47 per cent cases, the time the couple spent happily is only up to one year;

(*ii*) in 24 per cent cases, they did not have any happy time;

(*iii*) in 23 per cent cases, the couple had 1-5 years of happily-

[1]Elliott & Merrill, *Social Disorganization*, *op. cit.*, p. 442 (Who Obtains Divorce?).

married life; and

(*iv*) only in 6 per cent cases, they had happily-married time beyond 5 years.

This clearly shows that on the whole, the happily-married time in most cases has been too short, and those who had some years of happily-married life is very small in number (in all 29 per cent cases, that is, 1-5 years and beyond 5 years). If a couple lives together happily for a period of say five years, then, the chances of their parting is much less. The family is already established, children are born, and the family has taken its due place in the community as well. Kenkel has stated that "despite romantic notion of the delightful ecstasy of the early years of marriage, it is during these very years that the chances for divorce are the greatest."[2] He has further mentioned that half of all the divorces are granted to couples who have been married for six years or less, and 23 per cent to those who have been married for not more than two years.

INTERVAL BETWEEN MARRIAGE AND THE PETITION FOR DIVORCE

In the previous section, we have seen how many years the couple had happy married life. It was not the time between marriage and the divorce-petition, but just the happily—married time. In this section, we indicate the total interval between the time of marriage and the time of filing the petition for divorce. It is found that the maximum number of applications was filed during the interval 3-4 years after marriage (33.5 per cent). It is also found that during the 10-15 years interval, divorce-petitions were filed in 11 per cent cases. It is interesting to note that in a few cases, petitions were filed during the interval 20 years and above. On a further analysis, it is found that,

(*i*) in majority of the cases (55.5 per cent), divorce-petitions were filed during the interval up to 5 years;

(*ii*) in 25 per cent cases, the petitions were filed during the interval 5-10 years; and

(*iii*) in 19.5 per cent cases, such petitions were filed during the

[2]William, F. Kenkel, 1973, *op. cit.*, p. 324.

interval beyond 10 years.

A very significant conclusion arrived at by the researcher during the course of her study was that most of the marriages were already broken right in the first year of the marriage, but then, the spouses were either hesitant to go to the judicial court, or, had to wait for some time to approach the court because of the legal provisions in vogue at that time. However, after the 1976 amendment, divorce is availed of in an easier and quicker manner.

REACTION OF THE SPOUSES TOWARDS EACH OTHER AFTER THE START OF SERIOUS TROUBLES

Misunderstandings, quarrels and problems of even serious types are not uncommon in marital life. But how the parties react to each other after these problems is important in maintaining a marital relationship. There are several couples who quarrel with each other very often, but make up the quarrels also very soon. If there are sincere wishes and efforts on both sides to continue together, any problem can be overcome. What is detrimental to the marriage is either or both partners keep antagonistic views, and lack of sympathy and understanding for the partner, and especially an inability to accept one's faults and forgive those of the other spouse.

Reaction of the spouses towards each other after the start of the serious troubles has been ascertained. Annoyance was the most numerous reaction in respect of the husbands, while tolerance-satisfaction ('tried as much as possible') was the most numerous reaction in respect of the wives. In 9.5 per cent cases, the husbands' reaction was to persecute/murder the other spouse. 2 per cent husbands and 3.5 per cent wives were ashamed of the whole situation.

10 per cent of the husbands and 30.5 per cent of the wives revealed that they tried their utmost and then only gave up. They confessed that they suffered many inconveniences, difficulties and pains for the sake of continuing the marriage, and then gave up only when they were convinced that the marriage could not work at all. To take a typical instance, Mrs S. said, "I am from a poor family, and I know that my parents will not be able to support me and my children, if I chose to go back to them. I tried to continue. I wept, starved and threatened to commit suicide. But my husband

remained the same as he was. He did not want to mend any of his ways. At last, I decided to quit." It is worthwhile noting that the percentage of women who were eager to continue the marriage and who tried their best for the same was three times more than that of men. This, therefore, goes to the credit of female-spouses in the delicate and intricate phenomenon of divorce.

Our conclusion that comparatively less number of spouses tried sincerely to make up after the start of serious problems relating to their marriage. More women than men tried to continue in marriage in spite of problems.

REACTION OF THE PARENTS/RELATIVES ABOUT THE TROUBLES OF THE SPOUSES

The information collected in this behalf showed that the attitude of many parents towards their children's problems was not very helpful. 46 per cent of the parents of husbands and 9.5 per cent of the parents of wives tried to aggravate the marital problems of their children.

21.5 per cent of the husbands' parents and 60 per cent of the wives' parents tried to bring about reconciliation between the spouses. In many cases, it was found that the wives' parents were more eager than the husbands' parents to save the marriage. This is quite understandable, because most of the women were neither earning nor fit to earn. If they broke away from their husbands, the entire responsibility would come on the parents. In addition to all these, there was fear of criticism and stigma. These might have made the wives' parents relatively more interested in making efforts to continue the marriage. To quote an instance, one of the divorced husband's father confided to the researcher, "What is the harm that has come to my family due to my son's divorce? Practically, nothing. I got all my other children well-settled in spite of his divorce, and, he is also married with a nice girl soon after the divorce. But look at his wife's family. The divorce took place a few years ago. At that time, that girl had another marriagable sister. Still, she is unmarried." Divorce is stigma to any family, more so to the girl's family.

In conclusion, it may be said, that the wife's parents and relatives are more keen to continue the marital bond, as compared with the husbands' relatives. Due to this, more reconciliation efforts are made by the wives' parents. This is because of several reasons like (*i*) future prospects of a female divorcee are not very bright in Hindu society, (*ii*) most of the female divorcees are dependents, and hence become economic burden on their parents, and relatives, and finally, (*iii*) greater stigma is attached to a women's marital failure than a man's.

EFFORTS FOR RECONCILIATION

Efforts for reconciliation are mainly of two types, viz., (*i*) efforts by the judicial court, and (*ii*) efforts by others like parents, community leaders, etc.

Efforts by the Court

The extent to which a judge becomes successful in his attempts at reconciliation depends upon the parties with whom he has to deal, and also his personal interest in people, as well as the degree of the marital adjustment and maladjustment of the couple. Some judges take keen interest in the matter and bring about reconciliation in several cases. Mr D. who had once submitted an application for judicial separation said, "When Mr X. was the judge of the court, I had been to the court for the first time. But the judge talked and persuaded me and my wife to be reconciled. We, therefore, continued to live together." Some judges make it clear in the Divorce-decree that efforts for reconciliation were a failure.

In our study it was revealed that only in 34 per cent cases, the judges could make efforts for reconciliation. Even in them, reconciliation was futile, because, one or both the parties did not cooperate.

Efforts by Others

Besides the Court, others like parents, community leaders and several sources like letters, legal notices, etc., were also put into operation to achieve reconciliation. It is seen that parental efforts are of the highest incidence—27 per cent in case of husbands and 60 per cent in case of wives. Personal efforts rated next, and this included husbands' going personally to the place of wives to bring them back. Female respondents wrote letters to bring about reconciliation. 10 per cent of the husbands and 12.5 per cent of wives tried the intervention of caste/community leaders like punches.

Such leaders have a great hold on the people. Many a time, in marital matters, *panchayat's* decision was accepted. This was more so, in lower castes. 15 per cent of the husbands and 11 per cent of wives attempted to bring about reconciliation by serving the other party with legal notices. 45 per cent of the husbands and 29.5 per cent of the wives did not try any sort of reconciliation.

Thus, we find that besides the judge, several other persons/ agencies also made efforts for reconciliation, but they all proved futile, and the spouses pursued their cases of divorce. It was also noticed that some respondents made more than one method for bringing about reconciliation.

DURATION OF THE TRIAL IN THE COURT AND COURT EXPENSES

Our investigations indicated that in vast majority of the cases, it took time up to about 4 years. Only in 13.5 per cent cases, the court took time between 5 to 8 years. The prolongation of the case of some respondents was mainly due to the fact that the spouses concerned were indifferent. If a decree of divorce is granted in two parts (that is, a decree of judicial separation is granted first and then a decree of divorce is granted, or a decree of restitution of conjugal rights is passed and the parties did not resume cohabitation even after 2 years, hence a divorce is granted), the trial would take 2-4 years from the time of the first petition. Lawyers who deal with divorce cases have pointed out that in many cases 2-3 years is taken for decision, excepting those of mutual consent.

As for litigation expenses, it was revealed that on an average, a lower class case needed about Rs 500; middle class anything between Rs 1,000 and 2,000 and the upper class, Rs 2,000-3,000. The expenses mostly depended upon the duration of the trial. In cases of mutual consent, or when one party is not interested, the court expenses are very low. In several cases, husbands were made to pay court expenses and maintenance-allowance during the period of trial.

ATTENDANCE OF THE SPOUSES IN THE COURT DURING TRIAL OF THE DIVORCE CASE

In our study, in majority of cases (55.5 per cent) both the spouses attended the court. In the beginning, the parties made personal appearance and later usually engaged lawyers to represent and argue their cases. In a good number of cases (22.5 per cent), the wives refused to attend the court. In almost an equal number, the husbands did not attend the court mainly because they had no interest in the divorce case.

LIFE OF THE SPOUSES DURING THE PERIOD OF TRIAL

Matrimonial dispute cases may go on for years as shown in an earlier section of this chapter. The period of trial was extremely difficult for most of the respondents, especially females. It entailed much strain and anxiety. Some of the typical problems/situations faced by the respondents were:

(*i*) Uncertainty and anxiety about the future;
(*ii*) Much expenses;
(*iii*) Non-satisfaction of sex;
(*iv*) Disturbance in the home set up;
(*v*) Training, education and discipline of children;
(*vi*) Social stigma; and
(*vii*) Economic non-support.

Almost all respondents expressed the view that the post-divorce period is comparatively less disturbing than the trial period. The intensity of the problem varied from person to person, depending on various factors such as:

(*a*) the emotional make up or sensitivity of the person concerned;
(*b*) the support he/she received from parents and relatives;
(*c*) support received from friends;
(*d*) type of provision for economic needs; and
(*e*) employment or ability to be employed.

It was seen that the person who really desired divorce suffered less as compared with the other spouse who did not want it. A few had gone for divorce out of their exhaustion and intolerable circumstances. They would not have planned or even thought of what will be the future conditions, should a divorce decree was obtained.

For instance, Mrs L. said, "Life with my husband became so intolerable that I forgot everything. I was so exhausted physically and mentally, that all I wanted was some peace of mind and rest. I did not even think what I would do after he had left me." But several others went for divorce with definite plans.

In such a case, Mr D. said, "When I found that my wife is not very keen to come back, I immediately went to the Court. I thought it was better to finish off an unpleasant affair as early as possible, so that one can start afresh without wasting any more time."

The incidence of cohabitation during the pendency of the court case was inquired into. It was found that majority of the couples (92 per cent) were already separated when the trial started. Only in 8 per cent cases, some cohabitation took place. In a very peculiar case, the wife did not even know that proceedings were going on in the court against her. The husband tried to hide it from her. She thought that some other type of case was going on. Therefore, she continued to live with the husband even after the divorce was decreed. The husband did not want to make it known to her, because, his intention was never to leave her, but to legalize his relation with the second wife.

In some cases (13.5 per cent) the male spouse and in some other cases (5.5 per cent) the female spouse had already started cohabiting with the new spouse, before the final decree of divorce was granted, though it was illegal. Some spouses did not bother to have a formal remarriage, but just started living together or eloped with another.

Economic support of the female spouse during the period of trial was also inquired into. It was seen that in a good number of cases (51.5 per cent), the economic support came from husbands. It was as a result of payment of maintenance allowance ordered by the court. The amount was generally insufficient to meet the expenses of the wife and the children. But it was a great help when a woman had no other source of income. In several cases, this meagre amount was supplemented by their own earnings or assistance from parents.

From the foregoing information, we find that the period of trial of the divorce cases was really difficult for both the spouses, more so, for the wives.

ALIMONY

Alimony is defined as "an allowance required by a court to be paid out of the estate or earnings of a husband to his wife or by a former husband to his former wife, or by a wife to a husband."[3] There are temporary and permanent alimonies. Temporary alimony (pendete lite) is an allowance required from the husband to the wife before a divorce is granted. Permanent alimony is an allowance after divorce. The amount of the alimony and the length of time it must be paid vary according to the financial circumstances, health, age, and other factors decided by the court. It seems the theory of alimony has originated from the ecclesiastical court of England where it is laid down that "since at marriage the husband assumes the permanent obligation of supporting his wife, that duty naturally continues, if, for good reason, she chooses to live apart from him."[4]

The power of the court of ordering alimony *pendete lite* in a pending proceeding for matrimonial relief has been provided for by Section 24 of the Hindu Marriage Act, Section 36 of the Indian Divorce Act, and Section 36 of the Special Marriage Act. Under Section 24 of the Hindu Marriage Act, the relief has been extended to spouse of either sex, that is to say in an appropriate case, a husband also can claim alimony *pendete lite.*

In our study, it was found that 45.5 per cent wives were granted maintenance and/or court expenditure during the trials. Similarly, in 12.5 per cent cases, the wives were granted alimony on a permanent basis. No husband was granted maintenance or alimony, nor did they apply for the same.

As for the amount of the alimony, it varied between Rs 25 and Rs 425 per month. To conclude, it may be said that payment of court expenditure/maintenance/alimony is a healthy system, and it is found in urban Madhya Pradesh. However, it was found that in some cases, it was misused. That is, although the wive's, people were in a position to support the divorced women, or they had other sources of income, yet, maintenance-allowance was obtained. In a way, it is in favour of the female respondents and it helps to raise her status too. A man cannot easily get rid of his legally-married wife with or without children.

CUSTODY OF CHILDREN

One of the most pressing concerns in regard to divorce is the

[3]H.P., Fairchild, *Dictionary of Sociology*, 1944, p. 9.
[4]Elliott & Merrill, 1950, *op. cit.*, p. 430.

custody of children. In some cases, either the father or the mother does not wish to be burdened with young children, and is anxious to relinquish his or her rights. The child is thus spared with much unpleasant bickering. But he often gains this freedom from strife only at the expense of the permanent loss of one or the other parent. He must live in an incomplete household at least until his mother or father married again. More often, however, couples with children engage in a prolonged acrimonious controversy over their custody. The children then become innocent and bewildered pawns in a game played by their parents and the respective lawyers. When the case comes to court, it is the duty of the trial judge to settle the dispute and award the custody of the children to one or the other parent.

In the United States of America, it is the custom in most cases to grant the custody of minor children to the mother though the father must share in their maintenance. If the mother is not of good moral character, or is otherwise an unfit guardian for the children, they may be placed under their father's care.

According to Johnson, one of the worst aspects of divorce in the American society is "the frequency with which custody of children is divided. The divorced parents are often bitter towards each other, and one often embitters the children against the other."[5]

The question of custody of children has been dealt with in Section 26 of the Hindu Marriage Act, Section 38 of the Special Marriage Act and Section 41 to 44 of the Indian Divorce Act. Disruption of marital relations between the spouses is fraught with grave consequences to the welfare of minor children, and, accordingly, provisions have been made for safeguarding their interest and welfare. The relevant sections contemplate minor children only. Minority of the children will be determined with reference to the Indian Majority Act and, it is in relation to those children only who are minor that statute that the provisions of these sections apply. In making an order in respect of the custody of child, the welfare of the children is the paramount consideration, not the rights of the parents. The relevant portion of Section 26 of the Hindu Marriage Act, 1955 (amended up to 1976) reads as follows:

In any proceeding under this Act, the Court may, from time to

[5]H.M. Johnson, *Sociology*, 1961, *op. cit.* p. 175.

time, pass such interim orders and make such provisions in the decree as it may deem just and proper with respect to the custody, maintenance and education of minor children, consistently with their wishes, wherever possible.

Even though, under the Hindu Law, the father is the natural guardian of his child, and is preferred to its mother. Yet, in proper cases, a mother is appointed guardian. Ordinarily, the Court will refuse to give custody of the minor children to the guilty party, whether husband or wife. Even when the custody of the children is given to the mother, the guilty father may not be deprived of all control over the children. If neither the father nor the mother is fit and proper person to have the custody of the minor children the court will, in the interests of the children, place them in the custody of some fit and proper person.

In the present study, only 39 per cent of the couples had children. But in most of the cases, the parties had decided among themselves the custody of children without taking the issue to the judicial court. In some cases, the spouses did not show any interest in the children, and, therefore, the children were left with the other spouse. Only in 5 per cent cases, there was a dispute between the spouses regarding the custody of the child, and the matter was decided in the court. In about 4 per cent cases, the custody of the children was given to the mother, the reasons for upholding the claim of the mother in this connection being:

(*i*) The children were under five years of age;
(*ii*) It was the wish of the children themselves to remain with mother; and
(*iii*) the mother was the innocent party.

TRENDS OF DIVORCE CASES DURING 1968-1977

If we have a look at the statistics of divorce in the United States of America and the Europe, we notice, that there were different trends in the rate of divorce in different times. For instance,

(*i*) The rate of divorce was low before World War II;
(*ii*) The rate of divorce was high after the World War II; and
(*iii*) The rate of divorce was still higher in recent times.

The rate of divorce in England and Wales per 1000 population in 1911 was 0.07; it was 1.30 in 1950: and it became 4.70 in 1970, and it was 8.40 in 1973.[6]

It may have gone still higher in the 1980's.

In Sweden, the rate of divorce per 100,000 married women during 1901-1910 was 54.1, it became 505.5 in 1951-55 and 684.6 in 1970.[7] In the United States of America, divorce per 100 marriages in 1900 was 7.9; it became 17.4 in 1930; 23.4 in 1960, and 34.6 in 1973.[8]

It may still be higher in the 1980's. In countries like the United States, there are plenty of facilities and methods to have the statistics concerning marital disruptions and dissolutions. For instance:

(*i*) Compilation of divorce records at the county, state or national levels;
(*ii*) Collection of data through decennial and sample surveys made by the Census Bureau; and
(*iii*) Getting data directly from the divorces by means of questionnaires and interviews.

These facilities and methods we do not have yet in India, and, therefore, we are unable to say correctly, with the support of statistics what exactly is the trend. But with reference to our study, it is found that there are the following stages for divorce rates in India, especially with reference to the urban Hindus:

(*i*) Before 1955, that is, before coming into operation of the Hindu Marriage Act, there were very few legal divorces, except in some former States where divorce law came into operation even before 1955, e.g., Baroda, Madras and Bombay. During the pre-1955 period, most of the divorces were customary, undertaken through caste-panchayats.
(*ii*) During 1955 and 1970, there have been a few cases of divorce but not many.
(*iii*) During 1971-76, there were some more divorces; may be

[6]Robert Chester, *Divorce in Europe*; 1977, p. 77.

[7]Trust, Jan. *Divorce in Sweden*, in Divorce in Europe, edited by Robert Chester, 1977, p. 35.

[8]Kenkel, 1973, *op. cit.*, p. 314.

because of the spread of education and gradual awareness and awakening among the people that they can avail of the legal provisions and they started taking advantage of the same.

(*iv*) After 1976, many more cases started flowing in as a result of the Marriage Laws Amendment Act, 1976, where several amendments have been made, making matrimonial reliefs easier and quicker, more especially the provisions for divorce by mutual consent. (Section 13-B—Hindu Marriage Act).

Certain recent reports in the Press corroborate the above trend. For instance, it is reported that "seven years ago, only five divorce cases were filed each day in Delhi courts. Today, the number is 25. A similar increase is reported from most of the big cities."[9]

CONCLUSIONS

In this chapter, we have dealt with various processes and pro cedures in connection with the obtaining of divorce by the respondents concerned. Our general conclusions are:

1. In divorce cases, most of the procedures that are laid down under the Hindu Marriage Act 1955, as amended up to 1976, such as filing of the petition for divorce, making efforts for reconciliation, attending the court, presenting arguments and producing witnesses, waiting for the final decree with or without great strain and excitement and the custody of the child/children as allowed by the court.

2. Both the male and female respondents almost equally (43.5 per cent male and 41 per cent female) took courage to file the petition for divorce.

3. Most of the petitions were filed during the interval up to 5 years after marriage of the respondents (111 cases or 55.5 per cent). There have been some cases of divorce even after 20 or more years of happy married life, but it may be admitted that most of the marriages were already broken right in the first year of marriage.

4. There were different types of reactions of the spouses towards each other after the start of serious troubles, leading to the filing of divorce petitions. Many were annoyed, some were indifferent

[9]Kahkashan Naqvi, *Divorce an Increasing Phenomenon in India*, The Premier, July 19, 1982.

and some others felt that there was no other way out except divorce.

5. With regard to the reaction of the parents/relatives of the spouses about the troubles, it was found that some parents tried to reconcile, some tried to aggravate the situation, and some others remained ignorant or indifferent.

6. Efforts for reconciliation were made by the judges and others, but in most cases they were ineffective.

7. In most cases, it took up to about 4 years to decide the divorce case in the court. Expenses varied from Rs 500 in lower class to Rs 2,000 or more in upper class cases.

8. Most spouses attended the court during the course of the divorce proceedings.

9. The life of the respondents during the pendency of the court cases was really miserable, but many felt relieved after the decision of the court.

10. In majority of the cases, maintenance was paid by the husbands during the period of trial so that the wives had some support when the court cases were going on.

11. Custody of the minor children after the decree of divorce is a very delicate and, at the same time, important matter. Usually, the mothers have the custody of minor children. Dispute regarding children arose only in very few cases.

12. In analysis of the trend of divorce cases during the period 1968 to 1979 in our study showed that there are four stages of divorce trend in India. Out of these, in the fourth stage, that is, after the 1976 Amendment of the Hindu Marriage Act, the rate of divorce has increased much. However, we need more studies and analysis of data in our country, in order to assess the trend of divorce cases correctly.

Chapter 7

CONSEQUENCES OF DIVORCE: LIFE OF MALE AND FEMALE DIVORCEES AFTER DIVORCE, THEIR SOCIO-ECONOMIC STATUS

INTRODUCTION

THREE most important aspects of the study of divorce in any community or country are socio-cultural background of the couples in divorce, causes of their divorce, and the after-effects of divorce. Background and causes alongwith numerous aspects of marital adjustments/maladjustments we have already seen. In this chapter, we deal with the effects of divorce, more especially on the spouses. Their remarriage and the condition of children will be dealt with in the consequent chapters.

The consequences of divorce are many and grave. Between birth and death of a person, the most important event in life is marriage. Marriage changes the personalities, the attitudes and the life-style of men and women. Marriage is entered into with great hopes and expectations. Divorce is the failure of marital life, and, therefore, it has serious repercussions on the individual, family and the community. Many researches and observations have shown that the negative results of divorce are perhaps more than the positive ones. In a way, divorce brings about personal, familial and social disorganization. In divorce, it seems in the majority of the cases, "the effects are more severe for the wife than for the husband."[1]

[1]R.E. Baber, *op. cit.*, 1953, p. 497.

Divorce brings about the collapse of one's world. It also necessitates the reorganization of one's affectional life. There are close similarities in the bereavement and divorce situations. In both situations, there are (*i*) absence of the spouse, (*ii*) cessation of sex relationship with the spouse, (*iii*) usually (for the wife) a more difficult economic role, with lowered income and perhaps outside work to compensate, and (*iv*) the preservation of many old habit-patterns, even though some be broken. But, offsetting these similarities, at least for the women, is the fact that the divorce lacks the institutionalized patterns which shape and ease the reactions of the widow. As a consequence, "the divorce is placed in several acts of either underfined or incomparable roles."[2]

Divorce creates in a way a crisis situation. Of course, the intensity of the crisis is felt by different people in different ways, such as (*i*) men and women, (*ii*) young and old, (*iii*) marriage of short duration and those of longer duration. In cases where children present, the parent who retains the children experiences less of a crisis than the one who is cut off from both the former mate and children. Frequently, one member of a divorced couple may be more emotionally involved, more dependent, and suffer more emotional disturbance than the other, and this tends to prolong the crisis more for one than the other.

There are several types of adjustment to divorce such as

> (*i*) talking to others about one's divorce; (*ii*) continued association of the husband and wife after the divorce; (*iii*) involvement in a second marriage; (*iv*) attempts to control the life of the ex-mate; (*v*) idealization of early relationships with the ex-mate; (*vi*) an effort to drown one's sorrow by over-indulgence in drinking, sex, etc. especially by males; (*vii*) withdrawal from society temporarily; and (*viii*) moving to a new location.

Spatial separation is a means of adjusting to divorce. Moving to a different locality serves much the same function as in instances of bereavement where the bereaved separates himself from objects and relationships which remind him of the deceased.

Divorce represents a fundamental change in status and role for all concerned. This change is a crisis in their lives. Those with a

[2]William, J. Goode, *Problems in Post-divorce Adjustment*, American Sociological Review, 14: 394-401, June, 1949.

strong, well-integrated, or highly egoistic life organization may survive it with comparative ease. But such an adjustment is not possible for those with weaker personalities or for those who care to deeply. They cannot forget. They cannot immediately adjust to their new status and role.

According to some social scientists, as a result of the emotional crises to which they have been subjected, many divorcees develop symptoms of personality disorganization. These psychological manifestations include suppressions, repressions, regressions, ambivalent motivations, blockages, cleavage between lust and love, loss of self-confidence and ambition, doubts, indecision, nightmares, morbidly transferred attachments or aversions—all these and more.[3] These social scientists have also pointed out that divorce creates problems of sex adjustments, habit and economy, and finally came to the conclusion that "divorce is nearly always a tragedy, for, it generally means blighted faith, broken troth, and severe disillusionment."

Because of the adverse effects of divorce on the total society, the mounting rate of divorce is treated with great concern in countries like the United States of America where some writers have recently held that "divorce generally hurts and when that pain affects more than 15 million Americans, we are justified in regarding the situation as something of a national health emergency."[4]

Not all who are granted a divorce react in the same way. Some find it an extremely disorganizing experience; others are only mildly disturbed, still others feel a pleasant release. The intensity of trauma will depend upon a number of factors such as (*i*) the sensitiveness of the personality involved, (*ii*) the amount of love that is still left, (*iii*) the rapidity and degree with which the divorcee is able to find compensatory adjustment within society.[5]

The study of divorced Hindu women by Rama Mehta showed that many of the respondents especially of the lower middle class were ill-equipped, both psychologically and economically to create satisfactory life after divorce. The old values regarding respectability hampered them from being socially free. Indian orientation with its emphasis on female subordination, self-sacrifice, timidity

[3]*Cf.* Elliott & Merrill, 1950, p. 457.

[4]Pietropinto and Simenauer, *Husbands and Wives*, 1981, p. xvii.

[5]*Cf.* Christenses, Harold T., *Marriage Analysis*, 1958, pp. 567-71.

and modesty inhibited their capacity to stand on their own feet. Most of them were, for great part of their time, anxious and fearful of the future.

AGE OF THE SPOUSES AT THE TIME OF DIVORCE

The age at which a person gets the decree of divorce is an important factor in the adjustment, he is able to make after divorce. A person who is accustomed to a family and takes a divorce in a later age finds a very difficult time. By the advancement of age, habits, likings, behaviour and attitudes develop a definite trend and it is very difficult to change it later. Though the couple may have been having bitter fights and quarrels, people develop deep-rooted attachment too over the years. The problems and quarrels may prompt them to seek divorce, but, at the same time, they can also sense an opposite force within themselves which persuades them not to end such a long and intimate relationship.

People who break their marriage at an early age find comparatively less difficulty in readjustments They still have chances of finding a partner of their choice, their enthusiasm and energy to live is yet unfinished, their habits and interests are yet pliable and they exhibit a greater degree of adaptability. Though several other factors influence the post-divorce adjustment, age is a very important one.

The age at the time of divorce was investigated in the present study. Some of the important findings are:

(*i*) Vast majority of the men (65 per cent) are of the age group 26-35;

(*ii*) Vast majority of the women (67.5 per cent) are in the age group 21-30;

(*iii*) It would thus appear that the vast majority of the divorcees is still young, and, can afford to consider remarriage or other types of adjustments;

(*iv*) There are only 5 per cent women in the age group of 40 and above. In the same age group, the number of men is relatively more, that is, 14 per cent.

(*v*) About 42 per cent women got divorced between the ages of 20 and 25. This is the highest frequency in a single age group as far as the women are concerned. This is comparatively early age, and people who get divorced in this age have good chances to make fresh adjustments in life.

We conclude that majority of the divorced spouses are comparatively young, and are fit to remarry and settle in life, provided other factors are favourable to them.

TYPE OF FAMILY PROBLEMS FACED BY THE SPOUSES DUE TO DIVORCE

Various types of family problems faced by the divorced men and women were enquired and their responses indicated that

(*i*) The women were subject to much more criticism and neglect than men.
(*ii*) The men did not complain of economic hardship; while 27 per cent women had revealed this as an important problem.
(*iii*) The women did not have any problem to look after children while the men had.

Some illustrations of the different types of family problem may be given below.

One female divorcee said, "I could not pull alongwith my husband and hence broke off. But today, at my brother's place, I am treated no better than a servant. Many times, I feel that I did a great mistake by going for divorce. In the husband's house, with all problems, I had the status of a wife, but here, I am nobody."

Another young woman, Mrs S. said, "I am the only sister of three brothers. But what do they care for me? All of them are married, and have children. They care for their own families only. What happened to me is no concern of theirs."

One husband said, "I am the only male issue of my parents and they both were extremely fond of me. My father spent a lot of money and arranged a good wedding for me. But, when the bride refused to stay with me right on the day of wedding, my father was totally shocked. Soon, he had a heart attack, and passed away."

In a country like India, where close ties remain between parents and children till death, it is nothing unusual that parents consider their children's failures as their own and feel very unhappy about it. Vast majority of the marriages are arranged by parents themselves. Hence, marital failures are considered to be the responsibility of the parents rather than children. Our data also shows that parents were more unhappy about their famale offsprings than male. The reason is obvious: the future of a divorced woman is very bleak in our society.

PERSONAL PROBLEMS OF THE SPOUSES DUE TO DIVORCE

Divorce is a personal tragedy, for, marriage is mostly an intimate exclusive relationship between a male and a female. The extent of mental and emotional trauma that can be created by divorce cannot be explained sufficiently. Estrangement from the closest and the nearest person with whom a person must have lived for years, loss of economic and family security, a sense of inferiority or failure, fear of criticism, inability to face previous friends and associates, separation of children from one parent and consequent emotional problems in them, need to find out and settle a new establishment, break of a routine to which one may have been used to for years, sudden break in sexual life, etc., together create an extremely difficult situation for either partner.

Aldous has mentioned that, "the greatest amount of unhappiness occurred after two months the divorce was granted. Men who had always depended on their wives for physical maintenance now had to learn to take care of themselves. Those living in a joint family type organization were better prepared."[6]

Angela Reed describes the problems of divorce as "loneliness, frustration, guilt and despair for future, either apathy or overactivity socially or at work."[7]

Malcranzler has vividly expressed his own feelings after divorce as below:

"Suddenly, the consequences of what I have done, rushed in and terrified me. How could I, a family counsellor, of all people, end up in this predicament? What made me give up a 24 years of married life with an attractive, intelligent woman, and two delightful teenage daughters? Why, at the age of 50, was I leaving behind

[6]Joan Aldous, *Family Careers*, Developmental Change in Families, 1978, pp. 180-82.

[7]Reed, Angela, *The Challenge of Second Marriage*, London, 1973, Chapter 2.

a large comfortable home in a quietly genteel section of San Francisco? Even with my training and experience as a professional counsellor, I was not prepared for the emotional impact of divorce, when it hit me."[8]

The bitter experience of a woman, divorced after 12 years of married life, is given in the same book of Melcrantzler. In her own words: "I simply had to leave my marriage. It was intolerable. But now, I wonder if I did the right thing. At least, I knew who was I then. I was a wife, Mrs Somebody. Now, I am a zero. I can't get even credit on my own name."

During the course of the present study also, the investigator came across several men and women, who expressed their sorrow and bitterness in similar ways. The dependent nature of the divorcee is very clear in India. In our society, a girl or boy is treated as just a child, till the time he/she gets married. Many of them get married before they cross the threshold of childhood. Children are not given freedom to think or act independently. Even after marriage, the control of parents may continue as we see in the joint family system. An Indian divorcee, especially divorced female, finds it extremely difficult to pull on, if she does not get the support of her parents and relatives, because, she is never trained to live independently. Until she is married, her parents think and act for her. After marriage, this aspect is taken up by her husband or in-laws.

In our investigation, it was found that many of the divorcees were unable to express their personal problems eloquently. Some felt it is better to talk less about the matter, as talking about the same upsets them and stirs up bitter and painful memories. Some of the striking types of personal problems experienced by the divorcees are:

(*i*) Frustration;
(*ii*) Inferiority complex;
(*iii*) Shyness;
(*iv*) Loneliness;
(*v*) Economic hardship; and
(*vi*) Ill-health.

[8]Malcranzler, *Creative Divorce*, "A New Opportunity for Personal Growth", New York, 1973-74, pp. 4-5 (Emotional Truth of Divorce).

The worst problem is frustration. The next three types of problem in considerable frequency are inferiority complex, shyness and loneliness. Women were more frustrated than men. This is but natural, because, in India, the future of female divorcees is much more bleak as compared with that of male divorcees. Some of them were so frustrated that they did not want to continue to live and thought of committing suicide. A few instance may be narrated here.

One young woman confessed, "I was so depressed after the separation from my husband that I wanted to finish my life. I would have actually done that also, but for the sake of my daughter ..... helpless infant."

Another divorced woman, just in her early twenties revealed, "I was married when I was just 18. I stayed with my husband hardly for 3-4 months. Even in this short period, I do not remember to have spent even one day with him happily. He was always in an abnormal state due to drugs, and I did not experience the love and company of a man even for a day." Looking at her three-year-old daughter, she continued, "I have become a mother too, but in his company, I have never found an hour of enjoyment or happiness. Everything happened so unaware and all that I got is frustration and worry about the future of this child and mine."

Some men also had tales of woes. One middle-aged man, Mr H. said, "I was married for the last 13 years. All my youth, I have wasted toiling for my wife and her family. She had no brothers, and I had to look after all affairs of their family. Finally, I wanted to get separated from my wife's family. We got a new house constructed. When everything was finished, my wife wanted to drive me away. She was already in love with some man and I became a nuisance for her."

Inferiority complex is the second striking problem faced by the divorcees. This is a feeling of insufficiency or personal failure. If one partner was unwilling for divorce, the feeling increased all the more. In our study, the sense of inferiority complex was observed in almost equal frequency in both male and female divorcees. The feeling that there is something lacking in them and the other spouse left him/her to get a better partner was very much disturbing. One very beautiful upper class wife, who was left by her husband, because he fell in love with some one else disclosed "Till the day my husband met that woman, he was perfectly happy with me.

But, I cannot say, what is it that in her, which attracted him towards her so much that he left not only me but our three lovely children, his parents and wider family connections. She must be much more attractive than me."

Another divorced woman, who was also abandoned by her husband, because he fell in love with another woman said, "May be, she is prettier than me or she has better qualities. After all, I am only an ordinary girl brought up in an ordinary family in a small town; she, on the other hand, grew up in a large city, and has more experience with people and also worldly affairs."

Shyness is the third important problem experienced by the divorcees. In India, divorcee is treated with great social stigma, and he/she finds it extremely difficult to face people. Because of the caste affiliations, and constant social intercourse between members of a caste, even a very personal affair cannot be kept secret. Divorce is treated as a break from the traditional, approved norm and hence a social deviance, according to the members of the community. People start criticizing the divorcees indirectly, any many a time openly. Consequently, many divorcees avoid social contact, especially during the period immediately after the divorce.

A male divorcee disclosed, "I was so reluctant to face people that for several days, I did not go for work. I simply kept to my room feigning sickness."

One young woman said, "I do not go to attend any social function after divorce. I was divorced several years ago, but even today, I feel very difficult to face people. They treat me as if I have committed some crime."

Loneliness is yet another problem faced by the divorcees, males as well as females. Many have narrated their experiences but limitation of space does not permit us to describe them.

Two per cent males and 18 per cent females said that they were undergoing severe economic hardship owing to divorce and even their physical needs were not properly met.

Thus, vast majority of the male and female divorcees are facing various types of personal and emotional problems. Women suffer more than men. A small percentage of the divorcees felt happier after their divorce, because, they had a feeling of release from miserable situations.

SEXUAL LIFE OF THE DIVORCEES

One of the chief aims of marriage is regular sex satisfaction. Blocking of sex-satisfaction of the husband and wife is a serious problem in divorce. As a whole, the respondents were reluctant to speak about this rather delicate aspect, and, therefore. the researcher had to tap other sources also to gather reliable information on the subject.

Seventy per cent of the male and 35 per cent of the female divorcees were remarried, and so the problem of sex satisfaction and adjustment did not arise at all. 17.5 per cent of husbands and 43.5 per cent of the wives avoided sexual relations. 8 per cent of the male and 13 per cent of female divorcees indulged in illicit sex. Urban areas in Madhya Pradesh, like in other States, have prostitutes too to serve the unattached males who choose to go to them. As for the females who indulged in illicit sex, it was found that some of them had love affairs and found sexual satisfaction through their relationship with paramours. They try to keep it a secret as far as possible. A few divorced women were practising prostitution as part-time job. All these women except one or two were in regular jobs and were earning. But, illicit sex relation provided them additional income as well as sex-satisfaction. Some of them indulge in illicit sex through the contacts they get in the places of their employment.

2.5 per cent of the men and 1.5 per cent of the women are impotent and hence, incapable of normal sexual life. 1.5 per cent of the husbands and 3 per cent of the wives are mentally unfit, and hence incapable of normal relations with the opposite sex.

We conclude that majority of the divorced male and female spouses who are not remarried do not engage in sexual life. Facilities for sexual life for the single man are available, whereas there is no means open to women for the gratification of sexual urge. A small percentage of women entered into illicit sex relations, but such women are severely criticised by the community and the society in general.

PRESENT EDUCATIONAL STATUS OF THE RESPONDENTS

There is some difference between the standard of education of the respondents at the time of marriage and at the time of the data collection, that is, after divorce. The improvement in the level of education was possible for a number of reasons. The improved educational status was beneficial to the divorced women in particular in matters of employment.

Our data in this connection is given in Table 7.1.

TABLE 7.1

Comparative levels of education of the divorced spouses at the time of marriage and later on at the time of data collection

S. No.	level of education	Husband		Wife	
		At Marriage per cent	After Divorce per cent	At Marriage per cent	After Divorce per cent
1.	Uneducated or below Primary level	9	8.5	17.5	17.5
2.	Middle school	13.5	12.00	14.00	10.5
3.	Below Higher Secondary	12.00	12.00	7.00	5.00
4.	Undergraduate	19.00	13.00	33.5	17.5
5.	Graduate	24.00	29.5	17.00	27.00
6.	Postgraduate	22.5	25.00	11.00	22.5
	Total	100	100	100	100

Highlights of our data are:

(*i*) Both in the cases of males and females, the percentage of uneducated spouses has not changed;

(*ii*) In the case of women, the percentage of middle school educated ones at the time of marriage was 14, whereas now (at the time of data collection, after divorce) it has become 10.5. This means that 3.5 per cent women studied further;

(*iii*) Among men, the percentage of undergraduates has come down by 6 per cent, whereas among females by nearly 50 per cent.

(*iv*) 10 per cent of the females has become graduates after divorce;

(*v*) Women show much greater progress in education as compared with men.

It has been found that if a female spouses was a student at the time of marriage, her studies were interrupted by the marriage. Most of them thought of studying again only after facing adjustment problem with the husband, or, after being separated from the husband or after obtaining divorce. Divorce or marital problems have a direct bearing on the improvement in the women's education.

The women thought of educating themselves higher, mainly because, they felt that sooner or later, they may have to earn thier own bread.

OCCUPATION OF THE DIVORCEES AT PRESENT
(After Divorce—at the time of data collection)

The occupation of the spouses at the time of their marriage was already shown in Chapter 3 (Background of the Divorcees). Again, the occupation of the spouses at the time of divorce is given in Chapter 4 (Marital Relations and Adjustment before Divorce). Here, we deal with the occupation of the spouses during the post-divorce period.

It was seen that there is no substantial change in the occupational pattern of the males. But there is much difference in the occupation of the female spouses after divorce.

OCCUPATION OF THE DIVORCEE—WIVES AT THE TIME OF MARRIAGE, AT THE TIME OF DIVORCE AND AT PRESENT

Detailed data was collected in this connection. Our main findings are :

(1) There is much difference in the occupation of the females after divorce.

(2) There is increase in the number of women working as professors, for it was 0.5 per cent at the time of marriage, 1 per cent just before divorce and 4 per cent after divorce.

(3) There is great increase in the number of female office assistants also, for, it was 7.5 per cent at the time of marriage, 9 per cent at the time of divorce and 14.5 per cent during the post-divorce period. The number has almost doubled.

(4) Almost the same trend is found in the number of female divorcees working as school teachers also. It was 4.5 per cent at the time of marriage, 10 per cent at the time of divorce, and 18 per cent during the post-divorce period.
(5) The number of women working in the labour-category also registered a great increase, 0.5 per cent at the time of marriage; 3 per cent at the time of divorce and 7.5 per cent after divorce (post-divorce period).
(6) As a whole, the number of unemployed women steadily decreased in all the periods, that is, while it was 83.5 per cent at the time of marriage, it was 65.5 per cent at the time of divorce and 42 per cent during the post-divorce period.

Thus, during the post-divorce period, the incidence of working women increased much. The reasons are obvious after divorce, the women have to support themselves as their husbands separated. Even after remarriage, they did not want to discontinue working. When the women were facing problems or failing in one place (marital life), they were gaining elsewhere making adjustments and raising status.

SUPPORT OF THE FEMALE DIVORCEES IMMEDIATELY AFTER DIVORCE

Support immediately after divorce in the case of wives is an important affair, because, in the midst of trouble, anxiety and separation, such support was needed for their post-divorce adjustment in life. How did they support themselves, and who came for their rescue is discussed below:

(*i*) In large number of cases (34.5 per cent), the divorced wives supported themselves in the post-divorce period;
(*ii*) Next, (28.5 per cent) the parents of the wives supported;
(*iii*) 12.5 per cent wives received alimony;
(*iv*) In 19 per cent cases, there was very little support from any source, or no support at all. Those who did not have economic support what so ever had indeed a miserable life.

In several of these cases, the parents themselves were so poor that they could not take the responsibility of a married daughter with or without children. In some cases, the parents were unwilling to help their divorced daughters, because they were against their divorce. These women, therefore, had to pull on with severe economic strain, often on the charity of others and sometimes even starving.

HOW THE FEMALE DIVORSEES ARE SUPPORTED AT PRESENT?

It is found that in 35 per cent cases, the problem of support was met and overcome in a stable manner by remarriage. Then, in 43 per cent cases, they were supporting themselves mostly through employment. In 14.5 per cent cases, their parents were kind enough to extend support. In 5 per cent cases, alimony was received by them. In 1 per cent cases, unfortunately, no help was forthcoming from anywhere, and so, they were in the Destitute Home for Women, run by the Government of Madhya Pradesh. In some cases, the divorced wives were supported by the former husbands and in-laws.

We conclude that the economic condition of the divorced women was considerably better at the moment, as compared with the pre-divorce period or immediately after the divorce.

SENTIMENTS FOR THE EX-SPOUSE AND CONTACTS

One of the chief aims of marriage and family is emotional satisfaction. There are different types of emotions such as love, affection, sense of belonging and attachment. One of the seven functions of the family listed by William Ogburn is the affectional function. The affectional ties are broken in divorce. One of the distinctive features of the family described by MacIver & Page is its emotional basis, which is "based on a complex of the most profound impulses of our organic nature."[9] This emotional basis is shattered in marital disruptions and dissolutions. It is interesting to note that even after much conflicts, tensions and finally separation through divorce, some spouses retain soft sentiments for the other spouse. This phenomenon has been investigated in the present study of divorce among urban Hindus, and the relevant data is analysed on next page.

[9]R.M. MacIver, C.H. Page, *Society*, 1955, p. 240.

(*i*) As many as 35 per cent husbands had expressed sentiments like "still love", "repentent" and "no ill-feeling." 21.5 per cent wives had indicated identical sentiments. This means that in the inside of their hearts, they still cherished some good feelings about their ex-spouses.

(*ii*) At the same time, 65 per cent husbands and 78.5 per cent wives expressed sentiments like "don't care at all," "bitter feelings" and "hate intensely."

(*iii*) The second category of spouses seems to have had rather bitter and unforgiveable types of sentiments. By this, we may conclude that divorce was rather inevitable in majority of the cases that have been studied by us.

Some of the individual expressions of the respondents may be indicated now. One female spouse said, "I still hope, some day, he will come back to me. At least in his old age, he might remember the one whom he has mercilessly left just for a few years of vain pleasure. I am determined to wait till the last day of my life."

In ths same way, a totally frustrated husband said, "Though my wife has destroyed me many times and has almost ruined me, yet, I am ready to accept her, if some time she comes back."

Of course, it is but understandable that affection, love and attachment that the couples develop for each other might disappear temporarily due to strifes and conflicts, but come back to mind with fresh strength as the turmoil wears off. This investigator is led to believe that many more couples still preserve tender emotional ties towards their ex-mates though they are not prepared to proclaim it openly.

It was inquired of the respondents what sort of contacts they still maintain with their spouses. The data lead us to think that there are three categories of respondents:

(*i*) Those who have no contact at all;

(*ii*) Those who have some sort of contact, may be directly or indirectly, through children or any other way;

(*iii*) Reunited or reconciled.

In the first category comes 38 per cent of the couples. In the second are the vast majority of the couples, that is, 59 per cent. In the third category comes only a few couples (3 per cent). It was found that caste relationships have been helpful to the spouses to maintain indirect contacts.

TYPES OF ATTEMPTS AT RECONCILIATION EVEN AFTER DIVORCE

The data collected showed that

(1) In a few cases, reconciliation efforts are still going on and might be effected in the near future.

(2) In 3 per cent cases, reconciliation has already been effected and the couples have started living together.

(3) In vast majority of cases, no attempt was made for reconciliation.

Reconciliation even after long court cases and personal conflicts and bitterness seems to be a paradox. Yet, it was really attempted and established in a number of cases that are included in the present study.

HOW FRIENDS REACT TOWARDS THE DIVORCEES ?

Divorce is a personal tragedy. The anguish and pain one undergoes in personal life is often multiplied by the treatment he/she receives from the society. After having received such a great defeat and failure in personal life, many people shrink from other people altogether. Some avoid people for a long time and then try to come back gradually. Some, on the other hand, become aggressive for the sake of self-protection. In our study, it has been found that the treatment the divorcees received from their friends seems tolerable, as in vast majority cases (64.5 per cent) there was no substantial change in the attitude of friends towards the divorcees. Some sort of criticism was noticed in 26.5 per cent cases and avoidance in 5.5 per cent cases.

HOW PARENTS AND RELATIVES REACT TOWARDS THE DIVORCEES ?

There are mainly two types of reactions: (*i*) sympathetic or partially sympathetic, and (*ii*) opposed or indifferent. Majority of the cases in our study come under the first category. In the case of 13 per cent husbands and 9 per cent wives, the reaction of the parents/

relatives was almost nil, or not known. This shows that in most cases, the spouses received the sympathy of their parents and relatives. However, it is found that in the 'sympathetic' category, the number of husbands is more those that of the wives, which may lead us to think that parents/relatives were more sympathetic to the male divorcees than to the female divorcees. In all probability, the idea is that the parents thought that the women should have tried better and hard to bring about marital adjustment somehow or other. In those cases where the parents are "opposed or indifferent", it was found that the parents were convinced that it was their own children who were at fault, and not the other party.

REACTION OF THE COMMUNITY TOWARDS THE DIVORCEES

Reaction of the communities concerned towards the divorcees is very significant, because, it is the community which determines the status of the individual in the community. Status is a mental construct, a degreee of esteem or dis-esteem which people in a society display towards individual persons. Status is socially defined, that is, determined by factors outside the individual. The criteria of social approval and disapproval, esteem and dis-esteem, are contained in the social values, that is, the things which people consider important and worthwhile. Divorce has still not received the approval of most societies of the world, for, it" still represents failure in a highly-valued relationship."[10]

It has been pointed out that divorce, even with modern tolerance, involves a degree of public shame, for, "at best, divorce is a public confession of failure in a private, highly personal and highly intimate relationship."[11]

It is found that a wide variety of complications are introduced into the social relationships of both husband and wife after separation or divorce. Gossip in all its poisonous and malicious forms is an irritating and often dangerous bugbear to the divorced of either sex. Tongues wag, no matter how innocent he or she may be of any moral turpitude.

The respondents in our study belonged to a number of castes/

[10]Robert Chester, *Divorce in Europe*, 1977, p. 74.
[11]Paul H. Landis, *Social Policies in the Making*, 1947, pp. 359-60.

tribes/communities. The reaction of these communities towards the divorcees (husbands and wives) is discussed below:

(1) The incidence of severe criticism is very high among Hindu castes such as (*i*) Kayasth, (*ii*) Sonar and (*iii*) Kshatriyas, and the incidence of absence of such criticism was high among the (*i*) Harijans (scheduled castes), (*ii*) Tribals, and (*iii*) Brahmins (Maharastrian Brahmins). Thus a particular caste/community/tribe is an important determinant in the rate of approval/disapproval or divorce. Among the castes also, there are sub-divisions and regional variations. For instance, the Maharastrian Brahmin is entirely different from Madhya Bharat (Malwi) or Uttar Pradesh Brahmin. To be clear, all the Brahmins who said that there is no criticism in their community regarding divorce were Maharastrian Brahmins. Among the Kshatriyas also, two clear groups could be identified, that is, Marathas and local Rajputs. All the respondents who said that divorce is severely criticised in their community belonged to the Rajput community, and all the respondents who said that divorce is looked upon with mild criticism were Marathas. Among Vaisyas also, there are different groups. Four different groups were identified in our study, namely, (*i*) local baniyas, like the Agarwals and Guptas, (*ii*) Nemi community, (*iii*) Gujrati Baniyas, and the (*iv*) Sindhi baniyas. Divorce is severely criticised in the local baniya community, while only mild criticism was noticed among the Baniyas of Gujrat. No respondent belonging to the Kayasth community said that divorce is faced with mild criticism or no criticism.

(2) It has been noticed that social disapproval was more towards women divorcees than the males. Even today, the ideal Hindu wife is one who, under any sort of trial and temptation, will stick to her husband.

(3) The social attitude towards particular divorcee is very much dependent upon who is the aggrieved spouse and who is the guilty one. Usually, public opinion is in favour of the aggrieved spouse and against the offending one.

To conclude, it may be said that there is wide variation in social attitude towards divorce among the urban Hindus.

CONCLUSIONS

From this chapter, we may arrive at the following conclusions:

1. The post-divorce status of the divorcees is significant in the

sociological study of divorce among urban Hindus.

2. Vast majority of the men (65 per cent) are of the age-group 26-35, and the vast majority of the women (67.5 per cent) are in the age group 21-30. This shows that most of the divorced spouses are still young, and can remarry.

3. A good number of the divorced husbands and wives did not have much family problem as such after divorce. However, it was found that the women were subjected to much more criticism and neglect than men.

4. The divorced husbands and wives faced several personal problems like frustration, inferiority complex, shyness, loneliness, etc.

5. As for the sexual life of the spouses after divorce, it was found that majority of the males (70.5 per cent) and a good number of females (35 per cent) were remarried, and so, the problem of sex-satisfaction and adjustment did not arise seriously. 17.5 per cent of husbands and 43.5 per cent of the wives avoided sexual relations. None of the divorcees were inclined to speak much about their sex-satisfaction in the post-divorce period.

6. Women showed greater progress in education in the post-divorce period as compared to men. With their better education, women were able to take up employment to support themselves and children.

7. The incidence of the working women increased in the post-divorce period. This they could do with better education. These women took up jobs like college teachers, school teachers and office assistants. Improvement in education and consequent facility for employment helped the women to meet the crisis of divorce.

8. The female divorcees were supported in different ways immediately after divorce—34.5 per cent self-support; 28.5 per cent parental support and 12.5 per cent alimony. Some women did not receive any support and so were in great economic difficulty.

9. The problem of stable support in the post-divorce period was met by 35 per cent women by remarriage.

10. The divorced men and women had different types of sentiments for their ex-spouse, such as "still love", "repentent", "no ill-feeling", "bitter feelings" and "hate intensely." While a large number expressed favourable sentiments, majority of the spouses (65 per cent husbands and 78.5 per cent wives) expressed unfavourable sentiments.

11. Majority of the divorcees did not have any contacts with their ex-partners.

12. Vast majority of the divorcees did not make any attempts for reconciliation in the post-divorce period.

13. Somewhat tolerable and encouraging treatment was received by the divorcees from their friends.

14. Vast majority of the spouses received sympathetic or partially sympathetic treatment from their parents.

15. Different castes/tribes/communities reacted differently towards the divorcees, some highly critical and some less critical.

Chapter 8

DIVORCE AND CHILDREN

INTRODUCTION

THE three parts of a family are husband, wife and children. There are childless families also, but most families have children. Procreation and the perpetuation of the species is in fact one of the chief aims of marriage and family. According to the divorce statistics, in most of the families where divorce takes place, there is no child. Most divorces occur in the early period of marriage. But in some cases, young children are involved.

It has been held, that women and children are the worst sufferers of divorce, though husbands too suffer. Husbands can remarry; wives also can remarry after divorce, but then, where can the children go? American Sociology literature makes it very clear that divorce is a serious problem in that country, divorce affects the family organization, and at least some of the crime and juvenile delinquency are due to divorce, and its consequences.

Kingsley Davis has held that divorce is a more serious problem in single family than in joint family, in so far as the children are concerned.[1]

Kenkel has stated that in 1968, divorce in the United States of America involved 784,000 children. The average number of children per divorce-decree with children in 1968 was 2.20. Further, the average number of children involved in every 100 divorce-decree was 134.[2]

As regards the effects of divorce on children, there have been conflicting statements. There are estimates that 80 per cent of

[1] *Cf.* Davis Kingsley, Human Society, 1969, pp. 426-27.
[2] Kenkel, *op. cit.*, 1973, p. 33.

delinquent children in the United States are found in divorced homes. On the other hand, it is said that children adjust to the situations very quickly after a brief period of disturbance.

Divorce subjects the child to an abnormal family situation. Often his loyalty is divided and the attendant strain makes him miserable. He cannot understand why his father and mother both of whom may be very dear to him cannot continue to live together in his home. His timid questions are evaded and his protests disregarded. He is helpless to avert the catastrophe and sees his affectional world collapse about him. Children are happy in normal homes, be they rich or poor, frequently not even realizing it, if they are poor. They endure want more easily than parental discord. To them, the parental overpattern is like a sheltering tent; when it is rent as under, they stand starkly exposed to fear, loneliness and uncertainty. The protective adult pattern—taken for granted by children as they take for granted food and shelter—has failed, and they are assailed with a dread peculiar to children in the presence of strong emotions revealed by their elders. Even the play group and school life of children may be affected adversely by divorce. Baber has pointed out that one divorced woman noticed that her eleven-year-old son played only with two boys in the neighbourhood, one the son of a widow and the other the son of a divorcee. He seemed to avoid all the other children and when these two were not available, he played by himself. When asked, he said that he hated the others because they are always talking about their fathers.[3]

Unless the child is very young at the time of separation, considerable mental conflict tends to arise out of the fact that contacts with one parent are relatively infrequent. If this parent happens to be the favourite, the conflict is all the more severe.

Studies in the United States have shown that divorce also not infrequently leads the child to take a skeptical attitude toward marriage. This skepticism, however, comes into conflict with the natural tendency to seek contacts with the opposite sex and the wish to marry. The result is that the individual tends to enter marriage in a highly sceptical frame of mind, only to find all that he has feared. Thus, divorce is passed on from one generation to the other.

It is also seen that not always does divorce leads to disorganiza-

[3]R.E. Baber, *op. cit.*, p. 507.

tion of the child. Where remarriage occurs relatively early, the child may be quite, as well adjusted in the family. Divorce is but one of the many crises in life which call for readjustment.

It has been assumed until recently that divorce was apt to produce severe trauma in children. In a study of divorce in Detroit, however, the vast majority of 425 mothers who had been divorced for periods ranging from two to twenty-six months, believed that "both themselves and their children to be better off than before the divorce."[4]

In a study of about 4000 husbands and wives recently in the United States, it has been held that "people envision divorce not as a positive liberating factor, but as a step that will consign them to loneliness, financial insecurity, and alienation from children and former friends."[5]

Thus, we find that there are different views about the impact of divorce on children. In our study of divorce among urban Hindus of Madhya Pradesh, as will be seen later in this chapter, not too adverse effect was observed on children, on the whole, though there are exceptions.

CHILDREN BORN TO THE DIVORCEES

The number of children born to the divorced spouses was investigated and the findings are given below:

(1) 18.5 per cent divorcees had one child each; 9.5 per cent 2 children each and 8.5 per cent had 3 children each.

(2) In 58 per cent cases, the divorced couples had no children. In another 3 per cent cases, though children were born, they died.

(3) In the 42 per cent families where there were children, the average number of children per family was about 2.

The fact that majority of the couples did not have children goes to prove, among other things, that childlessness and divorce have inter-relationship. In other words, childlessness facilitated easy divorce. Further, in majority of the cases, the strain on the marital relationship started within the first year of marriage, and the natural love and affection found in a normal newly-wed couple was

[4]Paul B. Horton & Gerald, R. Leslie, *The Sociology of Social Problems*, New York, 1960, pp. 176-177.

[5]Pietropinto and Simenauer, *Husbands and Wives*, New York, 1981, p. xxvii.

absent in them. Of course, there are a few cases of impotency and a few cases where the couple could not have children, even after staying together for quite some time. There was a small percentage (2 per cent) of couples who had adopted some type of family-planning method and tried to put off child-birth to a later date. In all the other cases, the couples' cohabitation was either too short, or two hectic.

In most Indian homes, due to conservative attitudes of elders and inhibitions and shyness on the part of the youngsters, a couple takes some time to know each other and get adjusted to each other's emotional needs. If the relationship gets strained at the outset, this process is still lengthened, and a couple finds it difficult to adjust to each other. As we have seen earlier, sex relationship is not merely biological but it involves emotional and socio-cultural aspects of human life.

Child is considered to be the cementing factor which strengthens the marital and familial bond between the spouses. When a child is born, affection and attention of both the spouses are turned away from each other and centred on the child. In the same way, differences of opinion and problems are often forgotten with the coming of a child. The birth of a child is a unique experience in the life of any couple. Usually, both the parents experience thrill and pride in becoming a father or mother. It gives them a new sense of inter-communication, cooperation, mutual responsibility integration and a definite purpose in life. Now, they start feeling that they have to live together, if not for the sake of each other, at least for the sake of this new helpless dear creature. Birth of a child also affects the time-schedule of a couple. Before the arrival of the child, they have plenty of time and leisure together. With the coming of the baby, most of the mother's time is taken up by him and she hardly finds time to be with the husband. The chances for mutual fights are also automatically reduced. Grand-parents are also linked and they feel happy. With the birth of the new child, the position of the daughter-in-law in the family is confirmed. She now receive the status of the mother of a child of their family. If the child is a male, her status is still improved and strengthened, as, in the traditional Hindu family even today, a male child is preferred to a female child.

In the present study, in almost all cases, short duration of cohabitation was one of the most important factors responsible for the prevention of childbirth. In almost all cases, where there are more than one child, the couple stayed together for more than 5 years. In all these cases, the spouses, especially, the wives, confided that they tried their best to pull on with the other spouse and separated only when they found out that their peaceful stay together is an impossibility. As compared to this, childless couples separated rather easily and without much hesitation. Thus, the presence of children is an important factor in reducing marital and familial breakdowns.

In 2 per cent cases where 4 children per family were born, the couples lived together for many years, though in the midst of troubles and problems. In these cases, the couples had lived together for 20-40 years.

Fonseca's study in Bombay disclosed that couples having 2, 3 and 4 children comprise 14.3 per cent, 13.4 per cent and 6.4 per cent respectively, while those having only one child constitute 22.7 per cent, and those who have no children constitute 40.4 per cent of the total. She has pointed out that not only the absence of children, but also the economic problem of the couples led them to desert the spouses. In another sample of her study, Fonseca found that couples having two, three or four children comprise 10.1, 3.7 and 1.5 per cent respectively of those seeking redress in court, whilst those with one child constitute 21.3 per cent and those with no children 63.3 per cent. Couples with no children and those with only one child form the majority of those seeking redress in court.

Here, she concludes that "it appears that the failure to have children induces divorce and family instability, especially where there are other disruptive factors."[6]

In a study in the United States, Jacobson found that close to three-fifths of the divorced couples had no children.[7]

Our conclusions are that:

(*i*) There is interrelationship between childlessness and divorce, although there may be other factors too responsible.

(*ii*) Even those couples who have children, the number of children is smali. Thus, fewer children is also one of the factors that may be responsible for divorce.

[6]Mabel, Fonseca, *Counselling for Marital Happiness*, Bombay, 1966, pp. 55-56.

[7]Jacobson, Paul H., in *The Family*, edited by Winch & McGinnis, 1959, p. 523.

(*iii*) Shorter duration of stay together by the couples is the main reason for the absence of or for the few number of children.

WHO KEPT THE CHILDREN AFTER DIVORCE AND WHY ?

An analysis of the data in this connection showed that

1. In 79.5 per cent cases, the mother kept the children;
2. The father kept the children in 14.1 per cent;
3. In 3.8 per cent cases the father and mother jointly kept the children; and
4. In 2.6% cases, the children remained with the couples themselves as they are re-united.

Thus, we find that in vast majority of the cases, it was the mother who kept the children of the divorced spouses.

According to the Hindu Marriage Act, "the court may, from time to time, pass with interim orders and make such provisions in the decree as it may deem just and proper with respect to the custody, maintenance and education of minor children, consistly with their wishes wherever possible."[8] On several occasions, the court has decided that the "custody of the children should remain in the custody of the mother till seven;" (Jacob *v* Jacob AIR, 1973, SC 2090); "minor children in the interest of their welfare should remain in the custody of the mother" (Chandra Prabha *v* Prem Nath Kapoor, AIR, 1976, Delhi, 283) etc.[9]

In our study of the urban Hindus in Madhya Pradesh, it has been seen that majority (79.5 per cent) of the children (minor and grown up) were with the mother.

Let us now see why the children stayed with the mother. In 32 per cent cases, the children were too young, and, therefore, stayed with the mother. Some other children lived with the mother as the father declined to claim them, on account of alleged illegitimacy. In some other cases (15 per cent), the children were with the mother as they were so from the beginning. In another 15 per cent cases, the children stayed with the mother as the wife (mother) had not gone to the husband's place after the birth of the child. Yet, in some other cases (8 per cent), it was the choice of the children to remain with the mother. In another 8 per cent cases, the wife left the

[8]Hindu Marriage Act, 1955, Section 26.
[9]J.P. Bhatnagar, *Marriage and Divorce Laws*, 1977, pp. 95-96.

husband's place, taking the children along with her and refused to send them back later. The husbands also did not press the matter, because, they knew, they would not be able to take care of them alone. For instance, Mrs S.P. is a Bank employee, drawing a high salary. She had two children, a boy and a girl. When she separated from the husband, she took away her to children too, left the husband's house, and hired a house in the same town and started living separately. The husband tried to contact the children, but the wife did not allow. In another interesting instance, the wife left the husband's place, and started living with her five children, with her well-to-do paramour.

In 12.4 per cent cases, the husband did not bother about the children at all. Even before the separation or divorce, the father did not care for them. Many a time, they were provided by the mother alone. This was found in the lower class more often, but also in the middle class occasionally.

Mrs L., now a school teacher, said: "My husband had a small business and he was earning enough to pull on. But, he had such bad habits, that he spent whatever he earned on himself. I was left to starve, Often, I used to beg from my relatives or friends for food. I had a small child also then. There was no milk for it. He used to cry and cry, and then go to sleep. That time, I was also not earning. After the birth of my second child, I decided to study and do some work, so that I could feed the children." Similar was the case of a vegetable-seller.

Thus, we find that after divorce, the children are left with the mothers for various reasons, the important ones being that (*i*) the children are too small, (*ii*) children are usually under the care of the mother, (*iii*) father is not interested in the children, and (*iv*) the children themselves chose to remain with the mother.

However, in a small percentage of cases, the children were kept by the father for reasons such as

(*i*) the wives did not care for the children and went away;
(*ii*) the husband did not allow the children to go with the mother;
(*iii*) the child chose to be with the father; and
(*iv*) the husband kidnapped the child.

Thus, the children are left with the father only in rare cases.

WHO ACTUALLY SUPPORT THE CHILDREN OF THE DIVORCED SPOUSES?

Bringing up children is a very expensive affair in modern times. In several homes in urban areas, both the husband and wife earn and try to support and educate the children. After divorce, the care and economic support of children suffer much. In our study, it was found that in about two-third cases, where children were present, the mother or her people supported the children. In twenty per cent cases, the father or his relatives supported them. In a few cases, the responsibility of supporting the children was shared by mother's people, father, or step-father. Still, in another few cases, the children managed to support themselves as they were grown up.

We conclude that majority of the children of the divorced spouses are supported by the mother, father or their relatives. Though living in urban areas, the kinship ties are strong and so the divorced couples' children could be looked after reasonably well. Many mothers are gainfully employed and hence could support themselves and their children.

DIVORCEE-SPOUSES PRESENT CONTACT WITH CHILDREN

Blood ties are strong natural bond and can survive many adverse circumstances. Out of the cases where mothers kept children with them, it has been observed, that even after several years of divorce and remarriage, 41 per cent fathers perpetuate their contact with the children. In 49 per cent, there is no contact at all. In 10 per cent, once there was contact, but it has since been broken.

Relationship between two spouses can be terminated by a legal decree but relationship between a parent and child cannot be finished off, with any decree. In a country like India, where kinship ties are very strong, even today, father-child relationships cannot be obliterated so soon. Therefore, such ties were maintained in good number of cases as explained above.

The data reveals that about half of the fathers did not continue relationship with their children after they had been separated from them through the divorce process. This need not mean that they have forgotten their children immediately after divorce. Many of them, it was found, did not try to contact the children, merely because of guilt-feeling and because they did not want to face the divorced wife. Mr V.M. said, "I am divorced for the past five years. I have hardly met my children after that. I feel very guilty about not going to see them, and not taking care of them. But I cannot bear to meet my ex-wife again, and, if I try to see the children in the school or so, she will start the allegation that I am trying to kidnap them. She may even file a suit against me in the court of law. Such is her nature, and I am really scared of her." A few fathers did try to kidnap their children from their mothers' custody and some became successful in their attempt. This again makes it amply clear that fathers were not able to forget their children even after divorce. Of course, the kidnap attempts also must have been to disturb or harass the ex-wife. Depriving the mother of her children is a sure way of hurting a mother.

As mentioned earlier, in a few cases, the children were living with their fathers. Their mothers were asked if they contacted the children. In half of these cases, the mothers did not. In most of these cases, the wives had left the children and went away and they had deep guilt-feelings. One female respondent refused to accept the fact, that, she had children from a former marriage. In the remaining cases, the mothers kept up contact with their children.

From the foregoing discussion, we conclude that at least half of the divorced parents do not keep contact with their children due to a number of reasons and problems.

Personal visit by the spouse was the commonest method by which divorced persons maintained relationship with their children. These visits may be with or without the knowledge of the other spouse. In several cases, children themselves went to the other parent and met them occasionally. This also may be with or without the knowledge of the parent with whom they live now. Correspondence is another medium through which contacts are maintained. Relatives and friends also act as intermediaries.

In a few cases, the spouse who kept the children did not allow them to have any contact with the other spouse, and, hence, the relationship with the other parent could not be maintained.

KNOWLEDGE OF CHILDREN ABOUT THE DIVORCE OF THEIR PARENTS

It is very painful and embarassing for a child to know about his/her parents' failures and shortcomings. Everyone wants to be proud of his parents. In the eyes of children, father and mother are big and wonderful people who can do all things which they cannot do and who provide everything for him/her. People are eager to keep up this childhood illusions about their own parents. As one grows older, he becomes aware of the shortcomings and emptiness of the adult world around him. But, when failures of parents become too widely known, as in the case of divorce, a child feels helpless. He shrinks at the mention of his parents. Instead of being proud of his parents as son or daughter, he/she starts feeling ashamed of them. This, in turn, undermines the self-esteem and confidence of a child.

As a child grows up, he also notices that his family is essentially different from the families of his friends. Whereas in other families, the adults work together hand-in-hand for the welfare of the children, in his own home, he finds a single parent struggling hard in the midst of troubles and tribulations. The child may be deprived of many material things which a child of the normal family receives. Above all, he is denied the feeling of security he obtains with two parents to care for him and provide for him. He craves for the attention and love of the absent parent, though he may not express it verbally. In this connection, the non-fulfilment of the four basic wishes like response, recognition, new experience and security given by W.I. Thomas is very relevant. William Goode also has mentioned the "willed departures" on account of separation, divorce, annulment and desertion in connection with the different types of family disorganization and the consequent absence of role play for the children. On the top of all these, a child may face direct problems which makes him acutely aware of the fact that he is the child of a divorcee. Friends may tease and snear at his because of his parents. Friends may even ill-treat him when they know that he is defenceless. The tearful experience of a highschool boy in our study was narrated by his divorced mother: "In the school, whenever the children quarrel among themselves, my child is beaten badly. His friends tell him: 'You have no father to defend you.' My son is so very upset about this and he tells me of it with tears in his eyes."

The information gathered in our study regarding the knowledge of children about the divorce of their parents revealed that:

(*i*) In majority of the cases (64 per cent), the children know about the parents' divorce,
(*ii*) In some cases (12 per cent), the children have a vague idea about it, and
(*iii*) In 24 per cent cases, the children are too young to undetstand and discern matters like divorce of the parents.

ATTACHMENT AND LIKING OF CHILDREN OF DIVORCED SPOUSES TOWARDS PARENTS

It was inquired from the children which relatives they liked most now. Their answers disclosed that, most children have attachment and liking for their mother. Next comes the father, with 11.5 per cent children having attachment to him. Then, there are a few who are attached to grand parents, and some to both the parents, and in the same family, one child to one parent and the other to the other parent . . . An illustration may be given to the last category (that is, variation in the attachment of different children of the same family), Mrs S. is a teacher and she has two children, a 17-year old daughter and a 14-year old son. Both the children remained with the mother right from their birth. The mother only supported them all these years, as the father was extremely negligent in his paternal obligations. After the divorce, the mother kept both the children with her, and educated them. Since the last two years, the father meets the son on the way or in the school, and gives him gifts and eatables, with the result that the boy is very fond of the father, though he still continue to live with the mother. The daughter, however, hates the father intensely.

An illustration of the type of cases where the children have equal liking and attachment to both the father and mother may also be given. Mr and Mrs A. divorced each other after 18 years of marital life. They have three children at that time. All the three children were teenagers when the parents separated. Mrs A. kept the children after divorce, but the children go and meet the father very often. He also loves them and supports them just as he used to do before the time of divorce. In this section, our conclusions are:

(*i*) Children develop attachment to the person with whom they live and who takes care of their needs;
(*ii*) If the parents separate after the children are grown up, the children retain affection for both the parents; and
(*iii*) Irrespective of the implications of divorce, some of the parents/children retain love and affection for each other which may be rather natural on account of the blood affinities. Marital disruptions and dissolutions are the product of certain situations, but they need not come in the way of parent-child relationships.

RATING OF HAPPINESS OF CHILDREN OF THE DIVORCED SPOUSES

It has been attempted to rate the happiness of children of the divorced spouses. It was found that:

(*i*) Majority of the children (55 per cent) are not very happy. They are "unhappy" or "somewhat happy";
(*ii*) A small number (21 per cent) is happy;
(*iii*) The remaining children (24 per cent) are too young to express independent views.

The above information leads us to conclude that the happiness of children is much affected owing to the breakdown of the marriage of their parents. This may affect their personality and future life too adversely.

CONCLUSIONS

This chapter entitled Divorce and Children deals with the various aspects of the life of the children born to the divorced couples. Sociologists have laid much stress on this phenomenon. Studies elsewhere showed varying findings, that is, in some cases, it was found that the condition of children of divorced couples was far from satisfactory. In our study also, it is found that although the majority of the children are not quite happy, they live with their mother, father, or grandparents and receive education and training for future life. Divided loyalty of the children either to the father or mother is a striking phenomenon.

Another striking feature the researcher has observed in the course of her study is that in most of the homes, where children are grownup, they are well-adjusted and even accomplished young adults. Trials and tribulations, instead of hindering their progress, made them determined young people. Several of them retain memories of the painful experiences they have undergone in their childhood. But today, after several years, when they look back, they feel that the very adversities had taught them to be responsible people right from childhood. They filled them with an urge to work harder and excel in their own fields. Several of them were supported by their mothers alone and felt that they should share the burden of the home as early as possible. A middle-aged lady, Mrs S. said:

> When I left my husband's place, all my three children were below 10 years. Their every need was to be met by the small salary I was earning. But my children never complained. They have learnt to live within our limits. Today, all three of them are doing very well. The eldest son (26) is in a good job and is contemplating marriage, the middle one a girl of 23, is a research scholar, and youngest is a postgraduate student.

The children also confirmed that they never felt the absence of the father, and they may not have done any better, had he been present.

Another touching story is of a divorcee family, where the mother was forced to leave behind her three children with the husband. When she left the house, her eldest son was 12, and the youngest was 7, and the girl around 10. The youngest son, now a 21 years old postgraduate, described their life after the divorce of his parents. In his own words:

> Though my father was extremely cruel to my mother, he was deeply attached to us. He did not remarry because of us. Right from the day my mother left, the burden of the home fell on my sister, who was just 10 at that time. I was too young and could not help her much. But my brother, who was a couple of years elder to her, used to help. Of course, the father was very kind

and considerate and he helped us in our studies and all the other matters right after he got back from his work. In a couple of years, we all became well-adjusted to the new situation. My sister became an expert cook. I also started helping in small matters, and my elder brother could look after provisions and other important things. But alongwith all these, we never neglected our studies. All of us did extremely well in our studies. Today, my eldest brother is an engineer, sister a postgraduate and myself a First Class Commerce Graduate. I think the family circumstances forced us to work harder, right from our childhood and today, we all feel that adversities have helped us to go forward with determination.

In several other homes also, similar examples can be cited. Besides the above, some specific conclusions are given below:

1. The majority of the divorced couples have no children. Although childlessness may not be cited as a causation for divorce, yet, we may conclude that there seems to be some interrelationship between childlessness and divorce, or, at least, it can be said that the hindrance for divorce in the case of childless couples is less than in the case of child-having ones.

2. The number of children born to the couples in divorce is relatively small. The number of children per couple in the case of child-having couples is 1.88 (the mean number). The figure in respect of the total number of couples (that is, including both the child-having and childless couples) as 00.73. The fewer number of children is mostly due to the short duration of married life. It has been repeatedly mentioned by sociologists with reference to other studies that the highest incidence of divorce is observed within one or two years of married life. Horton and Leslie concluded that "the risk of divorce is considerably greater during the "first years of marriage than and any time thereafter. Most divorces are granted during the second or third years of marriage than any others."[10]

3. Most children are kept by the mother (79.5 per cent). Some of the important reasons for this are:

(*i*) The law and the decisions in various courts of the country are in favour of the mother to have custody of the child-

[10]Horton & Leslie, *The Sociology of Social Problems*, 1960, pp. 175-76.

ren, especially minor children;

(*ii*) the wife has always taken care of the children, and

(*iii*) The free choice of the children themselves was in favour of the mother.

4. In some cases, the husband kept the children, important reasons being (*i*) the indifference and negligence of the mother and (*ii*) keen desire of the husband to keep children.

5. The economic support of the children for their food, clothing and education was done, in majority of the cases by the mother (42.3 per cent) or mother's relatives (20.5 per cent). In a few cases, it was done by the father too.

6. In a fairly good number of cases (41 per cent) the divorced husbands do keep some contact with the children.

7. In majority of the cases (64 per cent), the children were aware of the fact that they belonged to divorcee-parents. Such knowledge did affect their emotional life, and, therefore, may have directly or indirectly affected their personality development as well as life patterns too. Studies elsewhere too indicated this.

Elliott and Merrill have correctly pointed out that the effect of divorce of parents "is a shock to the child's developing personality The child often does not know which way to turn."[11]

8. In most cases, the children were more attached to the mother and they had a liking for her, than anyone else. The data indicated that while 65 per cent of children were attached to mother, only 11.5 per cent had love and attachment to father.

9. The rating of the happiness of the children of the divorced couples showed that majority (55 per cent) of them are not really happy.

The statement that divorce does not disorganize children in all cultures alike is found correct in our study. The family in the western world is the nuclear or conjugal group composed of husband, wife and children. In such cases, when the husband-wife relationship is dissolved, the family no longer exists. In other cultures (like India) the consanguinous family or the joint family is based primarily upon blood kinship rather than marriage. In such cultures, the children remain with the family of the mother or father and consequently experience no drastic interruptions in

[11]Elliott & Merrill, 1950, *op. cit.*, pp, 464-65.

their way of life. The children of divorcees are ordinarily able to maintain permanent relationship with adults, who will perform the role of the missing parent. Uncles and aunts act as substitute fathers and mothers, and the continuity of the basic family relationship remains substantially unbroken. In this way, children are saved from the personal disorganization accompanying the rupture of the conjugal family. Kingsley Davis also held similar views in this matter. He writes: "The main concern over divorce in our (American) culture is a concern over the children. In our (American) small family system, the child of divorced persons has nowhere to turn except to one parent or the other. In contrast to a culture with a joint family system, our culture cannot provide a stable domestic milieu that continues after divorce. Divorce is, therefore, more serious for the child among us than among most cultures."[12] It is relevant to mention here that in our study of the urban Hindus in Madhya Pradesh, majority (70 per cent) of the couples belonged to joint family, that is, the couples lived with their parents, in-laws and other relatives. (See Chapter 3—Profile of Respondents). In Rama Mehta's study also, joint family patterns was dominant.[13] In Fonseca's study (Bombay) also, over 45 per cent of the respondents lived in joint or extended family environment.[14]

Our conclusion, therefore, is that the life of the children has definitely been affected by the divorce of their parents, but because of the traditional family and culture as a whole, they were protected from total disruption.

[12]Davis, Kingsley, *Human Society*, 1959, pp. 426-27.
[13]Rama, Mehta, *op. cit.*, 1974, p. 10.
[14]Mabel, Fonseca, *op. cit.*, 1966, p. 57.

Chapter 9

REMARRIAGE

INTRODUCTION

DIVORCE is the legal dissolution of marriage, that is, the termination of a particular marital tie with a judicial decree. Once the judicial decree of divorce is obtained, the parties involved are free to remarry. In the absence of a judical decree and legal and social recognition of the termination of the marriage and the approval for remarriage will be difficult. It is, therefore, with the intention of remarriage that many plan to go for divorce.

Remarriage is not unknown to society, for, a large number of societies, primitive and modern, permit the remarriage of widows and widowers.

There are several ways by which the divorced men and women readjsuet in life. One of the most successful solutions to the awkward problems of the divorced persons is a second marriage. In this status, it is easier to find a satisfactory role in ommunity life and to rebuild a normal family life, forgetting the unpleasant aspects of the earlier marriage.[1]

Of the 35 million married men in the United States of America, in 1948, about 4½ million (13 per cent) had been married more than once. Their median age at remarriage was 36.5 years.[2]

It is estimated that in the United States, large proportion (three-fourths) of the divorcees remarry. Some very interesting aspects of divorce and remarringe in that country are:

[1] *Cf.* Faris, Robert, E.L., *Social Disorganization*, New York, 1955, p. 429.
[2] *Cf.* Winch & McGinnis, *The Family*, 1959, pp. 418-19.

(*i*) There is a "swelling tide of remarrying divorces";

(*ii*) 70 per cent of the remarrying females and 75 per cent of the males had been previously divorced;

(*iii*) Americans are not merely interested in achieving the state of marriage; they are also eager to be successfully married, with divorce being an unintentional and unpremeditated outcome;

(*iv*) Some remarriages do fail, and, on the other hand, some divorced persons do achieve a successful remarriage, and perhaps for the 50 per cent or so which manage to survive, there is high level of happiness.[3]

According to some exploratory research undertaken by Locke and Klauaner, a hypothesis may be formulated about marriage after divorce as mentioned below:

> Divorced-remarried women are as good risks in their subsequent marriages as women marry only once, whereas, divorced re-married men are not as good risks as men who marry only once.[4]

This means divorced men are likely to adjust better than divorced women, in remarriages. However, this is to be substantiated by more researches.

Baber has stated the following aspects of remarriage:

(*i*) Estimates on the extent of remarriage after divorce have ranged all the way from one-third to four-fifths;

(*ii*) The probability of remarriage after divorce is very high;

(*iii*) Divorced or widowed men are even more likely to remarry than are divorced or widowed women, and this is true at every age;

(*iv*) Legal prohibition of immediate remarriage by divorcees might slightly affect the number of remarriages;

(*v*) In the United States remarriage have become very common;

(*vi*) Divorced men/women prefer to marry single women/men

[3]Monahan, Thomas, P., *The Changing Nature and Inslability of Remarriage* in Selected Studies in Marriage & Family, by Winch & Goodman, 1968, pp. 609-614.

[4]Locke, J., Harvey and Klausner, William, *Adjustment of the Divorced in Later Marriages*, in Readings in Marriage and the Family, edited by Landis & Landis, 1952, pp. 200-202.

rather than divorced/widowed;

(*vii*) In remarriage, divorces are benefitted by their past experience, so as to make remarriage more successful than the first—" after such a harrowing experience, one would expect that the average person would not deliberately expose himself to the possibility of its repetition without careful consideration."[5]

The Hindu Marriage Act, 1955, has made provision for remarriage by the divorcees. The relevant Section reads as under:

15. Divorced persons when may marry again:

When a marriage has been dissolved by a decree of divorce and either there is no right of appeal against the decree or, if there is such a right of appeal, the time for appealing has expired without an appeal having been presented or an appeal has been dismissed, it shall be lawful for either party to the marriage to marry again.

Before 1976, the parties had to wait for one year under section 15 which then said that:

It shall not be lawful for the respective parties to marry again unless at the date of such marriage at least one year has elapsed from the date of the decree in the court of the first instance.

With the Amendment of 1976 (Marriage Laws Amendment Act, 1976) the parties need not wait for a year. Thus, now

a marriage after dissolution of earlier marriage would be legal and valid even if the new marriage had taken place prior to the amendment of the Act and within one year of the dissolution of earlier marriage.[6]

INCIDENCE OF REMARRIAGE

In our study, majority of the divorced husbands (70.5 per cent) got remarried. At the same time, majority of the wives (65 per cent) could not get remarried.

[5]R.E., Baber, *op. cit.*, 1953, pp. 486-90.
[6]A.N., Saha, *Marriage and Divorce*, 1981, p. 310.

Thus, it is very clear that the percentage of women divorcees remarrying (35 per cent) is just half of the male divorcees (70.5. per cent). Care of children, emotional disturbance due to the failure in the first marriage, non-availability of proper mates for the second marriage unfavourable attitude, social stigma, etc., are some of the impotant factors hindering the remarriage of female divorcees in larger number. It is also found that many parents do not evince active interest in the remarriage of their daughters, whereas, to get them married in the first instance, they were extremely keen and even worried. Once the marriage ceremony is over, attitude of a typical conservative Hindu parent is that, now whatever happens, it is none of his responsibility. Everything will happen according to the pre-ordained will of gods, and, nothing else can be done. Marriage being treated as a sacrament, it is not to be broken at any cost. According to the traditional Hindu view, a woman has to remain a *pativrita* (devotee of the husband) under all circumstances, throughout life. Remarriage is considered even as a sin by the elders. Consequently, they are not supposed to show any activite interest in the remarriage of the daughters, though in their inner hearts, they might desire to re-settle the girls well.

Male divorcees remarry in greater number and with ease as compared to female divorcees. Relatively easy availability of partners, absence of responsibilities of children of the previous marriage, social acceptance of the rights of men for remarrige, etc., are some factors which enabled the males to remarry without much difficulty.

SELECTION OF THE NEW MATE

There are several ways in which the divorcees found new mates, as shown in the Table 9.1 (see on page 220).

It is seen that in respect of both husbands and wives, most of the new mates were found through parents and self-efforts including advertisements. We observe that the percentage of women is more than men in the self-seeking of mates in remarriage. Factors like education, employment, enlightenment, etc., of the women may have helped in this matter. Several of the divorcees took advantage of the matrimonial advertisement columns of newspapers to find mates.

TABLE 9.1
How the Present Mates were Found

S. No.	*How found*	*Husband per cent*	*Wife per cent*
1.	Parents	49	47.1
2.	Other relatives	5	2.9
3.	Friends	7.1	4.3
4.	Self-found (including through advertisement)	32.6	38.6
5.	Returned to former spouse and reunited	6.3	7.1
	Total	100.00	100.00

Interview with several remarried divorcees indicated that they were optimistic about future, and hoped that they will have a better life in future. For instance, some of them remarked:

> People say this and that about re-marriage. We have not listened to them at all. Had we listened, our lives would have been ruined for ever.

PRE-MARITAL CONTACTS WITH THE PRESENT PARTNER

Different types of pre-marital contacts, the male and female divorcees had, with their partners before remarriage. It was found that:

(*i*) In most of the cases (58.2 per cent husbands and 47.1 per cent wives) there was no pre-marital contact;
(*ii*) Love (12.1 per cent husbands and 28.5 per cent wives) and previous acquaintance (through friends and family) (18.4 per cent husbands and 14.3 per cent wives) are the two most frequent types of pre-marital contact;
(*iii*) In a few cases, contacts were possible on account of being neighbours.

A further analysis of the cases of love showed that love affairs were of mainly three types:

(*i*) In love with the spouse even before the marriage with the divorcee-spouse;
(*ii*) In love with the present spouse after marrying the divorcee-spouse but before being separated from him/her;
(*iii*) Fell in love with the present spouse after being separated from the divorcee-spouse.

It was observed that many of the love affairs were long-standing in nature, and were pre-marital. In several cases, such pre- and extra-marital affairs of the spouses were the main reason for divorce. 18.4 per cent divorcee-husbands and 14.3 per cent divorcee-wives married someone whom they knew early. This acquaintance was long-standing. Some of them was with children of the friends of parents.

If a man or woman is divorced owing to no fault of his/hers, the friends are particularly sympathetic and offer to help them as in the case of Mr P.S. a bank officer. He was married to a girl from a far off place. After the marriage, he found out that the girl had connections with a man and was still continuing it. He got a decree of divorce. One of the family friends had a very eligible girl. This girl was offered by her father immediately after the divorce proceedings were over. The couple got married soon and are very happy now.

In some cases, the present spouse was a friend of a brother, sister, sister-in-law, etc., and through these relatives they were well known to each other. In conclusion, it may be said that:

(*i*) Majority of the remarriages, especially of the males purely arranged ones;
(*ii*) As for love marriages, love affairs before divorce were more numerous as compared to those after divorce;
(*iii*) Female divorcees had more love marriages as compared to male divorcees;
(*iv*) Neighbours, friends and acquaintances were helpful in remarriage;
(*v*) The phenomenon of a woman having a living spouse entering into another marriage was not observed in our study.

WITH WHOM REMARRIED

An attempt was made to find out the type of people with whom the divorcees got married. The most significant data is shown in the Table 9.2.

TABLE 9.2

Whom the Divorcee-Spouses are Remarried

S. No.	*With whom remarried*	*Husband (per cent)*	*Wife (per cent)*
1.	Unmarried girl/Bachelor	80.2	30.00
2.	Widow/Widower without children	4.3	27.00
3.	Widow/Widower with children	0.7	25.80
4.	Former spouse	6.3	7.20
5.	Others	8.5	10.00
	Total	100.00	100.00

It would appear that vast majority of the remarrying men (80.2 per cent) found out unmarried women. A good number of divorcee-females (30 per cent) also could get bachelors for remarriage. Divorcee-males marrying widows with or without children were comparatively less in number, whereas divorcee-females married widowers with or without children in quite large number (27 per cent widower without children and 25.8 per cent widower with children). It was seen that in majority of the case of divorcee-women marrying bachelors, they had married below their social and economic status. There were a few interesting cases of re-union and also male-divorcees returning to their former mates.

Our conclusions are that (*i*) most of the divorcee-men get remarried to unmarried women, while (*ii*) in the case of divorcee-women, marriage with bachelors occurred mainly due to love affairs. Even in these cases, usually, they married below their status.

TYPE OF MARRIAGE CEREMONY FOR REMARRIAGE

Since marriage is a sacred sacrament among the Hindus, marital disruption and subsequent remarriage were not approved in the Hindu society. But, with modern changes in social and religious spheres of life, Hindus also seem to have accepted the inevitability of change in the institution of marriage.

Our data regarding the type of marriage ceremony for remarriage is shown in Table 9.3.

TABLE 9.3

Type of Marriage Ceremony for Remarriage

S. No.	*Type of ceremony*	*Husband (per cent)*	*Wife (per cent)*
1.	Religious ceremony	73	65.7
2.	Court Marriage	4.3	4.3
3.	Arya Samaj	2.8	5.7
4.	Started cohabitation without any ceremony (new mates)	14.2	18.6
5.	Resumed cohabitation with former/ divorced spouse	5.7	5.7
	Total	100.00	100.00

We find that most of the men (73 per cent) and women (65.7 per cent) had religious ceremony for remarriage. A few men and women preferred court-marriage. A considerable number of respondents (14.2 per cent males and 18.6 per cent females) started living with the new partner in life without any specific ceremony. Such cases were of elopement, or unions before getting legal divorce. Some of them went through some sort of marriage ceremony formally, after they had obtained legal divorce.

INTERVAL BETWEEN DIVORCE AND REMARRIAGE

The interval spent between the time of divorce and remarriage is significant. It was found that the interval varied from 0 to 10 years. The highest frequency in the case of men is of the interval 3 months to one year (32.7 per cent), and for women, it was 1-2 years (18.6 per cent). The next highest frequency is of cohabitation before the grant of divorce (22 per cent in the case of men and 17.1 per cent in the case of women). There are a few cases in which remarriage took place after 10 years of divorce. Thus, we find that majority of the remarriages occurred during the period 0 to 3 years. It may be stated here (as we have already mentioned earlier) that although majority of the men (70.5 per cent) got remarried, majority of the women (65 per cent) did not. With reference to the United States of America, it is stated that the median years before remarriage is 2.7. Further, most divorcees ultimately remarry and many marry quite soon after their divorce.[7]

CORRELATION BETWEEN THE PRESENCE OF CHILDREN (through the first marriage) AND REMARRIAGE OF THE FEMALE DIVORCEES

39 per cent of the women divorcees had children. Out of those who had children, 20.5 per cent got remarried. At the same time, 61 per cent women did not have children. 44 per cent of them got remarried. Thus, it is found that the incidence of remarriage is more among the women without children as compared with the women who have children. Presence of children discourage remarriage.

CORRELATION BETWEEN THE ECONOMIC CLASS AND REMARRIAGE

Our study revealed that the highest incidence of remarriage among men is from the lower class (92 per cent of the lower class men). The highest incidence of remarriage among women is from the upper class (46.6 per cent of the upper class women). Remarriage rate of lower class women was much less (45 per cent) as compared to men of the same economic class. Most of the women did not try to get remarried for unavoidable reasons like care of children and advanced age.

We conclude that the rate of remarriage among men of all classes is high as compared to women. The disparity between the remarriage rate of men and women is negligible among the upper class. The difference is much more among the middle and lower classes. Remarriage of men is a universal phenomenon among the lower classes unless very important reasons hindered it. Lower class women also remarry, whenever their family and personal circumstances are favourable. Social stigma of remarriage of particularly females was maximum observed in the middle class.

CHILDREN IN REMARRIAGE

Incidence of Child Birth in Remarriage

A good number of remarried men (58 per cent) and women (44

[7]Glick, Paul, C., Quoted by William Kenkel in *The Family in Perspectives*, 1973, p. 331.

per cent) have children through the second marriage. It is clear that the incidence of children is more among remarried male divorcees than among the female divorcees. It was also observed that those women who have no children or only one child in the first marriage have children through the second marriage. No female having more than one child through the first marriage had children in the remarriage. Among men, this difference was not noticed. Even after having 3 or more children through the first marriage, the men usually had children through the second marriage also.

The comparatively lower incidence of children among the remarried female divorcees may be due to various reasons such as the following:

(*i*) A good number of childbearing years are wasted in the prolonged processes of marital strife, divorce and remarriage. Many women got remarried after several years of divorce. By the time they are remarried, they may be well over 30 years of age. It is true that fertility in women decreases considerably as they advance in age.

(*ii*) If there are children from the first marriage, they are usually with the divorcee-wife. Even when she remarries, she continues to keep the children of the first marriage with her. Even if she leaves the children at her parents' place, she visits them frequently. The drive for motherhood is fulfilled in this way, and so, their desire to have children in remarriage is relatively less.

Number of Children Born in Remarriage

The number of children born in remarriage varied from one to six. The highest frequency is one child. 41.8 per cent of the remarried male divorcees and 55.77 per cent remarried female divorcees do not have children through the second marriage. More than three children are not born to any of the remarried female divorcees, although among the male divorcees, children up to 6 were observed. It was found that 17.5 per cent marriages are relatively recent, and, they have no children now; but they may have children in future. In a small number of cases, though married for a sufficiently long time, and the couples are young, children are not born. 6.5 per cent remarriages took place rather late, that is, either the husband or the wife is nearing old age, and the chances of childbirth are rather bleak. 2.5 per cent remarried couples do not relish children at all.

It has been calculated that the mean number of children born in remarriage per spouse is 00.96, say about one child.

HAPPINESS IN REMARRIAGE

Rating of happiness in remarriage is very significant, more so, because, the spouses in remarriage are those who have failed in marital adjustment elsewhere. They had divorced previously, because they were unhappy. In the second marriage, they have the opportunity to compare also—compare the happiness in the second marriage with that of the first. Four degrees of happiness in marriage were asked, that is, (*i*) very happy, (*ii*) happy, (*iii*) somewhat happy, and (*iv*) unhappy. The data gathered is presented is Table 9.4.

TABLE 9.4.
Degree of Happiness in Remarriage

S. No.	*Degree of happiness*	*Husband (per cent)*	*Wife (per cent)*
1.	Very Happy	16.3	20
2.	Happy	37.5	45.7
3.	Somewhat Happy	30.5	22.8
4.	Unhappy	14.2	7.2
5.	Again separated or divorced	1.5	4.3
	Total	100.00	100.00

If we combine the two degrees, namely, 'very happy' and 'happy', we find that 53.8 per cent husbands and 65.7 per cent wives or say majority of the remarried spouses were well-adjusted in remarriage. At the same time, only a small minority of the husbands (15.7 per cent) and wives (11.5 per cent) have been very unhappy or extremely unhappy in remarriage. Those husbands and wives who have rated their marital happiness as "somewhat happy" are just pulling on. 80 per cent of them belong to lower class or lower middle class, where economic hardship is a source of constant friction. The remaining 20 per cent are such cases where the respondent has lived with the former spouse for a good number of years. The necessity of finding a new spouse and adjusting again was rather strenuous for them. Majority of these respondents got unattractive spouses in the second marriage, as compared with the first. 14.2 per cent of the remarried husbands and 7.2 per cent of the wives were very miserable in the second marriage also. They are forced to continue only because of certain circumstances. In almost all these cases, the factors which destroyed the marriage formerly still persist. Cruelty of the husband and in-laws, non-support by the husband, poverty, bad character, etc., are some of the examples of such factors. As these were more or less permanent features in these cases, marital conflicts were inevitable. A few of the remarried husbands and wives are separated from the spouses in remarriage also.

Thus we come to the conclusion that majority of the remarriages are functioning very well and satisfactorily. Some cases are still unhappy owing to certain permanent factors. In a few cases, divorce has occurred again, because, the spouses had certain incorrigible tendencies.

William Goode has pointed out that "the percentage of failures is less among all second marriages than among all first marriages."[8] Monahan has held that:

> Some marriages are indeed an endless round of tensions and conflicts, until death does them part. On the other hand, some divorced persons do achieve a successful re-marriage, and perhaps for the 50 per cent or so which manage to survive there is a high level of happiness.[9]

According to Burgess & Locke:

> Marrying another person is, generally, the most satisfactory adjustment to divorce. Many divorced persons report that they are very happy with their second mates and that they hardly ever think of their first marriage.[10]

At the same time, Christenses has remarked that:

> Studies have shown higher divorce rates for divorce-marriages than first marriage—may be because they are more prone to divorce—the personal factors which destroyed the first marriage continue to exist.[11]

The above comments of different sociologists are relevant in connection with the findings of our study on divorce among urban Hindus. Many second marriages are very happy; mistakes made

[8]Goode, William, J., cited in *When You Marry* by E.M. Duvall and R. Hill, 1953, p. 291.

[9]Thomas, P. Monahan, *op. cit.*, p. 614.

[10]Burgess & Locke, *op. cit.*, 1950, p. 644.

[11]Christenses, Harold T., 1958, pp. 567-71.

in the first marriages are not always repeated, and people often attribute the success of their second marriage largely to experience gained in the first. Yet, there are a few failures in second marriage also.

PLAN OF THE SINGLE DIVORCEES FOR REMARRIAGE

The divorcee-husbands and wives who did not remarry were asked of their future plans. Near majority (49.2 per cent) of the husbands is planning for remarriage. Majority of the divorcee-women (63.8 per cent) has no intention to remarry. Yet, some men and women have not taken a decision in the matter. Divorced women with children do find it difficult to plan for remarriage. Some of the women are extremely bitter and frustrated with their first failure in marriage that they said they almost hate males, and will never want to get married. A typical example of a divorcee-woman may be given. She said, "I hate men. They are so unreliable and untrustworthy that I would never like to live with another man. I earn my living, and I am happy this way." The men who expressed no desire for remarriage are all typical characters. One husband revealed that he had never desired marriage. He wants to lead a lonely life now. He is rather relieved that the first wife left, because, he had no particular desire to cohabit with her. Another husband did not want to remarry only because of his children.

We may conclude by saying that some men and women would definitely remarry in future, while, some others will never, and will remain single.

DISINTEREST AND DELAY IN REMARRIAGE

The divorcee-men and women have several reasons for their indecision, non-planning or disinterest in remarriage. Not all have disclosed the reasons. Some of the reasons expressed by men are "just not interested", "disturbed with the previous marriage", overage, non-availability of suitable spouse and sexual incapacity. As for women, important reasons are: care of children, "too disturbed with the previous marriage", "just not interested", non-availability of suitable spouse, overage, and fear of criticism. However, in respect of women-divorcees, the researcher feels that it is not that they are not interested in remarriage, but that they cannot find a person willing to take care of their children as well. Mothers are deeply attached to their children, find it extremely difficult to separated from them.

With regard to the delay also, some of the reasons already mentioned for disinterest stand good. However, the two prominent reasons for delay are: non-availability of suitable mates and mental and emotional disturbances resulting from the previous marital failure.

CONCLUSIONS

In this chapter about remarriage of divorcee-spouses, we have seen different aspects of remarriage. In most of the sub-sections, we have given conclusions also. Yet, let us have certain general conclusions here:

1. Remarriage is one of the most successful solutions to the problems of divorced persons.
2. There is definite provision under the Hindu Marriage Act, 1955, for remarriage. According to the latest Amendments, remarriage can be effected immediately after divorce. Previously, one-year gap was needed.
3. In countries like the United States of America, about three-fourths of the divorcees remarry.
4. In our study, majority of the men (70.5 per cent) and a little more than one-third (35 per cent) of the women got remarried.
5. There are as many as six ways in which the spouses who remarried found their mates, the two largest ways being through parents and self-arrangement.
6. As for the pre-marital contacts with the partner, it was found that in most cases, there was no contact. Among different types of contact, "falling in love" was the most frequent type for men and women, although if we take men alone, 'previous acquaintance' was the most frequent. Interestingly, women divorcees had more love marriages as compared with males.
7. The divorcees preferred unmarried girls/boys (spinsters/bachelors) in second marriage.
8. Even in remarriage, some sort of religious ceremony was found.
9. Remarriage takes place usually during the period 0 to 3 years after divorce, in respect of both male and female divorcees. In the

United States, the interval between divorce and remarriage, according to several studies is about 3 years.

10. The incidence of remarriage among the women without children is more than that of women with children. The absence or presence of children born through the first marriage were one of the most encouraging or discouraging factors in remarriage in the case of women.

11. There seems to be some correlation between economic class and remarriage. The highest incidence of remarriage among men is from the lower class, and the highest incidence of remarriage among women is from the upper class. Remarriage rate of lower class women was much less. We also conclude that the rate of remarriage among men of all economic classes is higher than that of women.

12. A good number of remarried men and women have children through the second marriage. Incidence of children is more among male-divorcees than among female-divorcees.

13. As for the number of children in remarriage, our finding is that the mean number of children is about one.

14. Most of the divorcees who remarried have happy or very happy marital life. There are a few cases of unhappy condition and also separation or divorce.

15. As for those who have not yet remarried, it is found that near majority of the men is planning for remarriage, while in the case of women only 30 per cent. Divorced women with children find it difficult to plan for remarriage.

16. Reasons for the disinclination of the divorcee-spouses for remarriage shows that care of children, over-age, sexual incapacity, non-availability of suitable spouse, etc. are the most important ones. No doubt, the disinclination of the female divorcees for remarriage is due to the presence of chidren born to them in the first marriage.

17. There are several reasons for delay in remarriage, the most frequent being non-availability of suitable mate, and the emotional disturbance created due to the previous marital breakdown and failure.

The stigma arising out of divorce is still grave in a country like India. Educated, employed women may find it relatively easy, but even then, Hindu traditions may come in the way. Even widow-remarriage is not common in our society. Then what about remarriage of divorcees? In Rama Mehta's study, it was found that majority of the lower middle class women regarded remarriage as immoral, and it was rejected by them as an "unethical proposition."[12] The present researcher feels that since divorce has become easier and quicker after the Amendment of 1976, the rate of remarriage of divorcees also is likely to increase. William Goode's remarks are very appropriate here: "Remarriage is society's short answer to divorcee—the still possible happy ending for the men or women whose first marriage breaks up. Public opinion on the whole disapproves of divorce, dislikes its image, and tends to react strongly against the husband or wife who leaves a family to go off and marry someone else. Once the idea is a reality, however, the gossip has died down, society will accept more readily the person who remarries than the one who remains alone."[13]

[12]Rama Mehta, *op. cit.*, 1975, p. 21.
[13]William Goode, *Women in Divorce*, 1965, p. 201.

Chapter 10

SELECT CASE STUDIES

INTRODUCTION

A COMPREHENSIVE study of a social unit—be that unit a person, a group, a social institution, a district, or a community—is called a case study. Case data may be gathered exhaustively of an entire life cycle of a social unit or a definite section of it. Because of its aid in studying behaviour in specific precise detail, Burgess termed the case study method "the social microscope." Frederic Le Play, William Healy, Cyril Burt and others are some of the pioneers of case study method. Social scientists, in their study of human behaviour, strive to obtain a fundamentally real and enlightened record of personal experiences which would reveal in concrete detail a man's inner strivings, tensions, motivations that drive him to action, the barriers that frustrate him or challenge him, the forces that direct him to adopt a certain pattern of behaviour and to live according to a certain scheme and philosophy of life.

In the study of social problems, particularly, problems relating to the institution of family and marriage, it is found that case study method is extremely useful.

In problems like divorce, case study method can perhaps be considered as the best tool of study. Human nature and relationships are extremely complex and every individual react differently even in similar situations. Every divorce case is unique in the sense that the factors leading to divorce exhibit a different combination in each case. To understand the intricate problem of human adjustment and maladjustment in the most intimate relationship namely husband-wife relationship, detailed analysis of each case is necessary. The following 20 representative short case studies will give some amount of insight into the problem. Mr K. or Mrs V. are all initials of spouses and full names are withheld to conceal identity.

CASE STUDIES

Case Study No. 1 (Mr R.J. and Mrs A.J.)

Mr R.J. is a Jain by religion. He has studied up to B. Com. First Year Class. He is the eldest son of a family of 3 sisters and one brother. Only one sister is married and she is happily settled. Mr R. lives with his parents and younger sisters. He is employed in a factory and earns Rs 600 p.m.

Mrs A.J. belongs to a small family of one brother and a sister. Her father is a well-to-do farmer. The brother is younger to her and still unmarried.

The marriage between Mr R.J. and Miss A. was arranged by parents. The couple also knew each other well. Though A's. father was permanently residing in the village, he owned a house in the city also. All the family members used to come and stay there occasionally. Mr R.J.'s house is just opposite to her house, and hence, all the members of both the families knew each other well. The marriage was arranged quickly and the engagement lasted only 3 days.

As soon as Mrs A. reached her husband's home, she found that the situation was quite contrary to her expectation. Mr R.J. had four brothers. But all of them died very young and Mr R.J. was the only surviving male issue. Mr R.J.'s mother was extremely attached to him. The son was so much petted and over-protected that he was completely dependent on his mother. The mother ruled the home, and the father was an unimportant figure. Though Mrs A. was given a sufficiently large dowry, her mother-in-law started illtreating her, demanding more and more money or things from time to time. Mrs A's father fulfilled the demands many times, but the mother-in-law became more and more greedy day by day. Mrs A. was treated with extreme cruelty by her mother-in-law. She was asked to do all the household work from morning till evening. She was never given enough food to eat. The girl said, almost bursting into tears, that many days she went to bed hungry and spent restless nights due to the pangs of hunger. She was never allowed to meet any of the relatives or parents alone, though at least once a week, they all came to the house opposite and stayed overnight. The mother-in-law was superficially very cordial, and never gave out any sign that the girl was illtreated. This sort of affairs lasted for almost two years. The young girl got tired and frustrated and informed her parents. The parents took her away to their home. Mrs A. informed her parents that she will go back only if the husband's people promised to treat her well. She wanted that some important members of the caste should be called and a verbal agreement should be given in their presence. But the husband's people were unprepared for this. Mrs A. refused to go to her husband's place again, and, the parties separated. Though Mr R.J. and Mrs A. loved each other dearly, they could do nothing to save their marriage. No child was born to the couple. They stayed separately for about a year and then the wife went to the court for divorce. First a decree of judicial separation was granted on the basis of physical and mental cruelty, and, after two years, a decree of divorce was granted. The husband appeared in the court just once, but did not try to defend his case.

Mr R.J. is still working in the same factory as before. Though divorced for almost four years, he is not yet remarried. Indirect enquiry showed that the boy is finding it difficult to get another girl, because, the cruel treatment the mother-in-law had accorded to Mrs A. is known to all the community members.

Mrs A. is still very young. She is a very happy go lucky girl, and feels that she might find happiness again in future. After separation from husband, she continued her studies, and finished B.A. as well as B. Ed. Degrees. At present, she is working as a school teacher. Her father is looking for another suitable match, and she may be married off any time. She has no bitter feeling towards her ex-husband, but is sympathetic towards him. Yet, she feels, "A man should be capable of protecting his wife under all circumstances, whatever his parents say or feel." Her only regret is that her husband was not capable of that, though he loved her dearly.

This is a typical example of a marriage ending in divorce due to demand for more dowry and cruelty and interference of the mother-in-law coupled with weak personality of the husband.

Case Study No. 2 (Mr K. & Mrs L.)

Mr K. is a member of Harijan community (sweeper—scheduled

caste). He has 1 brother and 4 sisters. All the children had child marriage. Mr K. lost his father when he was but a child, and he being the youngest son, his mother is extremely attached to him.

Mrs L. also is a sweeper, belonging to the same community as that of K. She has 3 brothers and 4 sisters. All of them are married.

The marriage between the two was arranged when Mr K. was 10 years old, and the girl was only 5 years old. Both did not attend school. After child marriage also, Mrs L. remained in her own home for several years. When Mrs L. completed the age of 15 years, *gauna* was done, and she was brought to live permanently with her husband. Though belonging to low caste (sweeper) community, her family is respected because her father is a *panch* of the caste *panchayat* (member of the caste council), and they have a good house also. Mrs L. had never worked outside her home before coming to Mr K's house, though commonly sweeper girls start working at an early age, alongwith their parents, in houses and streets. Mrs L. was a good-looking young girl and she was fondled by her parents. When she came to her husband's place, she had to face entirely new circumstances. Her husband was completely under the thumb of his mother. The mother-in-law was employed as a sweeper in a hospital and had good earning. It was she who brought up Mr K., more so, because the father was dead for several years now. Mr K. felt very much obliged to his mother, and obeyed her blindly in all matters. Even his earnings were given to her only. When the daughter-in-law came to the house, the mother-in-law expected her to be her humble servant, and obey all her orders. She also asked the daughter-in-law to accompany her to the hospital and the streets to assist her in her work as a sweeper. Also, she wanted that Mrs L. should take her place in the hospital when she retires. Mrs L. did not comply with any of these demands. First of all, she was too young, and secondly, she was not used to much work. This irritated the mother-in-law very much. She started ill-treating and abusing the girl. She complained about the daughter-in-law's misbehaviour (disobedience) to her son. The infuriated husband beat up the girl many times. Thus, the home of Mr K. and Mrs L. became a scene of constant domestic discord.

Meanwhile, two children (a boy and a girl) were born to Mrs

L. The quarrels continued and increased in intensity day by day. Abuses and beating became a daily affair. The wife ran way to her home several times, but every time, the husband brought her back. When matters became intolerable, Mrs L's parents interfered and took away their daughter. Mr K's mother also was not to be defeated easily. She approached an advocate and sent a legal notice to Mrs L's parents, saying that if Mrs L. is not sent within a specified time, Mr K. will get married elsewhere. Mrs L's parents did not respond to this threat. Mrs K's mother was as good as her word. She found out another girl of the caste immediately and got her son married, "just to teach Mrs L. and her parents a lesson."

After the second marriage of Mr K., Mrs L. went to the court for divorce as well as for alimony. Both the parties fought the case for about two years. Mr K. lost the case. Mrs L. was granted a decree of divorce, and Mr K. was asked to pay Rs. 125 per month as alimony for the maintenance of his wife and children.

At present, Mr K. is working as a peon in a college. His mother is still working and earning. He has three children through the second wife. He feels that the second wife is much better because she has no pride, as she belongs to a poor family, and is very obedient to his mother. Yet, he says that he has nothing particularly against the first wife. His only complaint against her is that she did not obey his mother. "How can I go against my mother? After all, it is she who has brought me up." he says defensively.

Mrs L. is living with her parents. Now, she is employed as a sweeper in the Municipal Corporation and is earning well. Alongwith that, she is getting Rs 125 per cent as alimony. Hence, she has no economic problem.

Mr K confided to the researcher that though they are legally divorced, and Mr K. is remarried and has three children, his relationship with the first wife need not end. "In our community, such things are common. One of my uncles has five wives. He stays with all of them in turns," he said. Recently, Mr K. and Mrs L. are somewhat reconciled. Mr K. goes and meets the children sometimes. Mrs L. does not talk to him directly. Yet, she has agreed that she is willing to stay with him, i.e., not with his second wife and mother. "One of these days, I may arrange a separate house for her." Mr K. said laughing.

This case study clearly illustrates that marriage is treated as something very light, in a lower caste community. Too demanding mother-in-law, marriage at a very early age, domination of the husband by his mother, physical cruelty and illtreatment are the main factors that destroyed marriage in this case. The wife approached the court mainly because she wanted to receive alimony.

Case Study No. 3 (Mr H.G. and Mrs L.G.)

Mr H.G's parents died in early childhood, leaving him and his elder brother. The two brothers, then teenagers, migrated from Rajasthan to Indore in search of job and shelter. They came to a rich family and being members of the same community were given protection as well as job. Mr H.G. has no education and was living with one Mr R.P. as his household servant.

Mrs L.G. belongs to a middle class family in a suburban village near Indore. She has two brothers and two sisters. All of them are happily married. Both Mr H.G. and Mrs L.G. belong to Jain community.

The marriage between Mr H.G. and Mrs L.G. was arranged in a peculiar fashion. One day, a rich lady, Mrs R.P., approached Mrs L.G's parents saying that she had an adopted son for whom she was looking for a proper match. Mrs L.G's parents were flattered at the very thought of having connections with a rich and highly respected family. They said that they had a girl whom they wanted to marry off immediately. The very next day, Mrs R.P. arrived with the "adopted son". The young man was attired in a costly dress and was wearing even a diamond ring. Mrs L.G's parents were very anxious to get her married immediately. Mrs L.G. saw the boy. Though she was only a fifteen years old girl then, she plainly refused to marry this man. He looked very bulky and aged. She even threatened to commit suicide. But her father pressurised her, so much so that finally she agreed to marry the man. The marriage was arranged within seven days. Immediately after marriage, she was taken to Mr R.P's house. There she stayed with her husband for two-three days and then was taken to her parents house according to the custom of the community.

When the husband brought her back for permanent cohabitation, she found out the real state of affairs. She came to know that her husband was only a cook at Mr R.P's house. She and her husband had to share a small broken house with his elder brother's family. Mrs L.G. was still physically immature. Menstruation had not started yet; neither had she any secondary sex characteristics nor sexual interest. On the other hand, Mr H.G. was nearing 30 years of age. In the new house, Mrs L.G. had a typical routine. She was asked to get up early in the morning by the sister-in-law and was supposed to do cleaning of the pots, washing the clothes, sweeping the floor, etc. By the time, lunch was ready, she was asked to eat and go off to sleep. Her husband used to come after she slept. Again, in the afternoon, she was asked to finish the work early and was served dinner early and then put to sleep. Her husband came late in the night and left early in the morning. For days together, she never saw the husband because he came in after she had slept and went off before she got up. Gradually, her sister-in-law started taunting her saying that she was not a woman. She had no characteristics of a woman. That is why, her husband could not have any relations with her. Mrs L.G. was very upset at hearing these things. She went to her own home and said all these to her elder brother's wife. The sister-in-law understood that the girl has not yet attained puberty and hence asked her not to go to the husband's place for a year.

Mrs L.G. was sent to her husband's place after two years. Again, to her great distress, she found out that her husband continued his old routine and took no interest in her. Her sister-in-law also continued to treat her in the same way. But now, Mrs L.G. was a grown-up woman and started understanding the man-woman relationship. Gradually, she started noticing that her husband had illicit relations with his brother's wife and due to this only he did not take any interest in her. Mrs L.G. was frustrated more than ever. She went back to her parents with the new complaint. On closer enquiry, Mr H.G. accepted his crime and it was also revealed that he had an illegitimate son born through his sister-in-law before his marriage, Mrs L.G.'s parents interfered and it was decided that the couple will stay away from the brother and his wife. A small rented place was arranged for them by Mrs L.G's father. Things did not improve for Mrs L.G. even after this. Mr H.G. had started selling milk, but whatever he got he squandered elsewhere and Mrs L.G. was left to starve. Several times, he would not reach home even during night and Mrs L.G. used to sleep all alone, hungry in her dingy room. Occasionally, her parents used to visit her and give small help. With this, she survived. In the meanwhile, a baby girl was born to the couple, but Mr H.G. showed complete apathy to this new arrival. The mother and child were now left to starve and many a time, Mrs L.G. had to borrow and beg just to get a bit of milk for the baby. Once when the baby was just 7 months, the baby's constant hungry howls irritated Mr H.G. so much that he gave her an overdose of opium. The child would have died ; it survived since it received medical aid in time.

Mrs L.G. became pregnant again. Through out the pregnancy, she had no proper food and on top of that she had to worry day and night about feeding the other baby. When she started getting labour pains. Mr H.G. put her in an autorikshaw and said the rickshaman to go to the hospital. He said that he would be following on bicycle. Mrs L.G. reached the hospital, and waited in the rickshaw. Mr H.G. did not arrive. Her pains started getting stronger, and at last the rickshaw driver went and called the nurse to get Mrs L.G. to the hospital. In the hospital, she gave birth to a male child, but became unconscious due to exhaustion and starvation. Mr H.G. never bothered to find out what had become to his wife. After she had regained consciousness, she informed her people and they took her home. Thereafter, Mrs L.G. decided not to cohabit with Mr H.G.

Mrs L.G. was educated only up to Middle School, when she got married. Mrs L.G's parents asked her to study further. Thus, she had finished higher secondary and teachers' training. She got a job as a primary school teacher. With this small income, she started living independently, supporting herself and her children. But Mr H.G. was a constant source of harassment. Every now and then, he would go and ask for money and if she did not give, she was beaten up thoroughly. Once, she was stabbed by her husband. Once she had a tooth extracted and had severe bleeding and pain. The husband forced her to cook for him in spite of that. When she complained of severe pain, he gave some pill which made her unconscious. She was rescued by a neighbour.

Due to this sort of constant harassment and misery, Mrs L.G. decided to go to the court. After hearing her woeful story, the judge remarked in the judgement decree : "the story that has been narrated indicates callous neglect, deliberate refusal to cooperate, foorishness, a calculated, extracting and inconsiderate behaviour, want of affection and mean stinginess on the part of the respondent." She was granted a decree of judicial separation exparte. After three years, she again applied to the court, and got a decree of divorce.

Mrs L.G. is still working as a primary school teacher. Her daughter is 17 years old, and studying in college. The son is 14 years old and is a high school student. She has economic problem as the earning is small and she has to support two adolescent children, all alone. She is in her late thirties now. She is extremely desirous of getting remarried, but is very frustrated that she cannot find a suitable person. In her own words, "a person should be happy at least some time in life. I had never been happy till this day." She seems to be a broken person due to the excessive physical and mental torture she had undergone. Her colleagues describe her as "nervous and sometimes a bit crack." Mr H.G. is in his fifties. He has a small business of selling sweets. He still squanders money on drinking and women. Occasionally, he meets his son secretly and gives him small gifts. The boy has a soft corner for him, while the daughter hates him intensely.

From the above discussion, we can see that unplanned and unthoughtful marriage against the wishes of the wife, frauds used at the time of marriage, extramarital relations of the husband, coupled with his total neglect and cruelty towards wife and children, destroyed the marriage of Mr H.G. and L.G.

Note: Recently, Mrs L.G. met the researcher and informed her that she has now re-married. She still works as a teacher and her new husband is Graduate in Agriculture, employed in an organization. Further, a child is born through the second marriage. The son and daughter of the former marriage also stay with them.

Case Study No. 4 (Mr J.M. & Mrs U.M.)

Mr J.M. is a Punjabi Khatri. He is the younger of the two brothers in the family. They belong to a very rich business class family. They have even a market in their name in the Metropolitan city of 'I'. Mrs U.M. is also a Punjabi Khatri, though of a different subcaste. Mrs U.M. belongs to a well-to-do and sophisticated family. She has two brothers and two sisters. All of them are happily married.

Mr J.M's people met Mrs U.M. at a marriage party. The girl was extremely good-looking and Mr J.M's people liked her instantly. Mr J.M. also was present in the marriage. He also saw the girl and liked her much. Later, he came to know that she was a couple of years elder to him, and she is a graduate whereas he has done only High School. Mrs U.M. was not very keen on this marriage, but agreed, because of the persuasion of her parents and relatives. Mrs U.M's relatives were attracted toward Mr J.M's family on account of their high economic status.

They were engaged in marriage within a month of the initial meeting. The marriage took place after a year. In the meanwhile, the couple used to write to each other regularly, and had even met once or twice. The marriage was arranged with great pomp and show and the couple started living together at the joint family of Mr J.M.

Mrs U.M. was a very modern woman. A graduate from a prestigious institution, and having better education than all other members of her husband's family, she felt superior to everyone around and demonstrated it on all possible occasions. She could not adjust to the traditional life of the joint family; neither did she like the interference of the mother-in-law or sister-in-law. She did not like to be in *purdah*. She wanted to move around freely and attend parties and other social functions. She was used to free movements even before marriage as she was living in New Delhi, and had a very good job. Her family people also were very broad-minded, and did not put much restrictions on her. Mr J.M's parents, elder brother, sister-in-law, etc., were very much annoyed by Mrs U.M's behaviour, but Mrs U.M. was totally indifferent to all their protests. Mr J.M. was much in love with his beautiful wife, and was eger to fulfil her every wish. She persuaded him to separate from his joint family. They took a house on rent, and shifted there.

Mr J.M. was a businessman and had to leave the house early in the morning, and used to return only very late in the night. She was a very good cook and housekeeper and kept the house to the entire satisfaction of Mr J.M. Three children were born to them two boys and a girl. Mrs U.M. was a very devoted mother, and looked after the children with great care and love.

In the meanwhile, rumours started reaching Mr J.M's ears that his wife was leading an immoral life with other men in his absence. Though he did not want to listen to them, day by day, the rumours became louder. Mrs U.M's elder brother-in-law was a persistent visitor, and whenever he came, he used to stay on for several days. Mr J.M. used to be away during the day; the brother-in-law and Mrs U.M. used to eat, drink, and go for movies, together. Mr J.M. objected to this sort of affairs, but Mrs U.M. was not very mindful of him. She continued life in her own ways. Mr J.M. became totally frustrated with life. He was not able to take any interest in the business. Day and night, he wandered like a mad man, because, on the one hand, he was still very much in love with his wife, and, on the other hand, his suspicion about her grew stronger day by day. Because of his neglect, he lost all the business, and became a pauper. His mother was dead in the meanwhile. His father and brother refused to help him in any way, because, he had severed all connections with them on account of his wife. The frustrated, bankrupt man had no way left. His wife decided to go to her-parents, taking the children alongwith her. She promised to come back after he had re-established his business or he could join her and find a job there. Mr J.M. wandered around a few days in the hope of receiving some help from parents or relatives. But, none came to his rescue. He then decided to go to his wife's place, and try for some job. When he reached there, he was treated discourteously by his wife and her people. The lonely man left the place and came back to 'I' city. First, he started working as a daily-paid labourer. Later, he started selling tea on a cart. Gradually, he collected a small capital and started a very small business. He tried to bring back his wife and children. In the meanwhile, she had got into a very good job and hence refused to come back. The frustrated man went to the court and applied for a judicial separation, with the sincere hope of getting back his wife and children due to the threat of court case. But, Mrs U.M. did not bother to come to the court, nor did she defend herself. She had decided to separate from him for good. Mr J.M. got a decree of judicial separation ex-parte. After two years, he applied for a divorce. He hoped that at least the threat of being divorced will force Mrs U.M. to reconcile with her husband. He got a decree of divorce. But the unhappy man is more frustrated than ever. He confessed that even today, he loves his wife with all his heart, and is ready to accept her only if she would come back. The thought of his children is particularly painful for him. From the time of their separation, Mr J.M. used to meet them occasionally, and give them small amounts of money. But, after the decree of divorce, the wife refused to allow the children to meet him at all. Many times, he tried to meet them, but could not. He knows that the eldest son is an MBBS student, the girl a college student, and the youngest boy a high school student. They all are with the mother, and are doing well. According to Mr J.M., "the thought that I am separated from my children for ever makes me mad. I wander on the street in the hope that I might be able to see them per chance. But, now, long five years have passed. They all must be young men and women. Even if I see them, they may not recognize me. I also may not recognize them easily." He heaves a sigh of utter despair and continues, "Do you think there is anyone more unfortunate than me, who is denied even the pleasure of the sight of his children, who were dearest to him."

Mr J.M. stays all alone in a room and makes use of the some room as his office. He does his own cooking, and washing. Though desirous of remarriage, he has no courage to take the initiative and there is non to help him. The memory of his former wife and children haunts him day and night. His trade is just enough to sustain him and he does not make any effort to develop it further as he has no more ambition in life. He spends his lonely days either in the room or when he feels too lonely, he goes out for a week or two, just for change in travel.

Mrs U.M. is now an officer in a private firm and earns well. She keeps herself busy with her job and home. Though in her late forties, she is still a very charming woman. She has no plan to remarry and is completely adjusted with her present way of life.

The foregoing discussion makes it clear that factors like difference in cultural background, attitudes and temperaments of the husband and wife, higher education of wife, her extra-marital relations, etc., were the main factors which broke marriage.

Note: Mr J.M. has since remarried, after the interview with him. The second wife is a poor woman from a different community.

Case Study No. 5 (Mr S.H. & Mrs R.H.)

Mr S.H. is the third son of a large family of 8 brothers and sisters. His father was an employee of the State Govt. with moderate income. S.H's father got all his children educated.

Mrs R.H. is the second offspring of her parents, the elder and the younger also being daughters. Mrs R.H's father was first employed in Madhya Pradesh State itself. Later, he got a job in a foreign country and went there, leaving behind the children and wife. He used to come once a year to meet the family. Both Mr S.H. and Mrs R.H. belong to the Sindhi community, (included in 'Bania' community in our study), of the middle economic class.

Mr S.H. was a postgraduate and had a job with a reputed firm in another town. Mrs R.H's parents were residing in the same town earlier. Being members of the same community, they came in contact. S.H. was a regular visitor at Mrs R.H's place. The mother liked the boy very much, especially as she had no male child, and he used to help the family in several ways. Mrs R.H's parents contacted S.H's people and the marriage was arranged. Mrs R.H. had just finished her higher secondary examination and was only 16 years old, and Mr S.H. was 26 years at the time of their marriage. Soon the family shifted to a new city. Mr S.H. had picked up a quarrel with his employer and left the job. He also accompanied his wife's family.

Mr S.H. tried several jobs, but could not settle down anywhere. He then tried to practice Law, but did not prove to be a success. Finally, he decided to do some private trade. It was also a failure.

Mrs R.H. continued her education, and became a postgraduate in a social science subject. She is now a very pretty and accomplished young lady, wanting to have a career of her own. All these days, they were dependent on Mrs RH's parents as Mr S.H. did not have any regular income. Mrs R.H. tried jobs like Receptionist, Part-time Teacher, etc. Finally, she got into a permanent job in a nationalized Bank.

The differences between Mr S.H. and Mrs R.H. started becoming more obvious. Mr S.H. was now in his middle thirties, short-statured and below average in looks, with no career prospects, whereas Mrs R.H. was a blooming young women having high education and a settled job.

Mrs R.H. was never much attached to her husband. At the time of marriage, she was too young to realize the implications of marriage. But now she was different. She started realising that her marriage with S.H. was a mistake. His poor looks and failure in career irritated her.

In the meanwhile, she fell in love with a handsome young man.

Their relationship became intimate. Mr S.H. remained ignorant of his wife's amorous affairs for some time. Gradually, he came to know of it. Things became much wrose after Mrs R.H. gave birth to a baby boy. All these years, the couple had no child. Now, after the wife had started her extra-marital relations, she had conceived. Mr S.H. refused to accept this child as his son. He insisted to separate from the wife's family. They had already constructed a house in a colony and the couple shifted there. Mrs R.H's lover got married in the meanwhile, and had two children of his own, but he continued to visit Mrs R.H. One night, Mr S.H. saw his wife with her lover in the house. He reported the matter to the police. The conflicts between the spouses became more frequent and violent. Mr S.H. insisted that they leave for Bombay, which his wife refused. Mr S.H. wanted that the child be left with the mother of Mrs S.H. which was also refused by her, especially as she was extremely fond of the child. Their quarrels became a daily affair. This sort of affairs lasted for about a year. Finally, Mr S.H. left for Bombay, from where he started sending telegrams to Mrs R.H. urging her to join him immediately, on various pretexts. Mrs R.H. was not moved by any of these, as she was rather fed up of the marriage and wanted to terminate it at any cost. She went to the court after 12 years of the marriage, and applied for divorce on the basis of cruelty and extreme mental torture. In six months' time, she was granted a decree of judicial separation. Later, she applied again, and secured a decree of divorce. Mr. S.H. never came to the court.

At present, Mr S.H. is in Bombay, practising Law. He remarried and his second marriage also is reported to be a failure. Mrs R.H. is now staying separately with her little son, who is studying in primary school. Mrs R.H. has no economic problem as she is well-employed in the Bank and gets rent from the house too. She still continues relations with her lover but has no plan to remarry.

We conclude that, (*i*) marriage at an early age, (*ii*) absence of the father from home, (*iii*) failure of husband in his occupation, (*iv*) extramarital relations of the wife, (*v*) dissatisfaction of the wife, (*vi*) issue-lessness for several years and (*vii*) inferiority complex of the husband were some of the prominent factors leading to legal dissolution of marriage.

Case Study No. 6 (Mr G.L. & Mrs S.L.)

Mr GL is a Gujrati Jain settled in 'I' city, a tailor, earning about Rs 1500 per month. He is a graduate and has medium looks. The family belongs to middle class.

Mrs S.L. is also a Gujrati Jain, belonging to a family settled at 'I' for several years. She is a beautiful girl and is now a postgraduate.

Mrs S.L. was in love with an engineer-boy of the same caste. The boy also loved her very much and wanted to marry her.

As is the practice in the Gujrati community, the couple was given sufficient freedom to meet each other, and move around. Parents of both sides approved of the union wholeheartedly, but the final settlement and the matching of the horoscope was to be done. The horoscope did not match and both the lovers were very frustrated. The boy tried to produce a forged horoscope just to match with the girl's. The bride's parents having much faith in stars, came to know of it, and refused to have any connection with the boy in future.

Another mach, Mr G.L. was settled for Mrs S.L. The girl was not at all happy about this marriage and gave her consent very reluctantly. Her lover also asked her to go through the marriage just for the satisfaction of the parents. He promised to accept her if she came away from the husband's house immediately.

Mr G.L. and Mrs S.L. were engaged for about ten months. The couple used to meet each other and even visit each other's home. Mrs SL never seemed to dislike Mr G.L. though she never showed much love for him. The marriage was conducted with the usual pomp and show. The girl fell unconscious right in the marriage *shamiana* (tent) at the time of reception and was admitted in a Nursing Home for about a week. When recovered, she was sent to the husband's home, where she remained during the day and came away before night. She did so several days. Though married for four months, the couple did not cohabit even once. Mr G.L. and his parents pressurized her parents to send her. But the girl plainly refused to do so. Mr G.L. and his parents were be wildered at this strange behaviour of the girl. They contacted the community leaders and with their help tried to persuade the girl. The girl remained adamant and did not go. A caste panchayat (caste council) was called and a *Farkati* (agreement) was written. All the goods exchanged at the time of the wedding were returned.

Mr G.L. went to the court to confirm the divorce granted by the caste panchayat. The girl also appeared in the court and expressed her willingness for divorce. The parties were granted divorce immediately.

Mr G.L. got remarried and has a son. He still continues his job as a tailor. Mr G.L. has no problem at present, though he said that the time of the first marriage and divorce were periods of great distress for him and all members of his family. He is the only son of his parents. The unfortunate incident shook his aged father so much that he had a heart attack and died. Mr G.L. still feels that the untimely death of his father was due to his own marital problem.

Mrs S.L. is the eldest daughter of a family of three children. Her divorce has created lot of problem for the family. The parents feel that they may not get proper match for their son as well as the younger daughter. Mrs S.L. is still unmarried. Her lover ditched her and married another well-educated girl. She is extremely desirous of getting remarried, but is rather diffident about finding a proper match. She said in a frustrated and angry tone: "Though I have not lived with the man even for a day, I know, nobody will like to marry me now. In the eyes of the world, I am a divorcee and only a man who cannot get a proper wife will marry a divorcee." She has finished her postgraduation after divorce. She is still unemployed but plans to take up a job soon.

Thus, premarital love affair, coupled with the false promise made by the previous lover, led to the divorce in this case. Matching of horoscope was the only point which stood in the way of the love-marriage.

Case Study No. 7 (Mr R.V. & Mrs A.V.)

Mr R.V. is from a *Bania* (trading) community and medical doctor by profession. He was brought up in a large joint family and had two brothers and three sisters. All of them are happily married. His family belongs to middle income group.

Mrs A.V. also belongs to a middle class family of the *Bania* community, with four brothers and two sisters, all of whom are married leading happy life.

Theirs was an arranged marriage. Both the spouses liked each other before marriage. They had an engagement for a period of six months. They used to meet each other during that time. The couple stayed together at 'I' for 3 years.

After three years, the husband got an appointment as Doctor in the United States of America. He left promising to take the wife as soon as he got settled there. In the beginning, he used to send fervent letters very frequently from there. Gradually, letters became fewer, and they started revealing a disinterest toward Mrs A.V. She earnestly requested her husband many times to take her also abroad. In the beginning, he seemed eager about it. But later, he avoided the topic altogether. After about 4 years of her husband's departure, Mrs A.V. happened to see a letter of his, addressed to his younger brother, in which it was clear that he was living with an American girl and was no more interested in his wife in India. This letter was later produced in the court of Law for divorce. A part of the letter read like this:

> Since I left 'I' . . . I was very disturbed due to this new country with new customs and culture.
>
> It took me about two years to adjust myself to this new life. Now I am well settled. . .Regarding my personal life, as you are aware, to live lonely especially at such a distance is impossible. Luckily, I have come across a very beautiful and talented girl. Her name is. . . .We have been dating together and now we both have complete understanding among us. . . .K. and myself are living as husband and wife. . . .Please try to explain in indirect way to A. (wife), but be cautious that this secret is not disclosed to anyone else.

This letter naturally upset Mrs A.V. very much. Now, she realized the reason for her husband's disinterest in her. This news upset the relatives of both R.V. & Mrs A.V. so much so that R.V's father fell ill seriously and died within a month. R.V. was informed of his father's death and he came to perform some rituals connected with it. Now Mrs A.V. got a chance to talk to her husband personally. R.V. admitted that he was living with an American girl and hence would not be able to take her there. R.V. stayed only for a week and then left for the States. After his departure, Mrs A.V. applied for divorce on the basis that her husband was living in adultery. His letter was also produced in the court. R.V's brother also testified in the court in favour of his sister-in-law. Mrs A.V. was granted divorce immediately.

At present, Mrs A.V. is remarried with a widower, having three children. Mrs A.V. (now Mrs A.J.) has no child of her own, but she is happy and well-adjusted to the new family. Mr R.V. is still in the States and continues to live with the same girl from there.

In this case, factors such as the separation of the spouses for a long period soon after marriage, husband's life in a foreign country like the United States of America, his entanglement with another woman in an attempt to adjust to new culture and way of life, and the clear evidence for the same resulted in divorce.

Case Study No. 8 (Mr D.M. & Mrs S.M.)

Mr D.M. is an employee of the Life Insurance Corporation of India, a graduate, and belongs to a middle class Brahmin family. He has only 2 brothers and both of them happily married. Mr D.M. is a quiet and withdrawn person. His entire life is limited between the home and the office. Even with his colleagues, he keeps limited contacts. He looks an average person.

Mrs S.M. is a very pretty woman. Though educated only upto Middle Class, she is very social and likes to move around with people as much as possible. She belongs to a lower middle class Bengali Brahmin family. Her brothers and sisters are all married. It was reported that her sister's marriage was also not very pleasant.

Mrs S.M. got married when she was 22 and he was 27. She was not much satisfied with the match her father had selected for her, because of the husband's average look, but could not resist, because they were poor and dowry is a great problem among them.

In all the places the couple stayed, Mr D.M. faced problems due to his wife. His wife had very loose morals and wherever she stayed, she tried to establish undesirable contacts with men. Mr D.M. was forced to change houses several times in the same city because of the promiscuous behaviour of the wife. Mrs S.M. gave birth to four children, of which two died in early infancy.

Mr D.M. had a very handsme nephew. He was staying in a hostel and studying in a college. He used to visit the couple. Mrs S.M. started having illicit relations with this young man, though he was at least 10 years younger to her. In the beginning, Mr S.C. (cousin) used to come to D.M's house, and there had relationship with Mrs S.M. Gradually, Mrs S.M. started going to his hostel. Though married for several years and had given birth to four children, Mrs S.M. was very good looking and young Mr S.C. fell into her trap rather unwillingly. When Mrs S.M's visit to S.C. became more frequent, Mr D.M. came to know about it. He reprimanded his wife and asked her never to see his nephew again, but she was not worried about D.M. any more. She was strongly attracted to her lover and decided to join him permanently. She ran away from home, leaving behind her husband and children Mr S.C. was still a college student, and had no independent income of his own. She become pregnant through S.C. and he was much puzzled. Finding no way to get out of the situation, S.C. left the place. For about a year, two of them wandered here and there. In the meanwhile, Mrs S.M. gave birth to a child, the first fruit of their sinful union. The couple faced serious economic problems. S.C's parents and community disowned him. At last, S.C's father was persuaded to accept his son back.

Having eloped with his nephew and a child born to her through him, D.M. decided to divorce her. He applied for divorce and it was granted soon.

After a year of divorce, D.M. remarried. He has no child from the second marriage, but his children of the first marriage stay with him. He is somewhat adjusted to the new situation, but the memory of the former marriage and all the unhappy events disturbed him often.

Mrs S.M. (now Mrs S.C.) continues with her new husband, who is the nephew of her former husband. She has two children from the present union, a boy and a girl. Though in her middle forties, she is still an attractive woman. When the researcher approached her, she tried to hide the facts. Mr S.C., her present husband, is a broken man. Having left his studies, in the middle, he has no career. The crime he committed by forming illicit connections with his uncle's wife and then taking her away from him, is heavy upon his mind. Though only in his middle thirties and extremely handsome to look at, he appears a very unhappy and dejected man.

This case study shows that oversexuality and promiscuity of the wife, coupled with temperamental incompatibility between the husband and wife, led to the failure of the marriage.

Case Study No. 9 (Mr S.P. and Mrs N.P.)

Mrs N.P. belongs to a rich and prominent Maharashtriyan family with four brothers and four sisters, all of whom are in very good position. Her father had connections with the royal family

(Holkar family) and hence, the family was well-reputed right from the beginning. Mrs N.P. proved to be less intelligent and smart as compared with her brothers and sisters. With difficulty she had completed her High School, and could not study further, because of her poor intellect and lack of aptitude for studies. In the meanwhile, she fell in love with a man of another caste, and married him against the wishes of her parents. This marriage turned out to be very unfortunate because the man was extremely cruel and started treating her with great harshness. Mrs N.P. ran away from him and came back to her parents. She took the job of a school teacher and started living with her parents. Mrs N.P. was a very jolly person, and always remained happy even in her present condition. She had a job of her own. The family was well-to-do. Though erred once, her family treated her with love and kindness. She lived with them and had a care-free life. Nearly twenty years passed this way. By this time, all of Mrs N.P's brothers and sisters had finished their education, got married and settled in different parts of Madhya Pradesh or even outside the State. The father was no more. The huge family house was to be sold because there was none to maintain it. Mrs N.P's mother also became very old. Still they continued together.

Soon, Mrs N.P. lost her mother too. Suddenly, after many years, she realised her own position. She had no place to go and none to help her or to keep her company. She was nearing middle forties. A sense of lonelinesss and worry about future gripped her. She wanted to find some sort of company and protection. Being a person of simple mind and poor wits, she was exploited everywhere. The only help she had through mother also was lost. Mrs N.P. pondered over her condition and decided that she cannot continue to live alone. First, she thought of living with one of her brothers or sisters. When she reached the home of her sister, it was found that the sister's children were very hostile towards her. Next, she tried to live with a brother, whose wife treated her as an intruder and she was forced to leave. At last, she returned to her own place. She thought of marriage, though had crossed marriageable age. She decided to advertise. The man dealing with the matrimonial colum in the press was a widower, Mr S.P. He showed interest in her, and secretly contacted her instead of advertising. She was told by him that he came in response to her advt. She believed him. He visited her several times. They married in the court. Both hired a house. He was interested in her money and ornaments. Hardly had they stayed together for a couple of months, the man started asking for her money and ornaments. Her refusal resulted in harassment and persecution. After some fights, the husband left. After 3 years of marriage, she filed a petition in the court for divorce. The husband did not respond, and she was granted a decree of divorce without much delay.

At present, she is living alone and continues to work in the school. Though she has problems, she feels happier then the miserable time she spent with S.P. Her sisters' children help her occasionally. Her friends and colleagues testify that the unfortunate marriage she had with Mr S.P. turned her semi-insane, and many a time she behaves abormally.

Mr S.P. continues to live with his joint family. He has the same job in the Press, and has married off his female children born out of the first marriage. He has no particular problem now.

Thus, (*i*) postponement of marriage to a very late age, (*ii*) wrong calculations of dependence on relatives, (*iii*) conceited nature of the husband, and (*iv*) his concern not for her but only for her property and money resulted in the termination of a marriage.

Case Study No. 10 (Mr B.S. & Mrs H.S.)

Mrs HS belongs to a middle class South Indian Brahmin family, settled in a north Indian city. Her father died of TB many years ago. She is the eldest daughter in the family, with two brothers and two sisters. She completed Higher Secondary and Teachers Training and is working in a school as teacher. She had to help the brothers and sisters with her income. Nobody thought of her marriage at that time due to the financial problems.

When the brothers and sisters got married, they worried about the unmarried sister, and gave an advertisement in *Sarita*, a popular Hindi magazine. In response to this matrimonial advt., a young man, aged 40, working in the Army, came. Marriage was arranged according to the Arya Samaj rites. The man left after 2 days, promising to come back soon, with a convenient Army posting. After a few months, she was requested to join him in Darjeeling, where she went. The couple stayed in a hotel for a day. The next day, Mr BS went out promising to return in a few hours. He did not. She summoned her brother and searched for her husband.

They could not trace him, and the brother and sister returned. It was revealed later on that Mr B.S. was a fraud and cheat. He was married for many years and has five children. He has cheated others also like this. He was a dismissed person from the Army, and did not have any job. Not knowing the fact that Mrs H.S. and her brothers had known of the criminal nature of B.S. from other sources, he came to H.S's place. Her brother informed the Police and Mr B.S. was arrested and kept in Police custody.

Thereupon, Mrs H.S. approached the court for divorce. As the facts were too clear, the same was granted soon.

Mrs H.S. had not remarried. She still lives with her brother's family, doing the same job of a school teacher. The short-lived marriage is a disturbing memory to her even today.

Hurried marriage through matrimonial advertisements, without enquiring into the details and precedents of the man caused disastrous marital failure in this case.

Case Study No. 11 (Mr D.S. & Mrs A.S.)

Mr D.S. is the eldest son of a small family of 3 children. He is an income tax lawyer. They belong to the Gujrati Brahmin community permanently settled in a city in M.P.

Mrs A.S. is the only child of her parents. They are well-to-do and brought her up with great love and affection. She is also a graduate in Law.

The marriage was arranged through advertisement in newspapers. Before marriage, the couple had met each other and talked. Mr D.S. had made it clear that he could not go to Gujrat as she is settled in a city in M.P. The marriage was arranged in the traditional way. For about a year, they both had a very happy life. Later, she started telling him that she would like to be with her parents. She wanted him too to work there. Mr D.S. rejected this plea. The thought of permanent separation from her parents gnawed her heart. Parents also used to write to her almost daily, especially saying that they were very anxious to have her as well as her husband at their place.

In the meanwhile, Mrs A.S. became pregnant. As it was the custom, she was sent to her parents, this being the first delivery. A male child was born. Mr D.S. was very overjoyed at this. He went and saw his wife and child. After a couple of months, he went to bring his wife and child to his place, but they did not go, on one pretext or the other. He waited for another year and applied for a decree of restitution of conjugal rights on the plea that his wife left him without any reasonable cause. At last, the wife and her people agreed for divorce on the condition that the husband will not make any claim on his son. Mr D.S. was extremely upset at this proposal. But, he knew that this was the only way to end the case as well as his unsuccessful marriage, and start afresh. With considerable reluctance and sorrow, he gave in. The wife's party also agreed for divorce and thus a divorce decree was granted.

Mr D.S. got remarried after a year of divorce and has a female child too. But, the memories of the first marriage are still very much disturbing to him. He knows that his first wife was an extremely nice, gentle, cultured and talented girl. By losing her, he lost a lot of happiness and cherished dreams. In his own words, "My wife was an extremely nice and well-brought up girl. Her only fault was that she was the only child of her parents and was too much attached to them. She loved me deeply and I also was extremely fond of her."

Mrs A.S. is still with her parents. She is earning well in a private job. Her son is with her and he studies in school. Mrs A.S. has no intention to remarry. The parents of Mrs A.S. feel that they have not only a daughter but a grandson also to perpetuate their family.

The foregoing narration makes it clear how over-attachment to one's own parents, especially, of female spouse (mainly in the case of an only child) and the parents' reluctance to be separated from their only child can ruin a marriage, even when very cordial and harmonious relationship exist between the spouses.

Case Study No. 12 (Mr G.B. and Mrs V.B.)

Mr G.B. belongs to a middle class *kayasth* joint family. He has a diploma in Engineering and is employed as an engineer in a big cotton mill. He has two brothers, who are married and are somewhat happy.

Mrs V.B. belongs to the same community. She is from a well-cultured and sophisticated family. She has one brother and four-sisters, all of whom are happily married. Mrs V.B. is the second offspring of the family and she was a graduate when she got married.

Theirs was an arranged marriage. Though the couple saw each other before marriage and consented to marry each other, there was not much occasion for further contact.

Soon after marriage, Mrs V.B. found that her husband was a very ill-tempered preson. She was scared of him. His mother and elder brother's wife were jealous of Mrs V.B. because she was a very good looking girl coming from a family with superior status. Both these women started telling all sorts of things against Mrs V.B. to her husband. The husband used to get infuriated by these allegations (though most of them were false) and used to beat his wife mercilessly. This became a constant feature in the family within three years of the marriage. Mrs V.B. was extremely frustrated. The physical and mental torture was too much for her to bear. By this time, she had given birth to a son also. The future of the child, the prestige of her own family, and the staunch training received at her parental home, compelled her to continue at her husband's place in spite of all hardship. The couple had 3 children—two boys and a girl. Thereafter, she was all the more determined to continue with her husband, at least for the sake of their children. But her huband's cruelty increased day by day. Fourteen long years she suffered the inhuman treatment meted out to her by her husband. At the end of it, she lost all courage and strength. Now her children grew up, the youngest being 8 years. After a severe beating by her husband, one day Mrs V.B. left the house, never to return. She went to her parents, leaving the children with the husband, and started working as a teacher in a far off place and started living there all alone.

Mr G.B. never expected his wife to leave permanently. After every separation, she used to come back, at least for the sake of children But this time, she did not. Mr G.B. filed a suit against his wife, alleging that his wife was leading an adulterous life elsewhere and her father was helping her to continue in that. He also alleged that his wife had carried away cash, ornaments, clothes, etc. First, legal notices were sent to her and her father. Then the petition for restitution of conjual rights was filed. The wife, at the sametime, applied for judicial separation, in another court, on the basis of extreme cruelty by the husband. A third suit was filed by Mr G.B. against one Mr G.S. who was alleged to have relationship with his wife, Mrs V.B. A fourth case was yet filed by Mr G.B. alleging that Mr G.S., his wife's alleged lover, has used criminal intimidation against him. Further, it was alleged by him that his wife was pregnant through her lover. On the basis of all these, a decree of restitution of conjugal rights was passed. Later, a degree of divorce was also granted.

After divorce, Mr G.B., continued his life in the same house. He did not wish to remarry. The children grew up with him and looked after the household work. They were well educated also—the eldest boy an engineer, the middle girl a postgraduate and the youngest boy also postgraduate.

Mrs V.B. still continues as a school teacher. She has no intention to remarry. She is very unhappy because she is separated from her children. The children sometimes visit their mother without informing the father.

The researcher had occasion to talk with the children. They said that the father was really ill-tempered, but then he used to ask the mother to come back.

This is a typical example of a highly educated and well-to-do couple separating from each other due to severe marital disharmony. The major problems have been the temperamental defect in the huband's personality and the resultant extreme cruelty towatds his wife. The mother-in-law and sister-in-law were additional factors in making the rift complete. In spite of the wife's great desire to continue with her husband at least for the sake of her children, and in spite of the best and persistent efforts on her part, the marriage could not work, because of the non-cooperation and cruel treatment by the husband. The children must have undergone a lot of physical and mental anguish, because of the problems of their parents, but the remarkable thing about them is that they all are well-adjusted and accomplished young people today.

Case Study No. 13 (Mr P.P. & Mrs K.P.)

Mr P.P. is a Maharashtrian Brahmin. He lost his mother in childhood. His maternal grandmother brought him up and he is staying with them permanently. He is postgraduate, employed in a Bank. He is now 50 years old.

Mrs K.P. is also a Maharashtrian Brahmin with two sisters and three brothers. All, except the youngest brother, are married and are leading a happy life. Mrs K.P. is the eldest daughter, and is employed now as an officer in the Life Insurance Corporation.

Theirs was an arranged marriage. After the wedding, the couple lived with the husband's maternal grand-parents. Mrs K.P. did not like the arrangement at all. The grandparents were traditional. They tried to restrict her movements. The entire burden of maintaining the family was upon Mrs K.P. although she was employed in a full-time job. The husband did not offer any help in household matters. Even when a child was born, she had to look after the house and then work in the office also. Gradually, she had three children. She was a very active and talented lady, interested in games, stage-acting, music, poetry, writing and so on. But in her present way of life, she was almost imprisoned. When the children grew, she again started taking interest in her old hobbies. She was selected to represent LIC in Games Meet. Her grandparents-in-law were very much against this and with great reluctance she was granted permission to participate in these events. She was also an active member of the Maharashtrian cultural association. Mrs K.P. was selected to act the leading role in a drama. The grand-parents-in-law of Mrs K.P. was almost shocked at the liberties their grand-daughter-in-law was taking. They strongly objected. She did not bother about them and acted as heroine in the drama. There was much praise and criticism about her activities. Mr P.P. supported his grandparents views. By this time, he also developed some bad habits like drinking, eating outside the home, coming home very late, etc. This coupled with the activities of the wife caused serious conflicts between the husband and wife. Their relationship became perpetually strained. Each spouse started avoiding the other on all possible occasions. The grandparents-in-law persisted in their nagging and criticism. The perpetual tension became intolerable. One day, she left the house with all her three children. She hired a nearby house and started living separately. Mr P.P. tried to persuade her to come back, but she had left with the intention of breaking the marriage permanently. The children remained with her. They did not miss their father much, because, he never took active interest in them and for all their needs, they were dependent on their mother. The separation lasted for about 7 years before any legal proceedings started. He filed an application for judicial separation on the basis of desertion for several years. The wife did not contest. Thereupon, a decree of judicial separation was granted to him. After two years, a decree of divorce was also granted.

Mr P.P. could not remarry as he fell seriously ill after divorce. He is till suffering from some serious malady, and lives with his grandparents, though they are too old.

Mrs K.P. is an officer in the LIC. She earns well. She feels much relieved due to separation and divorce. She still continues with her cultural activities of the community, but looks after the children also well.

We conclude that (*i*) temperamental incompatibility and wide gap in the interests and attitudes of the spouses, and (*ii*) the interference of the in-laws broke the marriage.

Case Study No. 14 (Mr D.S.M. & Mrs K.A.M.)

Mr D.S.M. is a Rajput, son of a zamindar, and is still known as a "raja". He has one brother and two sisters, married and well-settled in life. Though his formal education is only up to Higher Secondary, he is well-cultured and refined in his tastes and dealings. He has a large agricultural farm and continues to live in the traditional '*haveli*' (big house).

Mrs K.A.M. is also a Rajput, brought up in *purdah*. Though not educated in school, she was taught by a governess at home and is well-versed in household management, music, and fine arts. She can also talk English fluently. She has widely travelled with her parents. Her brother and sister are highly placed in life. She is the youngest. Though she lost her mother when she was young, she was very much loved by her step mother and elder sister.

It was an arranged marriage. The couple had not met before. Both were handsome and accomplished young people. They lived in the joint family of D.S.M. The couple stayed together happily for about 10 years. They had two sons.

He used to spend lavishly, especially in drinking, hunting, and other matters. There was economic problem at home. D.S.M. demanded the jewellery of his wife which she refused as it is considered to be highly objectionable and shameful in the Rajput community. Fights started on this issue. She could not tolerate this and left the house, taking her small children and a small sum of money. Though she left home, she did not know where to go. She got down at the Railway station of 'I' city. She stayed at the railway-station itself for a day or two. Then, she hired a small hotel room just outside the station. She finished the money she had. She did not want to go back as this was considered to be a great humiliation for her. In the meanwhile, she came in touch with a low caste labourer working in the railways. He had a small quarter in the railway colony and promised to allow her to live there. Mrs K.A.M. shifted there. She had nothing to feed herself and her two children. Thereupon, the labourer started supporting her. He was unmarried Gradually, he started having relations with her, because, now, she was completely under his control.

Mr D.S.M. came to know about her presence here and persuaded her to return to the house, but she declined, and remained adamant. He filed a suit against the wife for divorce on the ground that she was living in adultery with another man. The wife never appeared to defend. A decree of divorce was granted to the husband, exparte.

The husband continues to live in his traditional home. He is remarried and has a child through the second marriage. He is happy and has no problem. The wife, Mrs K.A.M. is in a pitiable condition. She lives with the labourer of low caste and cohabit with him, though she never admits that she has relations with him. She lost one of her sons. He was lost and could never be traced. She suspects that he was kidnapped by her husband, but the husband refuses any knowledge about the boy. After she lost this child, she lost her mental equilibrium. Often, she wanders like a mad woman in search of the lost child. Her well-to-do sister keeps contacts with her and sends some money once a while. The other boy left with her, a handsome youth, has no hopes of his future. He had schooling only up to fifth standard; thereafter his education was disturbed. He wanders aimlessly on the railway platform, mingling with boys of other labourers. He told this researcher that once he tried to meet his father but his father refused to accept him. The boy came back and never tried to meet him again. Sorrow and despair overshadowed the youth's handsome features as he narrated this painful experience to the researcher.

This is a case of a high-born woman, drifting away from her family and husband, only to be lost in the hands of cruel fate, to be condemned to live a life of utter shame and degradation. The cause of initial trouble between the husband and wife was of course the extravagant habits of the husband and the proud unrelenting temperament of the wife. But stubbornness and pride of both the spouses, especially of the wife, destroyed the marriage and ruined her own life and that of her children.

Case Study No. 15 (Mr D.P. & Mrs I.P.)

Mr D.P. and Mrs I.P. are members of the Yadev community.

They were married some 40 years ago. Mr D. had small business and Mrs I. was only a housewife. Mr D. was educated up to Middle Class, whereas Mrs I.P. had not completed even primary school.

The couple had stayed together nearly 20 years, and five children (3 boys and 2 girls) were born to them. While she was yet living with her husband, Mrs I. started having relationship with a very rich Parsi gentleman. He used to visit her often and give her gifts. It is reported that right from the early days of the marriage, Mrs I.P. had relations with this man, and, probably, some of the children are fathered by him. After 20 years of marital life, Mrs I. left her husband taking all her children. She went to her lover's place, (Mr N.) and started living with him. The gentleman was very rich, and hence, had no problem in supporting Mrs I. or her children. The children were of various ages, ranging from 3 to 18. They were educated in good institutions. Both the girls are graduates and their step-father got them married. Two of the elder sons are married and have children.

Mrs I. went to the court after she had deserted the first husband for 20 years, and after having lived with the second man for several years. She testified in the court that she is separated from her husband for 20 years and hence desired a divorce. The eldest son, a thirty eight years old man, also appeared in the court to corroborate the story of his mother. Mr D.P. also appeared in the court and admitted that he is living separately for the past 20 years and he had no objection in granting a decree of divorce. Accordingly, a divorce was decreed.

Our investigations revealed that the divorce was sought only to avoid complications regarding inheritance of property. The sons were still going under the surname of their father, and could not become lawful heirs of the property of their stepfather, unless their mother was legally married to their step-father. After obtaining the legal decree of divorce, the couple had got another document made proclaiming them as husband and wife.

The divorce has not changed the status of the spouses at all. They were already living as spouses, although without legal marriage. The only benefit was to the children. They could become legal heirs of a considerably large estate. Mrs I.D. is continuing as Mrs I.N. for the past more than twenty years. Only very few people know of the real state of their affairs. To an outsider, Mrs I.P. always appeared a very genteel and respectable lady lawfully wedded wife of Mr N. The matter about divorce was kept as a great secret. No one knows about it except the parties concerned and the children. Mr D.P. is also continuing life with another widow of his own caste. He is completely adjusted with the new way of life. His previous marriage and children are forgotten. He is nearly sixtyfive and feels in the eve of his life, he need not think about the unpleasant past incidents and make life miserable. Mrs I never discussed the matter of her previous marriage with anyone.

This is a case of divorce, long after the marriage had ceased to exist for all practical purposes. The extramarital relations of the wife and her elopement with her lover had cut short the marriage long back. The divorce was only a farce to regularize certain material things.

Case Study No. 16 (Mr R.V. and Mrs V.V.)

Mr R. and Mrs V. belong to upper class families of Kayasth community. Both are postgraduates, and employed in well-paying jobs. Mr R.V. is the son of a high ranking government official, and has three sisters and one brother. All of them are happily married. Mr R.V. is the youngest son. He stays with his parents, elder brother and family and grandparents. He is very sociable and outgoing type and is very popular among friends. Mrs V.V. is the youngest daughter of a large family of ten brothers and sisters. Her parents are very old. The father was a medical doctor, but not practising at present. The brothers are all highly educated and employed in highly paid occupations. Two of her sisters are spinsiters. At present, Mrs V., her unmarried elder sister and old parents live together. The parents are extremely religious and Mrs V. was brought up in a strictly austere and conservative atmoshpere.

Their marriage was arranged by parents. But the couple used to meet and go out together. The boy was very jolly and good looking and hence Mrs V. almost fell in love with him. Mrs V. confesses that even during the period of engagement, Mr R. never showed keen interest in her. Many a time, he would promise to come and take her out, but would not. Even when he came, he always appeared very busy and hence not prepared to give any time for her. After marriage, the couple started living in the husband's joint family. The trouble between the spouses started soon after the marriage. Mrs V, though was only 23 years of age when she got married, was very rigid in many matters and was not prepared to make adjustments. The joint family of Mr RV was very unsuitable to Mrs V's taste. She was expected to work for the whole family. The burden of looking after the old grandmother-in-law was particularly irritating to the young wife. The interference and criticism of elder sister-in-law and mother-in-law worsened the situation. Mr R. also did not want to change any of his ways. He had a lot of friends and he was very fond of going out with them. He could not give sufficient time at home. He was fond of card game and used to sit up and play for hours together. Mrs V. had a particular aversion towards this game. All these matters caused continuous tension and irritation in Mrs V. Due to these, she used to go off to her parents very often. This Mr R. did not like it at all. Just after ten months of marriage, the couple separated from each other for good, as they both felt that a perpetual incompatibility existed between the two and they could not continue together. They jointly put in an application on the basis of mutual consent. The application was rejected first, because, it was put in even before one year of marriage. They waited for another six months and applied for divorce again which was accepted.

Within two months of divorce, Mr R. got married to a girl of another caste. They had worked together and thus he knew her also. Mrs V. now feels that Mr R.V. must have been in love with this girl and that could be the reason why he could not take sufficient interest in her, although she never suspected her husband's character. Mr R. refuses this allegation. Mr R. has a male child. He is very happy with his present marriage because the present wife, according to him, is very understanding and adjusting. She does not mind his preoccupation with the friends, but has established friendly relations with their wives and thus is able to enjoy their company, whenever she goes to their homes. At home also, she has made satisfactory adjustments with her in-laws.

Mrs V. is employed and is earning well. She is still very rigid in her views and due to this, she can hardly make friends anywhere she goes. Mrs V. is frustrated about her future. She feels that she should not go for remarriage, because, of her bitter experiences with the first marriage. She has a sort of distrust towards men in general.

This case shows that temperamental incompatibility of the spouses destroyed their marital happiness right from the early days of marriage. The cumulative effect of matters which may have little consequence individually can produce a serious end result like divorce. Lack of understanding and tolerance exhibited by many modern educated young people are detrimental to marital harmony.

Case Study No. 17 (Mr A.B. & Mrs N.B.)

They are Maharastrian Brahmins, and postgraduates belonging to well to do families. Mr A. is a probation officer in a bank and is earning Rs 2000 per month. Both the spouses have brothers and sisters, all of whom are happily married.

The marriage was an arranged one and the couples had opportunity to know each other.

Soon after marriage, the couple had gone on a honeymoon trip to cities like Bombay, Poona and Goa. Though she offered fullest cooperation, the husband never tried to consummate the marriage. They came back and started staying at the husband's place. They used to sleep in the same bed room, but the husband used to keep the doors and windows of the bed room deliberately open. He never tried to consummate the marriage. The young wife spent restless nights and was unable to bear the wilful refusal of the respondent to consummate the marriage. The wife told her mother-in-law about it. She tried many times to find out why he was not interested in coitus, but he was not ready to discuss the matter. The frustrated girl came away from the husband's house. After a few days, the husband came to meet her and handed over a letter personally in which he had stated that he was incapable of sexual life.

The girl was very much shocked and distressed at this revelation. To refresh her a little bit, she was taken to her maternal uncle's home. The husband went there and promised to behave better in future and brought her back. The couple started living together again. To the girl's great misery, she found no improvement in his attitude. Whenever she attempted to persuade him for intercourse, he was annoyed and misbehaved with her. Thereupon, she decided to end cohabitation and came back to her parents. The husband and mother came personally and took her back, giving fresh hopes and promises. So, the girl went back. Her sincere efforts to make him cooperate in sexual intercourse were a failure. On the contrary, he threatened to beat her, and made a remark that she is interested only in sex and she could get it anywhere and it was not necessary to marry for that purpose. The girl was appalled and crestfallen by this remark of her husband and retorted that she is no street girl and she has every right to expect sexual pleasure from her law fully wedded husband.

After this, (almost 3 years after marriage), Mrs N. realized that any amount of effort on her part cannot change her husband. She was just 22 at that time. She decided to put an end to this marriage for her own future. She came back to her parents home and took a small job just to divert her mind.

Then, she went to a gynacologist, and got herself examined. She procured a certificate to the effect that she was still a virgin and the marriage was not yet consummated. The doctor also certified that she is a perfectly-developed young woman capable of normal sex-life.

She approached the court for divorce. Divorce judgement was soon passed. In his decree, the judge observed: The doctor...had found her to be a virgo-in-tacta...the other important conclusion that the petitioner is perfectly developed lady with all secondary sex characteristics well developed...it is plain that it is not on account of any infirmity on her part that the respondent could have had any justification in not discharging one of the most important obligations of his marriage with the petitioner, namely, the consummation of marriage."

Mr A. has not remarried. Mrs N. is remarried, and she has a baby girl. She is very happy and contented with her second marriage. Her husband was a bachelor.

Thus, our plain conclusion is that the marriage between Mr A. and Mrs N. was disrupted due to a single factor, namely sexual incapacity on the part of the husband.

Case Study No. 18 (Mr V.M. and Mrs S.M.)

Mr V.M. and Mrs S.M. belong to the Malwi Brahmin community. Mr V. is the elder of the two brothers in a small family. He lost his mother when he was a small child. The father brought them up amidst a lot of problems. Mrs S. has two sisters and four brothers. Her family has better economic status as compared to that of Mr V.

Their marriage took place when he was 20, and she was 16. Right from the beginning, the problem of interference by the in-laws was there. Notwithstanding this, the marital life was happy for about five years and the trouble started only when he came in contact with another girl.

They had two children, a boy and a girl. On account of quarrels, the wife left for her parental home. Mr V. persuaded her to return. Again bitter quarrels ensued. Mr V. felt that the problems were due to the unnecessary interference of his in-laws and hence got himself transferred to another place. But things have not improved even in the new place. Mrs S. filed criminal suit against her husband. She left her husband because she was treated cruelly by him. By the time she was pregnant and gave birth to a female child. Mrs S. applied for maintenance on the plea that her husband had deserted her and she had no independent source of income. Mr V.M. applied for restitution of conjugal rights. He said that it was she who deserted him. Mrs S. also started fighting the case. First, the case was rejected for want of proof. The judge ordered:

> Merely showing that the parties are unhappy because of unruly temperament of a spouse or matrimonial wranglings would fall considerably short of the conduct which can amount to cruel treatment.
>
> Nor could it be sufficient to show that the other spouse is moody, whimsical, exacting, inconsiderate......

The parties remained separated. But the bitterness grew. Reconciliation was becoming impossible. He put in another application in the court and was successful in obtaining a decree of restitution of conjugal rights. By this time, the relationship between the spouses had disintegrated completely, and they had no desire to continue at all as husband and wife. The parties remained separated. The wife applied for maintenance and started getting it. The husband applied for the custody of children, but the court conferred the custody of children on the mother. After two years, Mr V.M. again applied for divorce. A divorce decree was granted in his favour, because, it was proved that there was no cohabitation even after two years of passing of the order of restitution of conjugal rights.

Mrs S. again fought for permanent alimony. Both the parties fought different court cases for long 8 years.

Mr V.M. got remarried within three months of divorce. He has two children out of the present marriage, and is very happy, though she belongs to a different caste.

Mrs S. is very unhappy in the present situation. Though she has a job, she is not able to maintain herself and the 3 children.

This is a case where temperamental problems of the husband and wife, interference of in-laws, extramarital interest of the husband, false allegations by both the parties and counter-allegations made married life miserable, ending finally in divorce.

Case Study No. 19 (Mr M.N. & Mrs V.N.)

Mr M.N. is a medical doctor, married in his early twenties and has two children. His brothers and sisters are married and well-settled in life.

Mrs V. belongs to the Sindhi community, while her husband a Kayastha. She lost her mother in childhood. Even as a child she had promiscuous tendencies, and was beaten brutally by father or brother for this reason. When she was undergoing training in Nursing, she came acorss Dr M.N. who wanted her because she was good-looking. They married and started living together, though she knew that he was already married with children. He left his wife and children with his parents and started living with the second wife. They lived together for five years. She wanted to have child, but he had vasectomy operation and could not procreate. This upset her. Quarrels ensued. He and she were transferred to several places from time to time. Wherever she went, she developed sex relations with other men. She used to drink also. She applied to the court for divorce on the plea that she was cheated by her husband, saying that he was unmarried. He told that she was not his legal wife and so, there is no question of divorce. Her application was rejected for the first time for this reason. She proved that they had undergone a marriage ceremony. Decree of divorce was also granted.

At present, Dr M. is with his former wife and children. Though there was a lot of unpleasantness between Dr M. and his wife on account of Mrs V. now they are reconciled, and happy. Mrs V. is working as a nurse and she leads an immoral life.

This is a case of love marriage, where a married man fell in love with a woman. Absence of childbirth was an important reason for the disatisfaction and frustration of the wife, leading to divorce.

Case Study No. 20 (Mr A.V. & Mrs K.V.)

Mr A. belongs to a middle class Bania joint family. He is a

graduate in law and is working as advocate in a city in MP. His brothers and sisters are married.

Mrs K. also is a Bania by caste. She lost her father when she was only eight years old. She has only one sister, younger to her, but mentally deficient.

They had court marriage. After marriage, she wanted to stay with her mother, as the father had died. The husband had no objection. But later on, people used to make fun of him for staying at the place of the wife. The husband told her to stay at his place, which she refused. He applied for divorce. In his petition, for divorce, he said that his wife was leading an adulterous life. The court case went on for some time, and finally, decree was passed in his favour.

After divorce, the husband became extremely frustrated. He lost interest in life. All tried for a reconciliation. Within three months of divorce, the spouses were again reconciled. They went to the court and remarried. At present, the couple is extremly happy, They have children too.

This is a case of divorce, in which the spouses, not willing for divorce, were forced to undergo the painful ordeal because of the interference of in-laws and others. This is also a typical example of the traditional attitudes and false prestige of members of the Hindu community which can create much problems for nothing. Further, this is a case showing how a couple can be reconciled even after divorce, by remarriage.

CONCLUSIONS

The case studies described above clearly indicate the different types of spouses involved in divorce, their socio-cultural background, chief factors leading to divorce and the consequences of divorce in their personal, familial and social life. Divorce, we have seen, is a very complex phenomenon, caused by a number of things working together.

The twenty cases studies represent the total number of cases studied by the researcher. Every case is different from the other, and therefore, general conclusions cannot be mentioned for all cases alike.

Case studies also prove that case study method indeed is very useful in the study of social problems like divorce.

Chapter 11

SUMMARY, CONCLUSIONS AND SUGGESTIONS

1. Divorce is related to marriage and family which are by far the most important and vital institutions of human society. Divorce is a decree of dissolution of marriage granted by the judicial court. Divorce is not simply the end of marriage but it means a lot more than that. It represents the end of the hopes that two people had for each other; it is the certificate that their relationship failed. Divorce is a social invention. While divorce is one of the forms of marital dissolution, there are other forms like death and separation.

Divorce is almost a new concept among the Hindus, for, the characteristic quality of a Hindu marriage was that it was a union for life. Hindu husband and wife are bound to each other, not only till death, but even after death, in the other world. It is said to be sacred and irrevocable.

Besides the customary divorce, the Hindu Law as such did not recognize divorce in any situation. Even if one of the spouses was guilty of infidelity, desertion or conversion to another religion, the other spouse could not get a release from such a marriage by means of divorce. It was in this background that the Hindu Marriage Act, 1955, came into being, enabling the parties to a Hindu marriage to seek dissolution of the marital ties. As a second step, under the impact of modern ideas of equality of the sexes, and human rights, the Marriage Laws Amendment Act, 1976, was passed. Consequently, the divorce laws have been made easier for the Hindus and have been liberalized to a great extent. The Hindu Marriage Act is applicable to all Hindus: Jains, Sikhs and others who are not Muslims/Christians/Jews are also included within the purview of this Act. Section 13 of the Act deals with the provision of divorce, while, Section 13-B has provided for divorce by mutual consent.

Legislation permitting divorce and separation will have far-reaching consequences in any society. This is particularly so in a country like India, where no divorce was permitted by law, more so, among the Hindus who still have a traditional outlook and way of life.

The impact of legal dissolution of marriage on the institution of family and the total society is a matter of difference of opinion. Some have stated that it will create disorganization, and, therefore, divorce is a symptom of social disorganization. Some others have held that divorce is a sort of adjustment and will help in the reorganization of the family. However, it has been seen that legislations favouring easy divorce in the Western countries (especially in the United States) have resulted in high rate of divorce, one-third of all marriages and in divorce. This will create problems for men, women, children, families and communities. American society seems to have realized this danger now. Certain latest studies in America have shown that "most married people basically are opposed to the concept of divorce."

As elsewhere, certain redeeming aspects of divorce in India would be that it would help to liberate the women from autocratic exploitation by males which had been going on for centuries. It will also enable to reorganize an irrevocably broken family. Instead of dragging a miserable family life, it is better to secure a divorce. Some studies in India have revealed that the Hindu women are in favour of legislation in respect of divorce. The modern woman is no longer prepared to accept a social code which recognized dominance of the male as binding on her. Further, the democratic ideal to which Indians are now committed by their Constitution and which has been defined as political, social, religious and economic equality lends force to the women's motivation to seek equality within the family and if not obtained, to break it. Modern education has inculcated in the Indian women a sense of her own identity. Several social legislations in India have furthered the women's movement in India, and added to her stature both economically and socially. Important ones are the Child Marriage Restraint Act, 1929 (Amended up to 1978), Hindu Succession Act, 1956, Dowry Prohibition Act, 1961, and the Hindu Marriage Act, 1955 (amended up to 1976).

A sociological study of Divorce among urban Hindus is very

significant, because, (*i*) no systematic study on the subject has been conducted so far in any University in India; (*ii*) Legislation on Marriage and Family pertaining to the Hindus is relatively recent. One has, therefore, to investigate and see how the legislation is being taken advantage of by the people, and what are its effects; (*iii*) The public is becoming more and more aware of the provisions of the Hindu Marriage Act about divorce, as can be seen from the newspaper reports. The results of this should be appraised scientifically.

The study is aimed at to find out the following:

(*i*) Marital adjustment and life of the couple before divorce.
(*ii*) Major causes of divorce.
(*iii*) How people obtained divorce—the processes and procedures they have adopted.
(*iv*) Consequences of divorce, especially on the socio-economic status and life of the spouses.
(*v*) The effects of divorce on children and, finally,
(*vi*) The patterns of remarriage of divorcee-spouses.

The hypotheses formulated in the study have been:

(*i*) Urban Hindus in India are taking advantage of the legislations made by the Government, particularly, the Hindu Marriage Act, 1955, for the final dissolution of marriage.
(*iii*) There may be adverse and far-reaching consequences of divorce, especially because the Hindus have been traditional in their outlook and marriage was treated as a sacred institution.
(*iii*) Most of the conflicts which lead to divorce sooner or later spring up in the early years of marriage, say, the first two or three years of marriage.
(*iv*) Children are the worst sufferers of divorce, and
(*v*) Remarriage of the divorced spouses, more particularly of the males, is taking in considerable number.

The 200 cases selected for the study represented a wide cross-section of the urban community in Madhya Pradesh, with regard to (*a*) socio-economic conditions, (*b*) caste/community/tribe, (*c*) occupation, (*d*) education, and (*e*) cultural background.

The sample selected for the study is major portion of the universe (total number of divorce cases) and, therefore, the sample has been considered adequate.

Different tools of data collection used in the study have been (*a*) Judicial Court Record (Case Files), (*b*) Schedule-cum-interview, (*c*) Case Study, (*d*) Observation, (*e*) Discussion with the lawyers dealing with divorce cases, and (*f*) Judicial Court attendance to watch the processes and proceedings of the divorce cases.

Our hypotheses have been tested and found correct. However, it is found that due to the traditional, joint family structure even among the urban Hindus, children are taken care of by the parents of the divorcees and, therefore, they are not too adversely affected, and many of the grown-up children are fairing well in life. When some of these young people were interviewed by the researcher, they seemed to retain the painful memories of the broken family situation they have encountered in their early or later childhood. Instead of being discouraged or overcome by the traumatic experiences these courageous people have fought adversities bravely. Some of them exhibit greater maturity, independence and self-reliance as compared to young people brought up in normal homes. Yet, the younger ones seemed to have problems of personality development due to the absence of parental, love, care and affection. The advantage of the joint family system in traditional societies like India to take care of the children of the divorced parents has been pointed out by several renouned sociologists like Kingsley Davis, Model Elliott and Fracis Merrill.

2. Chapter 2, deals with a theoretical discussion of divorce in various societies. Divorce procedures adopted by countries like England, France, Russia, China and America, both in olden and modern times, is briefly discussed. This is followed by a detailed discussion of divorce among the Hindus. The ancient Hindu views on marriage and the provisions for divorce in Hindu scriptures and texts is discussed. The modern critics and analysts of Hindu Law have concluded that Hindu marriage is a sacrament which means it is an urbreakable eternal bond. An outline of divorce among other religious communities of India namely Muslims, Christians and Parsis is also given.

The rate of divorce indicates that there has been high increase in divorce rate in Western countries from the year 1930. In India, though certain States like Kolhapur, Bombay, and Madras had enacted legislation permitting divorce among the Hindus, the impact was almost nil. Customary divorces used to be granted occasionally by caste *Panchayats*. After the Hindu Marriage and Divorce Act, 1955, has come into force, hesitant attempts to obtain legal relief for matrimonial problems have started very gradually. The number of cases steadily increased in the early seventies but a sudden rise in the number of divorce cases can be observed after the amendment of the Hindu Marriage Act in 1976.

3. The chapter, 'Background of the Spouses in Divorce' enables us to have an assessment of the social, economic, educational and cultural background of the respondents. Some of the important findings in this chapter are:

(*i*) Vast majority (70 per cent) of the spouses lived in joint families of different types, small and large, consanguinous families are thought to be more stable and sociologists have claimed that family disorganization is minimum in such larger family units. But our study shows that even in joint family situation, marital relations can disintegrate and end in divorce. In the studies of Fonseca (Bombay, 1966), and Rama Mehta (1975) also, it was found that majority of the cases of family disorganization and dissolution belonged to joint families.

(*ii*) Vast majority of the respondents (91 per cent men and 82 per women) are educated (46.5 per cent men and 28 per cent women are graduates or postgraduates). Various sociologists have considered education as an important criterion in rating of marital adjustment, satisfaction and happiness. In India, illiterate and traditional people (more of ruralites) still resort to customary divorce through caste and village panchayats and more and more educated people approach judicial courts.

(*iii*) As for the castes, communities or tribes of the divorcees, it is found that the highest number of them are from the Brahmin caste (41.5 per cent husbands and 40.5 per cent wives) hailing from different regions in India. There are also other castes and subcastes like the Vaisya (Bania—15 per cent men and women). Harijans (Sch. castes) formed 15.5 per cent of the male and female respondents. Tribals are 3.5 per cent, Jains 9 per cent males and 9.5 per cent famales, Sikhs 2.5 per cent and others 0.5 per cent. It was found that, out of the different types of Brahmins, Maharastrian Brahmins were more prone to divorce than others.

(*iv*) On the basis of economic class, it is found that 7.5 per cent belonged to the upper, 72.5 per cent middle and 20 per cent lower classes. The economic class was determined on the basis of (*a*) family income, (*b*) occupation of the respondents and, (*c*) ancestral economic status. The highest percentage (72.5 per cent) of divorce is from middle class.

(*v*) The respondents belonged to various occupations like elite Services, Doctors, Engineers, Advocates, Professors, Teachers, Businessmen, Office Assistants, Technical workers, Nurses, Farmers, Goldsmiths, Tailors, Drivers, Mill-workers, labourers, etc. The percentage of women working at the time of marriage was very low (16.5 per cent). Of all the occupations, the highest number (in respect of both men and women) was from the group 'Office Assistant.'

(*vi*) Correlation between caste and economic class revealed that there is much correlationship between upper or middle caste and upper or middle economic class. There is, however, no correlationship between lower caste and upper economic class or vice versa.

(*vii*) The correlation between caste and employment with regard to women showed that the tendency among unmarried women to work outside the home is more in castes such as Brahmins (particularly, Maharastrian Brahmins), Kayasth and Vaisya (particularly, Sindhi Bania), while, it is relatively less in castes like Kshatrias, Sonar and Yadev.

(*viii*) Similarly, the correlation between caste, community and tribe and education showed that the higher castes have better education as compared with lower castes, both among men and women.

(*ix*) As for religious training at home, it was found that Brahmins and Jains have better initiation into religion than others. There was very little or no religious training in respect of spouses of lower castes or tribals. Females received better religious training as compared with males. Further, as a whole, women are more riligious than men.

(*x*) The respondents belonged to different types of cultural background. But vast majority of them come from homes where traditions are still greatly encouraged. Conflicts between the traditional and modern cultures right in the family were found to be a significant factor in material disruptions.

Thus, it is seen that the social, economic, cultural and other backgrounds are important determinants in marital disruptions.

4. The chapter on Marital Relations and Adjustments Before Divorce is a detailed one. Several variables were taken and examined to see how the couples were having adjustment or maladjustment in relation to them.

(*i*) With regard to the type of marriage, it was found that majority of them (91.5 per cent) had arranged marriages. This proclaims that arranged marriages are no panacea for marital problems.

(*ii*) Majority (51 per cent) of the marriages was not well-though out or properly planned.

(*iii*) In vast majority of cases (93 per cent), there was engagement prior to marriage, though, in some cases, it was for a very short duration.

(*iv*) Majority of the men and women (86 per cent husbands and 87 per cent wives) did not have premarital relations with others. Thus, there is no correlation between premarital relation and divorce.

(*v*) As for premarital contacts between the spouses, vast majority (80 per cent) got an opportunity somehow or other to see, meet, talk, interact, etc., before the spouses really entered into the marital ties. This means, they were not just strangers. But, at the same time, they did not get much time for free communication or intimate interaction which would have led to better understanding of the other spouse.

(*vi*) The mean age at marriage in respect of husbands is 24.83 years and that of wives 19.13 years.

(*vii*) On an average, the husbands are older than wives by about 5 years, the exact mean age difference being 4.47 years.

(*viii*) The consent of the boys and girls was taken before marriage in most of the cases (72.5 per cent males and 55 per cent females). But, in majority of the cases, such consultation was meaningless, as the parents had already decided and asking for the consent of the boys/girls was just a formality.

(*ix*) The most frequent expectations of the husbands about wives were (*a*) to be good cooks, and (*b*) take care of the personal needs of the husband well.

As for the expectations of wives about their husbands, the most frequent expectations were (*a*) love and fulfilment of physical needs, (*b*) taking out for cinema, and (*c*) take care of them more than the relatives of the husbands.

(*x*) In most cases (91.5 per cent), dowry was paid, in cash or kind, or both.

(*xi*) As for the problems arising out of payment of dowry, it existed in 18 per cent cases. Some cases of cruelty were reported in this. The dowry problem is found mostly in communities like the Jain, Vaisya, and Brahmin. At the same time, there was not much problem due to dowry among the Harijans and Tribals. There is, thus, a correlation between caste and dowry, that is, the higher the caste or community, more the demand for dowry, and lower the caste or community the less demand for dowry.

(*xii*) Majority (75 per cent) of the spouses had good relation in the very early days of marriage (that is honeymoon period).

(*xiii*) A correlation between the education of the female spouses and the husband-wife relation during the early days of marriage showed that graduates and postgraduates had more intimate relation during the nuptial period as compared with less educated spouses. Also, housing conditions may be correlated with happiness in marriage, especially, the existence or absence of privacy and other facilities.

(*ix*) While majority of the husbands (64 per cent) preferred to live in joint family, majority of the wives did not. The husbands preferred joint family because it is constituted by their nearest kins, and hence, natural affection exists between the male spouse and his family members. For a woman, husband's close relatives can creat various problems. Interference of relatives, economic hardship, lack of privacy, exploitation and ill-treatment by in-laws, problem of time, inability to obtain economic independence, and lack of facilities to develop special interests or skills are some of the specific problems. It was found that the women in our study actually experienced several of these problems with much bitterness. Therefore, it can be safely concluded that joint family-living and non-adjustment by female spouses is a significant reason for marital maladjustment leading to marital dissolution.

(*xv*) There is some difference between the position of employment of women before and after marriage. At the time of marriage, only 16.5 per cent of the women were employed, but, after marriage, it became 34.5 per cent. This makes it very clear that 18 per cent of women took up employment after marriage. Several of these women were forced to take up jobs because either there husbands' earnings were too meagre or they did not support the families properly.

(*xvi*) In majority of the cases, the husbands' parents or the husbands themselves kept the purse (62 per cent). This also seems to have created problems of adjustment.

(*xvii*) The general economic condition of the majority of the couples was not satisfactory. This may have been a cause directly or indirectly responsible for marital conflicts and subsequently divorce.

(*xviii*) Majority of the husbands did not assist the wives in their household work (53 per cent). Non-participation in household work may be an indication of non-involvement in household affairs, which may result in marital maladjustment.

(*xix*) Spending the earnings of the couple for the use of the in-laws was a matter of difference of opinion between the spouses. Husbands' parents, unmarried sisters, and brothers were supported by the husband. This was not relished by several wives.

It may be concluded that several factors work together to create marital maladjustment. Thus, if joint family living, poor economic conditions, absence of freedom, demands of dowry, disparity in expectations and fulfilments and disagreement in the matter of spending money or supporting other members of the family, all these, or several of these work together, marital and familial maladjustments can occur.

5. Chapter 5 deals with the Causes of Divorce. The major causes of divorce discovered in our study are :

(*i*) Cruelty;

(*ii*) Interference by in-laws ;
(*iii*) Extramarital relations of the husband or wife ;
(*iv*) Education and economic independence of women ;
(*v*) Economic hardships in the family ;
(*vi*) Sexual maladjustments between the spouses ;
(*vii*) Mental problems created by several other factors ;
(*viii*) Unplanned and unthought of marriage ;
(*ix*) Child marriage ;
(*x*) Traditional and orthodox attitude of the males and in-laws towards the female spouse ;
(*xi*) Marriage against the wishes of the spouses ;
(*xii*) Unhealthy habits like alccholism, gambling and immorality ;
(*xiii*) Incompatibility of the spouses ;
(*xiv*) Making false impressions at the time of marriage ;
(*xv*) Marital unhappiness of parents and other siblings ; and
(*xvi*) Lonely sibling position of the husband or wife.

It should be reiterated that when several of these causes work together, the way for divorce is easily paved.

6. Various processes and proceedings of divorce are dealt with in Chapter 6, and our main canclusions are :

(*i*) The respondents followed most of the procedures that are laid down under the Hindu Marriage Act, 1955, such as
 (*a*) filing of the petition for divorce,
 (*b*) making efforts for reconciliation,
 (*c*) attending the court,
 (*d*) putting forward arguments and producing witnesses,
 (*e*) waiting for the final decree with or without great strain and anxiety, and
 (*f*) taking custody of the child/children as permitted by the Court.

(*ii*) Both the male and female respondents almost equally (47.5 per cent male and 45.5 per cent female) took courage to file the petition for divorce.
(*iii*) Most of the petitions were filed during the interval up to 5 years after marriage of the respondents (55.5 per cent).
(*iv*) As for reconciliation, in 34 per cent cases, the judges made efforts, but were of no avail. In the case of 27 per cent

husbands and 60 per cent wives, reconciliation efforts were made by their parents and relatives also.

(*v*) In most cases, it took up to about 4 years to decide the divorce cases in the court. The expenses varied from Rs 500 to Rs 2,000 per case.

(*vi*) Most spouses attended the court during the course of the divorce proceedings.

(*vii*) The life of the respondents during the pendency of the court cases was really miserable, but some felt relieved after the decision of the court.

(*viii*) There are a few cases of cohabitation during the pendency of the court case.

(*ix*) In majority of the cases (51.5 per cent), maintenance was paid by the husbands so that the wives had some support when the court cases were going on.

(*x*) In 12.5 per cent cases, the wives were granted alimony on a permanent basis. The alimony per month ranged from Rs 25 to Rs 425. None of the divorced husbands availed of this provision.

(*xi*) As for custody of minor children, although in 39 per cent cases the couples had children, only in 5 per cent cases, there was any dispute. Among them, in majority of the cases, the mother became the custodian of minor children for several reasons.

(*xii*) An analysis of the trend of divorce cases during the period 1968 to 1977 showed that there were four stages of divorce trend in India. Out of these, in the fourth stage, that is, after the 1976 Amendment of the Hindu Marriage Act, the rate of divorce has increased much. However, we need more studies and analysis of data in India in order to assess correctly the true picture of divorce cases.

7. The Consequences of divorce on the life of the male and female divorcees after divorce are dealt with in Chapter 7. Our chief conclusions are

(*i*) Vast majority of the men (65 per cent) are of the age-group 26-35, and the vast majority of the women (67.5 per cent) are in the age-group 21-30, which show, that most of the divorced spouses are still young and can remarry or make alternate adjustments and associations, like continuing education, getting into employment or developing hobbies.

(*ii*) The divorced husbands and wives faced several personal problems like frustration, inferiority complex, shyness, loneliness, etc.

(*iii*) The sexual life of the spouses after divorce showed that 70.5 per cent of the male and 35 per cent of the female divorcees were remarried, and the problem of sex-satisfaction and adjustment, therefore, did not arise. None of the divorcees was inclined to speak much about their sex-satisfaction in the post-divorce life.

(*iv*) Women showed greater progress in education in the post-divorce period as compared to men. With their better education, women were able to take up employment to support themselves and children.

(*v*) The incidence of the working women increased in the post-divorce period. They took up jobs like college teachers, school teachers and office assistants.

(*vi*) The problem of stable support of female spouses in the post-divorce period was solved by remarriage in 35 per cent cases. In 41 per cent cases, they were supporting themselves through employment. The economic status of divorced women was better in the post-divorce period as compared with the pre-divorce period.

(*vii*) The majority of the divorcees did not have any contacts with their former partners.

(*viii*) Vast majority of the divorced spouses did not make any attempt at reconciliation in the post-divorce period. However, in a few cases, reconciliation did work out, and in some cases, different types of efforts are being made to bring about reconciliation gradually.

(*ix*) Somewhat sympathetic or encouraging treatment was received from their friends by the divorced spouses.

(*x*) Vast majority of the spouses received sympathetic or partially sympathetic treatment from their parents during the post-divorce period.

(*xi*) Different castes, communities, and tribes reacted differently towards divorcees. Among some, (Kayasth and Rajput castes) there was high criticism, and some (Harijans, Tribals and Maharastrian Brahmins) had no criticism.

8. In Chapter 8, dealing with Divorce and Children, our main conclusions are:

(*i*) Majority of the divorced couples have no children. There seems to be some inter-relationship between childlessness and divorce. Absense of children must have hastened the couples' decision to end their marriage.

(*ii*) The number of children born to the couples in divorce is relatively small—147 children for 78 couples. That is, the average number of children per couple is 1.88. If we take the total number of families 200, it is seen that the number of children per family is 00.73. The fewer number of children is mostly due to the short duration of married life before divorce.

(*iii*) Most children in our study were kept by the mother (about 80 per cent).

(*iv*) In a fairly good number of cases (41 per cent) the divorced husbands keep contacts with the children.

(*v*) In majority of the cases, the children were aware of the fact that their parents were divorcees. Such knowledge did affect their emotional life and therefore may have directly or indirectly affected their personality development.

(*vi*) In most cases, the children were more attached to the mother.

(*vii*) Majority of the children are not very happy.

(*viii*) It may be said correctly that "divorce cannot disorganize children in all cultures." (Elliott & Merrill, 1950, p. 465). Kingsley Davis has also subscribed to this view. The reason is that in societies like India's, grand-parents and other relatives in the joint family look after the children of divorced couples. This seems to be relevant in our study, as 70 per cent couples had lived in joint families of some type before divorce, and several mothers have returned to their original joint families. One very encouraging aspect noticed is that the grown-up children of divorcees seem to be successful young adults today. Several of them are highly educated, placed in good occupation and happily married. Adverse circumstances have probably brought out the best in these young people.

9. In Chapter 9, we have dealt with Remarriage. Our conclusions are:

(*i*) Remarriage is surely one of the most successful solutions to the awkward problem of divorced persons.

(*ii*) There is definite provision under the Hindu Marriage Act, 1955, for Remarriage (Section 15). According to the latest Amendments, there is no need to wait for any particular period before entering into remarriage.

(*iii*) Majority of men (70.5 per cent) and a little more than one-third (35 per cent) women got remarried. Efforts by parents or themselves are the two most common methods by which the remarried couples found their mates.

(*iv*) In most cases, there was no premarital contact, with the present spouse.

(*v*) Interestingly, women divorcees had more love marriages as compared with male divorcees in their remarriage.

(*vi*) Most of the divorcee-spouses remarried unmarried boys or girls (Bachelors or spinsters). This is in tune with the findings in the United States too.

(*vii*) Most of them had religious ceremony in remarriage.

(*viii*) Majority of the remarriages took place during the period 0-3 years after divorce. (In America, the interval is 2.7 years).

(*ix*) Incidence of remarriage among the women without children is more than that of women with children.

(*x*) The rate of remarriage among men is more than among women.

(*xi*) Good number of remarried men and women got children in the second marriage also. The number of children per remarriage is one.

(*xii*) Most of the remarried couples were happy or very happy.

(*xiii*) Though there is considerable uncertainty about the remarriage of the remaining spouses, at least some of them will be married in near future.

(*xiv*) There are several reasons for delay in remarriage, the most frequent ones being non-availability of suitable mates and emotional disturbance due to the past marital failure.

(*xv*) The stigma arising out of divorce is still grave in India. Educated, employed women may face fewer problems after divorce, but even then, Hindu traditions and values come in the way. Even widow-remarriage is not very favourably looked upon. It is, therefore, but natural that divorcee-remarriage, with all the antecedents of a former marriage, marital problems and divorce will be frowned upon and condemned. The public opinion is gradually changing, and, it is hoped that in the days to come, the stigma of remarriage for divorcee-spouses will vanish. The present researcher is of the opinion that since divorce has become easier and quicker after the Amendment of 1976, the rate of remarriage of divorcees also is likely to increase. William Goode has appropriately said that, "remarriage is society's short answer to divorce—the still possible happy ending for the man or woman whose first marriage breaks up." (William Goode, Women in Divorce, 1965, p. 201). Goode has further commented that just as the stigma of divorce diminishes, the stigma of remarriage also will diminish.

10. A separate chapter is set apart for case studies in which we have dealt with 20 representative case studies, which forms 10 per cent of the total sample.

In a study of a phenomenon like divorce, case study method is perhaps the most useful method as it enables us to have an insight into individual cases. Every divorce case is unique in the sense that the combination of factors bringing about problems vary in each case. Human beings respond very differently even to similar stimulus and situations. For example, an average Indian bride accepts the dictums of her husband or in-laws unquestioningly whereas a highly educated modern female may react violently even to the mildest threat to her freedom and individuality. Certain matters which one person treats as a mild flaw and condons ungruntingly may prove to be a major source of problem for another. These things cannot be brought to light when we deal with entire sample. That is the reason why the author has included a few case studies in her study. It may be added that these 20 cases are typical cases and they do represent the entire sample with respect to caste, occupation, economic status and several other traits.

CERTAIN MORE GENERAL AND CONSPICUOUS CONCLUSIONS

Divorce is becoming more common in all castes of the Hindu society.

Fewer members of the lower castes or classes approach the Judicial Courts for obtaining divorce. Yet, different forms of marital disruptions like separation and desertion as well as customary divorce are common among them.

The joint family system which has served as an absolutely useful institution hitherto is creating problems of marital adjustment in the modern age. The female spouse's inability or unwillingness to fit into her traditionally defined role of a submissive daughter-in-law is the crux of the problem. Yet, joint families are helpful for spouses and their children to get adjusted in the post-divorce period.

Most of the Hindu castes still treat divorce as a social stigma and criticise individuals daring for it. However, in our study, it was found that Maharastrian Brahmins are an exception. Divorce and Remarriage are more common among them as compared to others.

The idea that marriage is a sacred bond and hence irrevocable has never existed among the lower castes and tribals. They treat marriage as a means to fulfil certain biological, social and economic necessities, and hence, break in marriage is not met with much stigma or criticism. Moreover, vast majority of them are illiterates, belonging to poor classes where satisfaction of the basic physical needs is the top-most priority and emotional or affectional aspects of marriage is not stressed.

Educated women have higher expectations of their marriage. Education has widened their horizons and ability to think and rationalize. They are unwilling to subject themselves to the indignities their sisters have suffered for centuries in the name of religion and moral values. On the other hand, modern, educated, Indian women are prepared to break the chains of tradition, which have kept them under captivity for ages. They are determined to assert themselves, first of all, in their own families, and divorce is a proof that where their rights are threatened, they are ready to finish off such a union. Not all divorced women belong to this category. Many are victim of exploitation condemned to lead a life of utter sorrow and despair for the remaining days.

Despite higher education and employment of women, love marriages are comparatively few in number in urban India. The main reason for this appears to be marriage at relatively earlier age. By the time the girls mature, parents have already fixed their marriage. In many Indian cities, chances for free mixing of sexes are few and hence young people do not get to know each other intimately. Many young girls do not dare to enter into close relationship with the opposite sex for fear of criticism. It is also noticed that most of the Indian males are still traditional in their outlook in matters of marriage, and they depend upon elders for the selection of bride.

The early days of marriage are extremely important and crucial in relation to marital adjustment. In many cases, it is noticed that marriages are disrupted right at this phase. In our culture, the couple is not allowed much privacy in the honeymoon period or even later. As a result, the young people take longer time to know each other. Continuous interruptions from relatives usually delay this process and many spouses separate under exterior pressures even before they had a fair chance to know and understand each other.

Each divorce case is to be analysed separately as every marriage has its unique features and the process of adjustment and maladjustment differ from case to case. Human beings, their personality and responses they make are all highly complex and individualistic and, therefore, generalizations on such matters may not be very appropriate.

Divorce is usually a product of multiple factors—personal, familial, and environmental—at work simultaneously.

With the changes in legislation, public opinion, weakening of tradition and religion, as well as emancipation and economic independence of women, divorces and remarriages are likely to increase.

Divorce is a process of readjustment. When marital tensions and discord continue persistently, family undergoes a process of disorganization. Divorce brings about the ultimate break in the family, ending this continuous strife. It also enables the parties to start afresh by getting remarried. The divorcees themselves have agreed that the pre-divorce stage of disharmony and indecision is much more problematic than the post-divorce phase.

Except in cases of mutual consent, divorce is still a cumber some and costly affair. Many a time, it is observed that a spouse who is not interested in legal decree or remarriage can prolong a case for years, thus, wasting precious years of youth of the other spouse. In several such cases, after years of fighting, the interested spouse has settled the matter through intermediaries, by offering compensations of different types, and got the decree passed in the court.

After divorce, men face relatively fewer problems as compared with women. The Indian society is still partial in its attitude towards men. Men are economically independent. In most of the cases, they continue in their joint family; as a result, home management or even care of children pose no great problem.

Remarriage rate is much higher in men. Several of them did not wait for a legal decree of divorce and started living with another spouse with or without a marriage ceremony. In our country, to find a mate for a male of any age is still easy, but to find a suitable partner for a divorcee-female is extremely difficult. On top of these, in most of the cases, where children were present, it was the mother who kept the children. The care of the children was an important deterrent in divorcee-female's remarriage.

Divorce is more common among childless couples. Child acts as a cementing factor between the spouses. Many spouses especially females tolerate hardships and problems for the sake of children. In the absence of children, the motivation to stay together under stress and strain is considerably lessened.

Divorce results in acute emotional problems. Longer, the duration of a marriage, greater is the trauma produced. In this aspect, women suffer much more than men. Home is the most significant part in an average Indian women's life. When this is shattered, she sinks into despair. Many women are just housewives and they have no place to go and nobody to talk to. Parents, relatives and community members also may be highly critical, whereas in the case of men, they spend their time in day-to-day work, in the company of their friends or in pursuit of hobbies. As a result, the emotional trauma is less acutely felt by them.

Divorcees prefer to remarry single spouses. This was so more in the case of males, but a good number of female divorcees also married bachelors.

Children of divorcees do suffer in various ways. In poor homes, their physical needs are not even met. Even in middle and upper class families, younger children suffer, if not physically, at least emotionally, due to the absence of one parent.

Reconciliation and reunion even after divorce are not very uncommon. This shows that, at least some divorces took place in haste or due to external interferences, and as time passed, these differences were made up by the parties.

After studying 200 cases of divorce in much detail, the researcher feels that the real reason for divorce in many cases is lack of understanding and communication between the spouses. Marriage is an intimate relationship between a man and a women. If real love and understanding exist between two people, difficulties and problems are overcome. A wife who is deeply attached to her husband and who receives love and sympathy from her husband will undergo any number of hardships to perpetuate that love. A man who loves his wife, and is loved by her, will do everything to protect and cherish her. Such a union connot be shattered by temporary problems. Where the husband-wife relationship itself is not very deep, problems are magnified, external influences become a threat to the relationship, and the relationship gradually disintegrates, ending in ultimate rupture. The only way to prevent divorce is to encourage a young people to understand each other and communicate freely so that tensions do not pent up and create irrevocable situations.

SUGGESTIONS

As a result of the present study, it is felt that in order to prevent and resolve the problem of divorce, we ought to give some useful suggestions. Our suggestions are as follows:

1. There is great need for marital and familial counselling. There must be Marriage and Family Bureaux accessible to all kinds of people. In a team of counsellors, there must be Sociologists, Psychiatrists, Social Workers, Doctors and Priests.

2. As in the United States, there must be Family Courts in India also, in order to deal with various cases of marital and familial disputes. These courts will be very helpful in hearing and deciding matrimonial disputes without unnecessary delay. It is gratifying to note that the matter of enactment of legislation for the establishment of family courts was recently discussed in the Indian Parliament.

3. Marriage should be entered into after sufficient thought and planning.

4. In no case, marriage against the wishes of the spouses concerned should be entered into.

5. The basic instruction regarding sex and marriage as well as family living should be imparted to the youth in schools, colleges

and other institutions.

6. As the success of marriage depends much on ability to make adjustments, both the spouses should make all efforts in this direction.

7. Too high expectations in marriage are utopian or unachieveable, and therefore, should not be insisted upon.

8. Unnecessary interference by parents and in-laws should be avoided. After marriage, the couple should be allowed freedom and privacy.

9. When a marriage is irrevocably broken, it should be ended.

10. Social security measures be put into operation by the Government to look after unattached women and their children, so that they do not become destitutes or orphans after divorce.

11. There must be social education and awakening among lower castes, classes, and tribes for healthy married life.

12. The dowry cases exploitation should be seriously dealt with.

13. All Hindu marriages must be registered, whether they are held at home, in temple or anywhere else.

14. Physically unfit people should not enter into marriage. Physical check up of the parties entering into marriage is advisable.

15. Provisions of the legislation for divorce should not be misused. There must be restricted use of the legislation so that the interests of the individuals, families and communities are protected in a healthy manner.

16. Better and greater efforts for reconciliation must be made by courts as well as other agencies.

17. Scientific and sociological researches be conducted about the causes, effects and trends of familial maladjustments and disruptions in India.

18. Legislations in other communities (e.g., Christians, Parsis, etc.) should be revised and made uptodate.

19. Prolonged and protracted court proceedings, delaying relief to the aggrieved spouse should be avoided. In many cases, it is found that a substantial part of the youth is depleted due to court cases. By the time the final decree is received, the spouses are already in the middle age and their energy and enthusiasm to start a new life dwindle.

20. Public opinion about divorce and remarriage, especially in the case of female spouses should undergo change.

APPENDIX I

Table showing the correlation between caste and employment of women before marriage.

S. No.	*Caste/community/tribe*	*Working women*		*Non-working women*		*Total No.*	*Per centage*
		No.	*per cent*	*No.*	*per cent*		
1.	Maharastrian Brahmin	16	36	28	64	44	100
2.	Other Brahmins	6	16.2	31	83.8	37	100
3.	Kshatriya	1	14	6	86	7	100
4.	Vaishya	3	10	27	90	30	100
5.	Kayasth	2	25	6	75	8	100
6.	Khatri	1	25	3	75	4	100
7.	Sonar	—	—	4	100	4	100
8.	Yadev	—	—	3	100	3	100
9.	Harijan	—	—	31	100	31	100
10.	Tribals	—	—	7	100	7	100
11.	Jain	2	10.5	17	89.5	19	100
12.	Sikh	1	20	4	80	5	100
13.	Others	1	100	—	—	1	100
		33		167			

200: 100 per cent

APPENDIX II

Table showing the correlation between Caste/Community/Tribe and education of the respondents.

S.	Caste/	HUSBAND			(Percentage)				WIFE (Perencetage)						
No.	community/ tribe	PG	Gr	UG	B.HS	Mid	BP/ UE	Total	PG	Gr	UG	B.HS	Mid	BP/ UE	Total
(1)	(2)	(3)	(4)	(5)	(6)	(7)	(8)	(9)	(1)	(2)	(3)	(4)	(5)	(6)	(7)
1.	Brahmin	12	12.5	9.5	4	2	1.5	41.5	6	0.7	19.5	3.5	3	1.5	40.5
2.	Kshatriya	1	1.5	1	0.5	0.5	—	4.5	0.5		0.5	—	1	1.5	3.5
3.	Vaishya	3.5	3.5	3	2	2.5	0.5	15	1.5	2	7.5	1	2	1	1.5
4.	Kayasth	2	2	—	—	—	—	4	0.5	3	0.5	—	—	—	4

(1) (2)	(3)	(4)	(5)	(6)	(7)	(8)	(9)	(1)	(2)	(3)	(4)	(5)	(6)	(7)
5. Khatri	1	—	0.5	—	—	—	1.5	0.5	1.5	—	—	—	—	2
6. Sonar	—	0.5	—	—	1	—	1.5	—	0.5	1	—	0.5	—	2
7. Yadev	—	—	0.5	—	1	—	1.5	—	—	—	—	0.5	1	1.5
8. Harijan	—	—	2	3.5	4.5	5.5	15.5	—	—	—	2	3.5	10	15.5
9. Tribal	—	0.5	—	0.5	1	1.5	3.5	—	—	0.5	—	0.5	2.5	3.5
10. Jain	2	3.5	1.5	1	1	—	9	1.5	2	4	0.5	1.5	—	9.5
11. Sikh	1	—	1	0.5	—	—	2.5	0.5	0.5	—	—	1.5	—	2.5
12. Others	—	—	—	—	—	—	—	—	0.5	—	—	—	—	0.5
Total	22.5	24	19	12	13.5	9	100	11	17	33.5	7	14	17.5	100

APPENDIX III

Age of the divorced sp ouses at the time of their marriage

S. No.	*Age group*	*HUSBAND*		*WIFE*	
		No	per cent	*No*	per cent
1.	Under 10 years	2	1	6	3
2.	11—15 years	6	3	18	9
3.	16-20 years	17	8.5	96	48
4.	21-25 years	82	41	62	31
5.	26-30 years	67	33.5	14	7
6.	31-35 years	20	10	2	1
7.	36-40 years	4	2	1	0.5
8.	41-45 years	1	0.5	1	0.5
9.	46-50 years	1	0.5	—	—
	Total	200	100	200	100

APPENDIX IV

Table showing the occupation of the spouses at the time of divorce

S. No.	*Occupation*	*HUSBAND*		*WIFE*	
		No.	per cent	*No.*	per cent
1.	Central Civil Services	2	1	—	—
2.	Doctor	6	3	4	2
3.	Engineer	5	2.5	1	0.5
4.	Advocate	8	4	—	—
5.	Professor	6	3	2	1
6.	Officer	10	5	1	0.5
7.	Business	34	17	3	1.5
8.	Office Assistant	43	21.5	18	9
9.	School Teacher	12	6	24	12
10.	Military Service	4	2	—	—
11.	Technical Worker	9	4.5	2	1
12.	Beautician	—	—	1	0.5
13.	Nurse	—	—	2	1
14.	Farmer	8	4	—	—
15.	Goldsmith	2	1	—	—
16.	Tailor	2	1	—	—
17.	Driver/Conductor	2	1	—	—
18.	Mill Worker	6	3	2	1
19.	Vegetable Seller	2	1	1	0.5
20.	Peon/Ayah	8	4	2	1
21.	Labourer	9	4.5	6	3.00
22.	Others	6	3	—	—
23.	No regular work (including students)	16	8	131	65.5
	Total	200	100	200	100

APPENDIX V

Table showing the factors responsible for starting serious conflicts between husbands and wives.

S. No.	*Factor*	*Percentage*
1.	Cruelty	11.5
2.	Husband interested in other women	11.00
3.	Wife interested in other men	4.00
4.	Interference of in-laws/relatives	8.00
5.	Husband has no regular job/does not support	9.5
6.	Husband suspicious	5.5
7.	Sexual maladjustment	5.00
8.	Wife is a bad character	5.00
9.	Mental problems	5.00
10.	Alcoholism/drug addiction	3.5
11.	Dowry problem	3.5
12.	Wife goes off to parents	3.00
13.	Incompatible nature	2.5
14.	Marriage by fraud/duress, etc.	3.5
15.	Husband not interested in home	2.5
16.	Husband previously in love with someone else	2.00
17.	Unsuitable partner	2.00
18.	Wife too much interested in career/hobbies	2.00
19.	Wife previously in love with someone else	5.1
20.	Poverty	1.5
21.	Husband deserted for food	1.5
22.	Constant quarrels	1.5
23.	Wife pregnant through someone else	1.00
24.	Wife does not want to live in joint family	1.5
25.	Ill-health	1.00
26.	Other factors	2.00
	Total	100

APPENDIX VI

Table showing the complaints of husbands and wives against each other in order of their frequency

S. No.	*Complaints of Husband*	*Frequency*	*Complaints of Wife*	*Frequency*
1.	Poor management of home and income	90	Cruelty	99
2.	Insufficient income	68	Insufficient income	91
3.	Wife non-adjusting	52	Interference of in-laws	83
4.	Interference of in-laws	50	Husband quarrelsome	81
5.	Wife quarrelsome	50	Squanders money	67
6.	Interested in other men	45	Husband not affectionate	54
7.	Incompatible nature	39	Husband's vices	45
8.	Wife not affectionate	39	Husband interested in other women	43
9.	Wife goes off to parents/wants to stay with parents	34	Husband demands dowry	36
10.	Wife extravagant	33	Desertion	35
11.	Wife nagging	30	Incompatible nature of husband	32
12.	Desertion by wife	29	Husband suspicious	30
13.	Wife breaks away from joint family	27	Husband unemployed/ lazy	28

14.	Poor education/intelligence/ manners of wife	21	Husband has no interest in home	27
15.	Wife misbehaves with parents/relatives	21	Husband stingy	26
16.	Wife too much interested in her own work	18	Husband misbehaves/insults	25
17.	Sexual maladjustment	17	Lack of freedom	25
18.	Wife unsubmissive	16	Objectionable friendship	22
19.	Objectionable friendship	15	Selfish & inconsiderate	21
20.	Poor looks of wife	11	Inferior education/ intelligence/ social status of husband	20
21.	Immorality	10	Sexual maladjustment	20
22.	Wife mentally unfit	7	False information about job, income, education, wealth, etc. of husband	16
23.	Poor health of wife	6	Unsocial/ill-mannered	15
24.	Wife barren	6	Husband comes home late	14
25.	Illegitimate pregnancy of wife	5	Interference in hobbies	11
26.	Interference in hobbies	5	Husband criticizes/nags	11
27.	Undisclosed physical defects	3	Poor looks	9
28.	False information about wife (age, etc.)	3	Forced to lead immoral life	7
29.	Wife suspicious	3	Husband polygynous	5
30.	Wife tried to murder husband	2	Husband mentally unfit	4
31.	Wife alcoholic	1	Husband considerably older	4
32.	Forced marriage	1	Tried to kill wife	4
33.			Threatens suicide	2
34.			Poor health	2
35.			Husband crippled	1

APPENDIX VII

THE HINDU MARRIAGE ACT, 1955[1]

(ACT NO. XXV OF 1955)

CONTENTS

CHAPTER I—PRELIMINARY

[1]Received the assent of the President on the 18th May, 1955 and published in the Gazette of India, Extraordinary, dated May 18, 1955, Part II, Section 1.

CHAPTER V—**Jurisdiction and Procedure**

CHAPTER VI—**Savings and Repeals**

Preamble

An Act to amend and modify the law relating to marriage among Hindus.

Be it enacted by Parliament in the sixth year of the Republic of India as follows:

CHAPTER I—**Preliminary**

1. **Short title and extent**—(1) This Act may be called the Hindu Marriage Act, 1955.

(2) It extends to the whole of India except the State of Jammu and Kashmir and applies also to a Hindu domiciled territories to which the Act extends outside the said territories.

Comments

The Hindu Marriage Act, 1955, which became Law of the country on May 18, 1955, witnessed in 1976 for the first time drastic changes. What necessitated these changes is evidence from the S.O.R. appended to the Marriage Law Bill. The S.O.R. runs as below:

Statement of Objects and Reasons—The Hindu Marriage Act, 1955 (25 of 1955), became law on the 18th May, 1955. It applies to all Hindus, Buddhists, Jains or Sikhs. It applies also to all other persons who are not Muslims, Christians Parsis or Jews unless they establish that they were not governed by Hindu Law, custom or usage prior to the Act.

Since the passing of the Hindu Marriage Act, various suggestions for amending the same as well as the Special Marriage Act, 1954, were received from some Members of Parliament and the general public. The Special Marriage Act, 1954, being a civil law applicable to all, has necessarily to keep pace with any reform of matrimonial laws. The Law Commission was requested to examine the matter and they have presented the Fifty-ninth Report which contains their recommendations. The Bill seeks to amend both the Acts aforesaid so as to implement, with necessary modification, the recommendations contained in the Report. The Committee on Status of women in India have generally supported the amendment proposed by the Law Commission and suggested, *inter alia*, the incorporation of a suitable provision for mutual consent in the Hindu Marriage Act more or less on the lines of a provision in that behalf in Section 28 of the Special Marriage Act. It is, however, felt that when once the parties have chosen to move the Court for divorce by mutual consent, it is not necessary to make them wait for a further period of one year to obtain relief. This period of waiting is, therefore, proposed to be reduced from one year to six months. The Committee has further suggested that having regard to the frequent violations of the provisions of the Child Marriage Restraint Act, it is necessary to provide in the Hindu Marriage Act, a suitable provision conferring the right of repudiation of girls who are subject to such marriages, whether the marriage was consummated or not. The right of repudiation is proposed to be conferred on such girls subject to their exercising the same before attaining the age of 18 years. To avoid multiplicity of litigation and consequent delay, it is also proposed to apply the amended law in relation to all pending proceedings under the relevant Acts. Notes on clauses appended to the Bill indicate the charges proposed to the statutes. The objects of the legislation are mainly, (1) to liberalise the provisions relating to divorce; (2) to enable expeditious disposal of proceedings under the Act; and (3) to remove certain anomalies and handicaps that have come to light after the passing of the Acts.

The Bill seeks to achieve the above-mentioned purposes.

2. **Application of the Act**—(1) This Act applies:

(*a*) to a person who is a Hindu by religion in any of its forms or developments, including a *Virashaiva*, a *Lingayat* or a follower of the *Brahmo*, *Prarthana* or *Arya Samaj*;

(*b*) to any person who is a Buddhist, Jain or Sikh by religion; and

(*c*) to any other person domiciled in the territories to which this Act extends, who is not a Muslim, Christian, Parsi or Jew by religion, unless it is proved that any such person would have been governed by the Hindu law or by any custom or usage as part of that law in respect of any of the matters dealt with herein if this Act had not been passed.

Explanation—The following persons are Hindus, Buddhists, Jains or Sikhs by religion, as the case may be:

(*a*) any child, legitimate or illegitimate, both of whose parents are Hindus, Buddhists, Jains or Sikhs by religion;

(*b*) any child, legitimate or illegitimate one of whose parents is a

Hindu, Buddhist, Jain or Sikh by religion and why is brought up as a member of the tribe, community, group or family to which such parent belongs or belonged; and

(*c*) any person who is a convert or re-convert to the Hindu, Buddhist, Jain or Sikh religion.

(2) Notwithstanding anything contained in sub-section (1) nothing contained in this Act shall apply to the members of any Scheduled Tribe within the meaning of Clause (25) of Article 366 of the Constitution unless the Central Government, by notification in the official Gazette, otherwise directs.

(3) The expression 'Hindu' in any portion of this Act shall be construed as if it included a person who, though not a Hindu by religion, is nevertheless a person to whom this Act applies by virtue of the provisions contained in this section.

Comments

The scope of the Act has been widened to include almost every citizen of India who is not a Muslim, Christian, Parsi or Jew by religion. The explanation appended to the section gives a brief, a fairly complete picture of persons, belonging to the cult of Hinduism, Buddhism or Jainism, who come within the scope of the Act.

Hindu Law applies even to convert to Hinduism and it does not necessary for the application that a person should be a Hindu by birth—(1967) 2 Mad LJ 334.

3. **Definitions**—In this Act, unless the context otherwise requires:

(*a*) the expression "custom" and "usage" signify any rule which having been continuously and uniformly observed for a long time, has obtained the force of law among Hindus in any local area, tribe, community, group or family:

Provided that the rule is certain and not unreasonable or opposed to public policy; and

Provided further that in the case of a rule applicable only to the family it has not been discontinued by the family;

Comments

Merely going through certain ceremonies with intention that parties be taken to be married, will not make ceremonies prescribed by law or approved by custom; Departure from essentials cannot be said to have become a custom as contemplated by this Sec. 3 (a) —A.I.R. 1965 S.C. 1564.

Saptapadi ceremony is essential—custom not requiring saptapadi must be proved to supersede shastra—1969 Cr. L.J. 836.

(*b*) "district court" means in any area for which there is a city civil court, that court, and in any other area the principal civil court of original jurisdiction, and includes any other civil court which may be specified by the State Government, by notification in the official Gazette, as having jurisdiction in respect of the matters dealt within this Act;

(*c*) "full-blood" and "half-blood"—two persons are said to be related to each other by full-blood when they are descended from a common ancestor by the same wife and by half-blood when they are descended from a common ancestor but by different wives;

(*d*) "uterine blood"—two persons are said to be related to each other by uterine blood when they are pescended from a common ancestress but by different husbands:

Explanation—In clauses (c) and (d), "ancestor" includes the father and "ancestress" the mother;

(*e*) "prescribed" means prescribed by rules made under this Act;

(*f*) (*i*) "*Sapinda* relationship" with reference to any person extends as far as the third generation (inclusive) in the line of ascent through the mother, and the fifth (inclusive) in the line of ascent through the father, the line being traced upwards in each case from the person concerned, who is to be counted as the first generation;

(*ii*) two persons are said to be "*Sapindas*" of each other if one is a lineal ascendant of the other within the limits of *Sapinda* relationship, or if they have a common lineal ascendant who is within the limits of *Sapinda* relationship with reference to each of them;

(*g*) "degrees of prohibited relationship"—two persons are said to be within the "degrees of prohibited relationship"—

(*i*) if one is lineal ascendant of the other; or

(*ii*) if one was the wife or husband of a lineal ascendant or descendant of the other; or

(*iii*) if one was the wife of the brother or of the father's or mother's brother or of the grandfather's or grandmother's brother of the other; or

(*iv*) if the two are brother and sister, uncle and niece, aunt and nephew or children of brother and sister or of two brothers or of two sisters.

Explanation—For the purposes of clauses (f) and (g), relationship includes—

(*i*) relationship by half or uterine blood as well as by full blood ;

(*ii*) illegitimate blood relationship as well as legitimate ;

(*iii*) relationship by adoption as well as by blood, and all terms of relationship in those clauses shall be construed accordingly.

4. Over-riding effect of the Act—Save as otherwise expressly provided in this Act—

(*a*) any text, rule or interpretation of Hindu Law or any custom or usage as part of that law in force immediately before the commencement of this Act shall cease to have effect with respect to any matter for which provision is made in this Act;

(*b*) any other law in force immediately before the commencement of this Act shall cease to have effect in so far as it is inconsistent with any of the provisions contained in this Act.

Comments

The vital role played by custom and usage in Hindu jurisprudence has been done away with, save as otherwise expressly provided for in the Act.

Section 4 was intended to provide that Provisions of Act were to override all statutory and customary laws to the extent that they dealt with or were in consistent with matters dealt worn by the Act—A.I.R. 1958 Bom. 116 (F.B). "Matter for which provision has been made in this Act"—release of wife by husband under local Custom —Held not matter provided for—A.I.R. 1978 Punj. and Har. 115.

CHAPTER II—Hindu Marriage

5. Conditions of a Hindu Marriage—A marriage may be solemnized between any two Hindus, if the following conditions are fulfilled namely:

(*i*) neither party has a spouse living at the time of the marriage;
[1][(*ii*) at the time of the marriage, neither party:
(*a*) is incapable of giving a valid consent to it in consequence of unsoundness of mind ; or
(*b*) though capable of giving a valid consent, has been suffering from mental disorder of such a kind or to such an extent as to be unfit for marriage and the procreation of children ; or
(*c*) has been subject to recurrent attacks of insanity or epilepsy.]
(*iii*) the bridegroom has completed the age of [2][Twenty one years] and the bride the age of [2][Eighteen years] at the time of the marriage ;
(*iv*) the parties are not within the degrees of prohibited relationship, unless the custom or usage governing each of them permits of a marriage between the two ;
(*v*) the parties are not *Sapindas* of each other, unless the custom or usage governing each of them permits of a marriage between the two;
(*vi*) [* * * *][3]

Comments

In Hindu Law marriage is treated as a "Sankara" or a Sacrament. Act merely amends and codifies law relating to marriage among Hindus. It restains its nature as a religious Sacrament—I.L.R. (1967) Guj. B. 22.

Act imposes obligation on a Hindu Husband not to enter into a second marriage during subsistence of the first. A second marriage by husband will, therefore, infringe the wife's right to monogam-

[1]Cl. (ii) subs. by the Marriage Laws (Amendment) Act, 1976.
[2]Subs. for the words [Eighteen years] and [Fifteen years] by Act 2 of 1978, vide Sec. 6, Sch.
[3]Cl. (vi) omitted by Act No. 2 of 1978, Sec. 6 Sch.

ous married life and she can ask for an injunction to restrain her husband from entering into a second marriage—1965 All. W.R. 410 Marriage of a girl below 15 years—marriage not vitiated. Such contravension may only result in punishment under section 18, but the marriage continues to be valid—A.I.R. 1977 Orissa 36, 1969 A.L.J. 623.

A custom and usage permitting a marriage between parties in this degrees of prohibited relationship such as of cousins, cannot be inferred much less established from one single instance in the past—(1970) 2 Mad. L.J. 477 (DB) Marriage between first cousins—Marriage not valid under the Act—(1963) 65 Punj. L.R. 121.

[[1]6. Guardianship in marriage—[* * *]

Note—Section 6 omitted by Act No. 2 of 1978. The original section reads as follows:

[6. Guardianship in marriage—(1) Wherever the consent of a guardian in marriage is necessary for a bride under this Act the persons entitled to give such consent shall be the following in the order specified hereunder, namely—

(*a*) the father;
(*b*) the mother;
(*c*) the paternal grandfather;
(*d*) the paternal grandmother;
(*e*) the brother by full-blood; as between brothers the elder being preferred;
(*f*) the brother by half-blood as between brothers by half-blood the elder being preferred;

Provided that the bride is living with him and is being brought up by him;

(*g*) the paternal uncle by full-blood ; as between paternal uncles, the elder being preferred;
(*h*) the paternal uncle by half-blood, as between paternal uncles by half-blood, the elder being preferred:

Provided that the bride is living with him and is being brought up by him—

(*i*) the maternal grandfather;
(*j*) the maternal grandmother;

[1]Sec. 6 omitted by Act No. 2 of 1978, Sec. 6, Sch.

(*k*) the maternal uncle by full-blood, as between maternal uncles; the elder being preferred;

Provided that the bride is living with him and is being brought up by him.

(2) No person shall be entitled to act as guardian in marriage under the provisions of the section unless such person has, himself completed his or her twenty years.

(3) Where any person entitled to be the guardian in marriage under, the foregoing provisions refuses or is for any cause unable or unfit, to act as such, the person next in order shall be entitled to be the guardian.

(4) In the absence of any such person as is referred to in sub-section (1), the consent of a guardian shall not be necessary for a marriage under this Act.

(5) Nothing in this Act shall affect the jurisdiction of a court to prohibit by injunction an intended marriage, if in the interest of the bride for whose marriage consent is required, the court thinks it necessary to do so.]

7. **Ceremonies for a Hindu marriage**—(1) A Hindu marriage may be solemnized in accordance with the customary rites and ceremonies of either party thereto.

Where such rites and ceremonies include the *Saptapadi* (that is, the taking of seven steps by bridegroom and the bride jointly before the sacred fire) the marriage becomes complete and binding when the seventh step is taken.

Comments

The *Homa Kanyadana* and the *Saptapadi*, these are more important marriage rites prevalent among vast majority of Hindus. The ceremony of *Saptapadi* before the sacred fire (*Homa*) has been held essential for a valid Hindu marriage under the present Act in sub-section (2) of section 7, marriage becomes complete as soon as the seventh step is taken.

Comments

Custom—In the case of High Class Brahmins, Khatris, and Rajputs, the marriage ceremony is completed with Ganesh Puja, in a few cases vedic rites are performed. All other communities, that is, those are not Brahmins, Khatris, and Rajputs, perform their marriage by merely giving meals to the marriage party and where they are very poor a mere deed is executed. Where the parties are Harijans and there is ample material on the record to show that meals were served to the marriage party then the marriage must be to have been solemnized according to Custom—A. I. R. 1977 Noc 275 (Him. Pra.).

8. Registration of Hindu Marriage—(1) For the purpose of facilitating the proof of Hindu marriage, the State Government may make rules providing that the parties to any such marriage may have the particular, relating to their marriage entered in such manner and subject to such conditions as may be prescribed in a Hindu Marriage Register kept for the purpose.

(2) Notwithstanding anything contained in sub-section (1) the State Government may, if it is of opinion that it is necessary or expedient so to do, provide that the entering of the particulars referred to in sub-section (1) shall be compulsory in the State or in any part thereof, whether in all cases or in such cases as may be specified and where any such direction has been issued, any person contravening any rule made in this behalf, shall be punishable with fine which may extend to twenty-five rupees.

(3) All rules made under this section shall be laid before the State Legislature, as soon as may be, after they are made.

(4) The Hindu Marriage Register shall, at all reasonable times be open for inspection, and shall be admissible as evidence of the statements therein contained and certified extracts therefrom shall, on application, be given by the Registrar on payment to him of the prescribed fee.

(5) Notwithstanding anything contained in this section the validity of the Hindu marriage shall, in no way, be affected by the omission to make the entry.

CHAPTER III—Restitution of Conjugal Rights and Judicial Separation

9. Restitution of conjugal rights—[1][**] When either the husband or the wife has, without reasonable excuse withdrawn from the society of the other, the aggrieved party may apply by petition to

[1]Figure (1) omitted by the Marriage Laws (Amendment) Act, 1976.

the District Court for restitution of conjugal rights and the court, on being satisfied of the truth of the statements made in such petition and that there is no legal ground why the application should not be granted, may decree restitution of conjugal rights accordingly.

[1][*Explanation*—Where a question arises whether there has been reasonable excuse for withdrawal from the society, the burden of proving reasonable excuse shall be on the person who has withdrawn from the society.]

[2][* * *]

Comments

What would be the "reasonable excuse" cannot be reduced to formula and would vary with time and circumstances and will have to be determined by court in each individual case in light of features peculiar to it. Reasonable excuse, cannot, therefore be equated with legal ground, and court cannot grant a decree for restitution of conjugal rights if there is reasonable excuse for husband or wife withdrawing from society of other even though ground for judicial separation or for nullity or for divorce has not been made out—A.I.R. 1966 All. 150.

10. Judicial Separation—(1) [3][Either party to a marriage, whether solemnized before or after the commencement of this Act, may present a petition praying for a decree for judicial separation on any of the grounds specified in sub-section (1) of section 13, and in the case of a wife also on any of the grounds specified in sub-section (2) thereof, as grounds on which a petition for divorce might have been presented.]

(2) Where a decree for judicial separation has been passed, it shall, no longer, be obligatory for the petitioner to cohabit with the respondent, but the court may, on the application by petition of either party and on being satisfied of the truth of the statements made in such petition, rescind the decree if it considers it just and reasonable to do so.

[1]Explanation inserted by the Marriage Laws (Amendment) Act, 1976.
[2]Sub-section (2) omitted by ibid.
[3]Sub-sec. (1) of Sec. 10 Subs by the Marriage Laws (Amendment) Act, 1976.

Comments

Irritating idiosyncrasies of the wife rendering husband's life unhappy—Not a ground for granting decree for Judicial Separation—A.I.R. 1964 M.P. 28 (DB)

Proof of a single Act of adultery is sufficient for decreeing judicial separation 1970, All. W.R. 749.

CHAPTER IV—Nullity of Marriage and Divorce

11. Void marriages—Any marriage solemnized after the commencement of this Act shall be null and void and may, on a petition presented by either party thereto [1][against the other party] be so declared by a decree of nullity if it contravenes any of the conditions specified in clauses (*i*), (*iv*) and (*v*) of Section 5.

Comments

Marriage solemnized after commencement of this Act in contravention of the provisions of Section 5, shall be declared null and void by the court on petition by either party to the marriage. Strangers have no such right to petition the court.

12. Voidable marriage—(1) Any marriage solemnized, whether, before or after the commencement of this Act, shall be voidable and may be annulled by a decree of nullity on any of the following grounds, namely:

[2][(*a*) that the marriage has not been consummated owing to the impotence of the respondent ; or]

(*b*) that the marriage is in contravention of the condition specified in clause (*ii*) of Section 5; or

(*c*) that the consent of the petitioner where the consent of the guardian in marriage of petitioner [was required under Section 5, as it stood immediately before the commencement of the Child Marriage Restraint (Amendment) Act, 1978] the consent of such guardian was obtained by force [3][or by fraud as to the nature of the ceremony or as to any

[1]The words in brackets Subs. by the Marriage Laws (Amendment) Act, 1976.
[2]Cl. (*a*) of Sec. 12 Subs. by the Marriage Laws (Amendment) Act, 1976.
[3]The words in brackets in cl. (*c*) Subs. by Act No. 2 of 1978.

material fact or circumstance concerning the respondent]; or

(*d*) that the respondent was, at the time of the marriage, pregnent by some person other than the petitioner.

(2) Notwithstanding anything contained in sub-section (1), no petition for annulling a marriage—

(*a*) on the ground specified in clause (*c*) if sub-section (1) shall be entertained, if—

(*i*) the petition is presented more than one year after the force had ceased to operate or, as the case may be, the fraud had been discovered; or

(*ii*) the petitioner, has, with his or her full consent, lived with the other party to the marriage as husband or wife after the force had ceased to operate or, as the case may be, the fraud had been discovered;

(*b*) on the ground specified in clause (*a*) of sub-section (2) shall be entertained unless the court is satisfied—

(*i*) that the petitioner was at the time of the marriage ignorant of the facts alleged;

(*ii*) the proceedings have been instituted in the case of a marriage solemnized before the commencement of this Act within one year of such commencement and in the case of marriage solemnized after such commencement within one year from the date of the marriage; and

(*iii*) that marital intercourse with the consent of the petitioner has not taken place since the discovery by the petitioner of the existence of [1][the said ground].

Comments

Petitioner must prove that mental or physical condition of respondent from time of marriage till institution of proceedings was such as to make consumation of marriage a practical impossibility—A.I.R. 1970 S.C. 137.

13. Divorce—(1) Any marriage solemnized, whether before or after the commencement of this Act, may, on a petition presented by either the husband or the wife, be dissolved by a decree of divorce on the ground that the other party—

[1]Subs. by the Marriage Laws (Amendment) Act, 1976.

[1][(*i*) has, after the solemnization of the marriage, had voluntary sexual intercourse with any person other than his or her spouse; or

(*i-a*) has, after the solemnization of the marriage, treated the petitioner with cruelty; or

(*i-b*) has deserted the petitioner for a continuous period of not less than two years immediately preceding the presentation of the petition; or]

(*ii*) has ceased to be Hindu by conversion to another religion; or

[2][(*iii*) has been incurably of unsound mind, or has been suffering continuously or intermittently from mental disorder of such a kind and to such an extent that the petitioner cannot reasonably be expected to live with the respondent.

Explanation—In this clause,

(*a*) the expression "mental disorder" means mental illness, arrested or incomplete development of mind, psychopathic disorder or any other disorder or disability of mind and includes schizophrenia;

(*b*) the expression "psychopathic disorder" means a persistent disorder or disability of mind (whether or not including sub-normality of intelligence) which results in abnormally aggressive or seriously irresponsible conduct on the part of the other party, and whether or not it requires or is susceptible to medical treatment; or]

(*iv*) has [3][* * *] been suffering from a virulent and incurable form of leprosy ; or

(*v*) has [3][* * *] been suffering from venereal disease in a communicable form; or

(*vi*) has renounced the world by entering any religious order; or

(*vii*) has not been heard of as being alive for a period of seven years or more by those persons who would naturally have heard of it, had that party been alive;

[4][*Explanation*—In this sub-section, the expression "desertion" means

[1]Cl. (*i*) Subs. by ibid.

[2]Cl. (*iii*)Subs. by the Marriage Laws (Amend.) Act, 1976.

[3]The words (for a period of not less than three years immediately preceding the presentation of the petition) omitted by the Marriage Laws Amendment Act, 1976

[4]Expl. inserted by the Marriage Laws (Amendment) Act, 1976.

the desertion of the petitioner by the other party to the marriage without reasonable cause and without the consent or against the wish of such party, and includes the wilful neglect of the petitioner by the other party to the marriage, and its grammatical variations and cognate expressions shall be construed accordingly;

(*viii*) [* * *][1]

(*ix*) [* * *][1]

(1-A) Either party to a marriage, whether solemnized before or after the commencement of this Act, may also present a petition for the dissolution of the marriage by a decree of divorce on the ground—

(*i*) that there has been no resumption of a cohabitation as between the parties to the marriage for a period of [2][one year] or upwards after passing of a decree for judicial separation in a proceeding to which they were parties; or

(*ii*) that there has been no restitution of conjugal rights as between the parties to the marriage for a period of [3][one year] or upwards after the passing of the decree for restitution of conjugal rights in a proceeding to which they were parties.

(2) A wife may also present a petition for the dissolution of her marriage by a decree of divorce on the ground—

(*i*) in the case of any marriage solemnized before the commencement of this Act, that the husband had married again before such commencement or that any other wife of the husband married before such commencement was alive at the time of the solemnization of the marriage of the petitioner; or

Provided that in either case the other wife is alive at the time of presentation of the petition; or

(*ii*) that the husband has, since the solemnization of the marriage, been guilty of rape, sodomy or [4][bestiality; or]

[5](*iii*) that in a suit under Section 18 of the Hindu Adoptions and Maintenance Act, 1956, or in a proceeding under Section 125 of the Code of Criminal Procedure, 1973 (or under the corresponding Section 488 of the Code of Criminal Procedure,

[1]Cls. (*viii*) and (*ix*) delected by Act No. 44 of 1954.

[2]Words in brackets subs. by Marriage Laws (Amendment) Act 1976

[3]Words in Brackets Subs. by Marriage Laws (Amendment) Act, 1976.

[4]Subs. by the Marriage Laws (Amendment) Act, 1976.

[5]Cls. (iii) and (iv) inserted by the Marriage Laws (Amendment) Act, 1976.

1898), a decree or order, as the case may be, has been passed against the husband awarding maintenance to the wife notwithstanding that she was living apart and that since the passing of such decree or order, cohabitation between the parties has not been resumed for one year or upwards ; or

(*iv*) that her marriage (whether, consummated or not) was solemnized before she attained the age of fifteen years and she has repudiated the marriage after attaining that age before attaining the age of eighteen years.

Explanation—This clause applies whether the marriage was solemnized before or after the commencement of the Marriage Laws (Amendment) Act 1976.]

Comments

Divorce was unknown to old Hindu Laws of Marriage, Section 3 introduces a very vital and dynamic change in the Hindu Laws of Marriage. Both the husband and wife have been given the right to petition the court for divorce on any one of the grounds mentioned in the section. The provisions of this section have also been given retrospective effect. It is significant to note in this connection that the conditions laid down for divorce are fair and reasonable.

Mere severance of all connections with wife by husband because of his ill health and allowing her to remarry any person she likes cannot amount to divorce in this meaning of Section 13 because divorce which could result in dissolution of solemnized marriage has to be obtained by one of the two parties on presentation of petition, from competent court—A.I.R. 1965 All. 464.

"Living in Adultery"—"Living in adultery" means a continuous course of adulterous life as distinguished from one or two lapses by virtue--A.I.R. Guj 33.

Desertion—The two essential conditions which must be there before the spouse can be held guilty of desertion—(1) the factum of separation and intention to bring cohabitation permanently to an end—A.I.R. 1971 Raj 140.

Cruelty—Cruelty is wilful unjustifiable conduct of such a character as to cause danger to life, limb or health bodily or mentally as to give rise to reasonable apprehension of such a danger—A.I.R. 1978 Raj. 140.

[1][**13-A. Alternate relief in divorce proceedings**—In any proceeding under this Act, on a petition for dissolution of marriage by a decree of divorce, except in so far as the petition is founded on the grounds mentioned in clauses (*ii*), (*vi*) and (*vii*) of sub-section (1) of Section 13, the court may, if it considers it just so to do having regard to the circumstances of the case, pass instead a decree for judicial separation.

13-B. Divorce by mutual consent—(1) Subject to the provisions of this Act a petition for dissolution of marriage by a decree of divorce may be presented to the District Court by both the parties to a marriage together, whether such marriage was solemnized before or after the commencement of the Marriage Laws (Amendment) Act, 1976, on the ground that they have been living separately for a period of one year or more, that they have not been able to live together and that they have mutually agreed that the marriage should be dissolved.]

(2) On the motion of both the parties made not earlier than six months after the date of the presentation of the petition referred to in sub-section (1) and not later than eighteen months after the said date, if the petition is not withdrawn in the meantime, the Court shall, on being satisfied, after hearing the parties and after making such inquiry as it thinks fit, that a marriage has been solemnized and that the averments in the petition are true, pass a decree of divorce declaring the marriage to be dissolved with effect from the date of the decree.]

14. No petition for divorce to be presented within three years of marriage—(1) Notwithstanding anything contained in this Act, it shall not be competent for any court to entertain any petition for dissolution of marriage by a decree of divorce, [1][unless at the date of the presentation of the petition one year has elapsed] since the date of the marriage:

Provided that the court may upon application made to it in accordance with such rules as may be made by the High Courts in that behalf allow a petition to be presented [2][before one year has elapsed] since the date of the marriage on the ground that the case is one of exceptional hardship to the petitioner or of exceptional depravity on the part of the respondent, but if it appears to the

[1]Subs. by the Marriage Laws (Amendment) Act, 1976.
[2]Sec. 13-A and 13-B inserted by the Marriage Laws (Amendment) Act, 1976.

court at the hearing of the petition that petitioner obtained leave to present the petition by any misrepresentation or concealment of the nature of the case, the court may, if it pronounces a decree, do so subject to the condition that the decree shall not have effect until after the [1][expiry of one year] from the date of the marriage or may dismiss the petition without prejudice to any petition which may be brought after the expiration of the said one year upon the same or substantially the same facts as those alleged in support of the petition so dismissed.

(2) In disposing any application under this section for leave to present a petition for divorce before the [2][expiration of one year] from the date of the marriage, the court shall have regard to the interests of any children of the marriage and to the question whether there is a reasonable probability of a reconciliation between the parties before the [3][expiration of the said] one year.

Comments

This section is enacted to discourage young spouses from taking recourse to legal proceedings in frivolous and irresponsible manner—Petition under Section 13 presented within three years—Petition with amended plaint filed at expiry of statutory period of three years—Amendment allowed and condonation granted—A.I.R. 1967 J. & K. 89; A.I.R. 1959 Mad. 423.

15. Divorced persons when may marry again—When a marriage has been dissolved by a decree of divorce and either there is no right of appeal against the decree or; if there is such a right of appeal, the time for appealing has expired without an appeal having been presented or an appeal has been presented but has been dismissed, it shall be lawful for either party to the marriage to marry again.

Comments

Marriage within one year from the date of dissolution of marriage—Marriage held valid in Amendment is retrospective—A.I.R. 1978 Mad. 161.

[1]See. 13-A and 13-B inserted by the Marriage Laws (Amendment) Act, 1976.
[2]Subs. by the Marriage Laws (Amendment) Act, 1976.
[3]*Ibid.*

[1][* *]

[2][**16. Legitimacy of children of void and voidable marriages**—(1) Notwithstanding that a marriage is null and void under Section 11, any child of such marriage who would have been legitimate if the marriage had been valid, shall be legitimate, whether such child is born before or after the commencement of the Marriage Laws (Amendment) Act, 1976, and whether or not a decree of nullity is granted in respect of that marriage under this Act and whether or not the marriage is held to be void otherwise than on a petition under this Act.

(2) Where a decree of nullity is granted in respect of a voidable marriage under Section 12, any child begotten or conceived before the decree is made, who would have been the legitimate child of the parties to the marriage if at the date of the decree it had been dissolved instead of being annulled, shall be deemed to be their legitimate child notwithstanding the decree of nullity.

(3) Nothing contained in sub-section (1) or sub-section (2) shall be construed as conferring upon any child of a marriage which is null and void or which is annulled by a decree of nullity under Section 12, any right in or to the property of any person, other than the parents, in any case where, but for the passing of this Act, such child would have been incapable of possessing of acquiring any such rights by reason of his not being the legitimate child of his parents.]

Comments

Every child born of void marriage cannot be deemed legitimate under Section 16 where decree of nullity has not been obtained—A.I.R. 1964 Mad. 118.

Children born of void or voidable marriage are legitimate until decree of nullity or of annulement is passed by Court—A.I.R. 1967 Pat. 277.

17. Punishment for bigamy—Any marriage between two Hindus solemnized after the commencement of this Act is void if at the date of such marriage either party had a husband or wife living, and the provisions of Sections 494 and 495 of the Indian Penal Code

[1]Omitted by the Marriage Laws (Amendment) Act, 1976.
[2]Sec. 16 Subs. by ibid.

(Act XLV of 1860) shall apply accordingly.

Comments

Unless marriage is 'celebrated or performed with proper ceremonies and in due form' it cannot be said to be 'Solemnized'. It is, therefore, essential for the purpose of Section 17 that marriage to which Section 494 I.P.C. applies on account of provisions of the Act, should have been celebrated with proper ceremonies and in due form. Merely going through certain ceremonies with intention that parties be taken to be married, will not make the ceremonies prescribed by law or approved by any established custom—A.I.R. 1965 S.C. 1564.

18. Punishment for contravention of certain other conditions for a Hindu marriage—Every person who procures a marriage of himself or herself to be solemnized under this Act in contravention of the conditions specified in clauses [1][(*iii*), (*iv*) and (*v*)] of Section 5 shall be punishable—

(*a*) in the case of the contravention of the conditions specified in clause (*iii*) of Section 5, with simple imprisonment which may extend to fifteen days, or with fine which may extend to one thousand rupees or with both;

(*b*) in the case of contravention of the conditions specified in clause (*iv*) or clause (*v*) of Section 5, with simple imprisonment which may extend to one month, or with fine which may extend to one thousand rupees, or with both; [* * *][2]

(*c*) [* * *][3]

CHAPTER V—Jurisdiction and Procedure

[4][**19. Court to which petition shall be presented**—Every petition under this Act shall be presented to the District Court within the local limits of whose ordinary original civil jurisdiction.

[1]Subs. by Act 2 of 1978.
[2]Omitted by Act 3 of 1978.
[3]Cl. (*c*) omitted by Act 2 of 1978. Original cl. (*c*) an as follows:
"in the case of a contravention of the conditions specified in clause (*vi*) of Section 5, with fine which may extend to one thousand rupees."
[4]Section 19 Subs. by the Marriage Laws (Amendment) Act, 1976.

(*i*) the marriage was solemnized, or
(*ii*) the respondent, at the time of the presentation of the petition resides; or
(*iii*) the parties to the marriage last resided together; or
(*iv*) the petitioner is residing at the time of the presentation of the petition, in a case where the respondent is, at the time, residing outside the territories to which this Act extends, or has not been heard of as being alive for a period of seven years or more by those persons who would naturally have heard of him if he were alive.]

Comments

"Last resided together"—meaning of—there must be intention on part of parties to reside together A.I.R. 1978 All. 18.

20. Contents and verifications of petitions—(1) Every petition presented under this Act shall state as distinctly as the nature of case permits the facts on which the claim to relief is founded [1]and except in petition under Section 11 shall also state] that there is no collusion between the petitioner and the other party to the marriage.

(2) The statements contained in every petition under this Act shall be verified by the petitioner or some other competent person in the manner required by law for the verification of plaints, and may, at the hearing be referred to as evidence.

21. Application of Act V of 1908—Subject to the other provisions contained in this Act and to such rules as the High Court may make in this behalf all proceedings under this Act shall be regulated, as far as may be, by the Code of Civil Procedure, 1908 (Act V of 1908).

Comments

Court can pass decree directing husband to return to wife her ornaments and other articles—In view of Section 21 all powers of a Civil Court are available to the court which dealing with the proceeding under the Act—A.I.R. 1972 All. 153.

[1]Subs. by the Marriage Laws (Amendment) Act, 1976.

[1][**21-A. Power to transfer petitions in certain cases**—(1) Where—

(*a*) a petition under this Act has been presented to a District Court having jurisdiction by a party to a marriage praying for a decree for judicial separation under Section 10 or for a decree of divorce under Section 13, and

(*b*) another petition under this Act has been presented thereafter by the other party to the marriage praying for a decree for judicial separation under Section 10 or for a decree of divorce under Section 13 on any ground, whether in the same District Court or in a different District Court, in the same State or in a different State,

the petitions shall be dealt with as specified in sub-section (2).

(2) In a case where sub-section (1) applies—

(*a*) if the petitions are presented to the same District Court, both the petitions shall be tried and heard together by that District Court ;

(*b*) if the petitions are presented to different district courts, the petition presented later shall be transferred to the District Court in which the earlier petition was presented and both the petitions shall be heard and disposed of together by the District Court in which the earlier petition was presented.

(3) In a case where clause (*b*) of sub-section (2) applies, the court or the Government, as the case may be, competent under the Code of Civil Procedure, 1908 to transfer any suit or proceeding from the District Court in which the later petition has been presented to the district court in which the earlier petition is pending, shall exercise its powers to transfer such later petition as if it had been empowered so to do under the said Code.

21-B. Special provision relating to trial and disposal of petitions under the Act—(1) The trial of a petition under this Act shall, so far as is practicable consistently with the interests of justice in respect of the trial, be continued from day to day until its conclusion unless the court finds the adjournment of the trial beyond the following day to be necessary for reasons to be recorded.

(2) Every petition under this Act shall be tried as expeditiously as possible and endeavour shall be made to conclude the trial within six months from the date of service of the notice of the

[1]Secions 21-A, 21-B and 21C, inserted by Marriage Laws (Amendment) Act, 1976.

petition on the respondent.

(3) Every appeal under this Act shall be heard as expeditiously as possible and endeavour shall be made to conclude the hearing within three months from the date of service of notice of appeal on the respondent.

21-C. Documentary evidence—Notwithstanding anything in any enactment to the contrary, no document shall be inadmissible in evidence in any proceeding at the trial of a petition under this Act on the ground that it is not duly stamped or registered.]

[1][**22. Proceedings to be in camera and may not be printed or published**— (1) Every proceeding under this Act shall be conducted *in camera* and it shall not be lawful for any person to print or publish any matter in relation to any such proceeding except a judgment of the High Court or the Supreme Court printed or published with the previous permission of the Court.

(2) If any person prints or publishes any matter in contravention of the provisions contained in sub-section (1), he shall be punishable with fine which may extend to one thousand rupees.]

23. Decree in proceedings—(1) In any proceeding under this Act, whether defended or not, if the court is satisfied that—

(*a*) any of the grounds for granting relief exists and the petitioner, [2][except in cases where the relief is sought by him on the ground specified in sub-clause (*a*), sub-clause (*b*) or sub-clause (*c*) of clause (*ii*) of Section 5] is not in any way taking advantage of his or her own wrong or disability for the purpose of such relief, and

(*b*) whether the ground of the petition is the ground specified [3][* *] in clause (*i*) of sub-section (1) of Section 13, the petitioner has not, in any manner, been accessory to or connived or condoned the act or acts complained of or where the ground for the petition is cruelty the petitioner has not in any manner condoned the cruelty, and

[4][(*bb*) when a divorce is sought on the ground of mutual consent, such consent has not been obtained by force, fraud or undue influence, and]

[1]Sec. 22 Subs. by the Marriage Laws (Amendment) Act, 1976.

[2]The words in brackets in Sec. 23 (1) (a) Ins. by the Marriage Laws (Amendment) Act, 1976.

[3]Certain words omitted by Marriage Laws (Amendment) Act, 1976.

[4]Cl. (bb) inserted by ibid.

[1][(*c*) the petition not being a petition presented under Section 11] is not presented or prosecuted in collusion with respondent, and

(*d*) there has not been any unnecessary or improper delay in instituting the proceeding, and

(*e*) there is no other legal ground why relief should not be granted, then, in such a case, but not otherwise the court shall decree such relief accordingly.

(2) Before proceeding to grant any relief under this Act, it shall be the duty of the court in the first instance, in every case, where it is possible so to do consistently with the nature and circumstances of the case to make every endeavour to bring about a reconciliation between the parties:

[2][Provided that nothing contained in this sub-section shall apply to any proceeding wherein relief is sought on any of the grounds specified in clause (*ii*), clause (*iii*), clause (*iv*), clause (*v*), clause (*vi*) or clause (*vii*) of sub-section (1) of section 13]

[3][(3) For the purpose of aiding the court in bringing about such reconciliation, the court may, if the parties so desire or if the court thinks it just and proper so to do, adjourn the proceedings for a reasonable period not exceeding fifteen days and refer the matter to any person named by the parties in this behalf or to any person nominated by the court if the parties fail to name any person, which directions to report to the court as to whether reconciliation can be and has been, effected and the court shall in disposing of the proceeding have due regard to the report.

(4) In every case where a marriage is dissolved by a decree of divorce, the court passing the decree shall be given a copy thereof free of cost to each of the parties.]

Comments

Wife obtaining decree for judicial separation. Husband after two years seeking divorce under Sec. 13 for failure of resumption of cohabitation—Husband entitled to divorce—A.I.R. 1977 Delhi 178.

[1]The words in clause (c) Subs. by Marriage Laws (Amendment) Act, 1976.
[2]Proviso to sub-section (2) inserted by ibid.
[3]Sub-sections (3) and (4) inserted by ibid.

[1][**23-A. Relief for respondent in divorce and other proceedings**— In any proceeding for divorce or judicial separation or restitution of conjugal rights, the respondent may not only oppose the relief sought on the ground of petitioner's adultery, cruelty or desertion, but also make a counter-claim for any relief under this Act on that ground; and if the petitioner's adultery, cruelty or desertion is proved, the court may give to the respondent any relief under this Act to which he or she would have been entitled if he or she had presented a petition seeking such relief on that ground.]

24. Maintenance pendente lite and expenses of proceedings— Where in any proceeding under this Act it appears to the court that either the wife or the husband, as the case may be, has no independent income sufficient for her or his support and the necessary expenses of the proceedings, it may, on the application of the wife or the husband, order the respondent to pay to the petitioner the expenses of proceeding, and monthly during the proceeding such sum as, having regard to the petitioner's own income and the income of the respondent, it may seems to the court to be reasonable.

Comments

Maintenance pendente lite and expencess of the proceedings—The reason for enacting the provisions in Section 24 is obviously that a wife or husband who has no independent income sufficient for her or his support or enough to meet the necessary expenses of the proceedings may not be handicapped—A.I.R 1959 M.P. 187.

25. Permanent alimony and maintenance—(1) Any court exercising jurisdiction under this Act may, at the time of passing any decree or at any time subsequent thereto, on application made to it for the purpose by either the wife or the husband, as the case may be, order that the respondent shall, [2][* * *] pay to the applicant for her or his maintenance and support such gross sum or such monthly or periodical sum for a term not exceeding the life of the applicant as, having regard to the respondent's own income and other property of applicant [3][the conduct of the parties and other

[1]Sec. 23-A ins. by ibid.

[2]The words (while the applicant remains un-married) omitted by the Marriage Laws (Amendment) Act, 1976.

[3]The words in brakets Subs. by ibid.

circumstances of the case] it may seem to the court to be just, and any such payment may be secured, if necessary, by a charge on the immovable property of the respondent.

(2) If the court is satisfied that there is a change in the circumstance of either party at any time after it has made an order under sub-section (1), it may, at the instance of either party, vary, modify or rescind any such order in such manner as the court may deem just.

(3) If the court is satisfied that the party in whose favour an order has been made under this section has remarried or, if such party is the wife, that she has not remained chaste, or, such party is the husband, that he has had sexual intercourse with any woman outside wedlock. [1](It may at the instance of the other party) vary, modify or rescind any such order in such manner as the court may deem just.

Comments

Relief of alimony being ancillary and incidental is available even after the marriage is dissolved—A.I.R. 1977 Delhi 174.

26. Custody of children—In any proceeding under this Act, the court may, from time to time, pass such interim orders and make such provisions in the decree as it may deem just and proper with respect to the custody, maintenance and education of minor children, consistently with their wishes, wherever possible, and may, after the decree, upon application by petition for the purpose, make, from time to time, all such orders and provisions with respect to the custody, maintenance and education of such children as might have been made by such decree or interim orders in case the proceedings for obtaining such decree were still pending, and the court may also, from time to time revoke, suspend or vary any such orders and provisions previously made.

27. Disposal of property—In a proceeding under this Act, the court may make such provisions in the decree as it deems just and proper with respect to any property presented, at or about the time of marriage, which may belong jointly to both the husband and the wife.

[2][**28. Appeals from decrees and orders**—(1) All decrees made by

[1]Subs. by ibid.
[2]Sec. 28-A Subs. by Marriage Laws (Amendment) Act, 1976.

the court in any proceeding under this Act shall, subject to the provisions of sub-section (3), be appealable as decrees of the court made in the exercise of its original civil jurisdiction, and every such appeal shall lie to the court to which appeals ordinarily lie from the decisions of the court given in the exercise of its original civil jurisdiction.

(2) Orders made by the court in any proceeding under this Act, under section 25 or section 26 shall, subject to the provisions of sub-section (3), be appealable if they are not interim orders, and every such appeal shall lie to the court to which appeals ordinarily lie from the decisions of the court given in exercise of its original civil jurisdiction.

(3) There shall be no appeal under this section on the subject of costs only.

(4) Every appeal under this section shall be preferred within a period of thirty days from the date of the decree or order.]

[1][**28-A. Enforcement of decrees and orders**—All decrees and orders made by the court in any proceeding under this Act shall be enforced in the like manner as the decrees and orders of the court made in the exercise of its original civil jurisdiction for the time being are enforced.]

CHAPTER VI—Savings and Repeals

29. Savings—A marriage solemnized between Hindus before the commencement of this Act, which is otherwise valid, shall not be deemed to be invalid or even to have been invalid by reason only of the fact that the parties thereto belonged to the same *gotra* or *Pravara* or belonged to different religions, caste or sub-divisions or the same caste.

(2) Nothing contained in this Act shall be deemed to affect any right recognized by custom or conferred by any special enactments to obtain the dissolution of a Hindu marriage whether solemnized before or after the commencement of this Act.

(3) Nothing contained in this Act shall affect any proceeding under any law for the time being in force for declaring any marriage to be null and void or for annulling or dissolving any marriage or for judicial separation pending at the commencement of this Act,

[1]Section 28-A inseated by ibid.

and any such proceeding may be continued and determined as if this Act had not been passed.

(4) Nothing contained in this Act shall be deemed to affect the provisions contained in the Special Marriage Act, 1954 (43 of 1954) with respect to marriage between Hindus solemnized under that Act, whether before or after the commencement of this Act.

Comments

'Inter Caste' marriages are made valid with retrospective effect under section 29(1)—A.I.R. 1960 All. 446.

30. Repeals—The Hindu Marriage Disabilities Removal Act, 1946 (XXVIII of 1946), the Hindu Marriage Validity Act, 1949 (XXI of 1949), the Bombay Prevention of Hindu Bigamous Marriage Act, 1946 (Bombay act XXV of 1946), the Bombay Hindu Divorce Act, 1947 (Bombay Acts XXII And XXIII of 1946)), the Madras Hindu (Bigamy Prevention and Divorce) Act, 1949, (Madras Act VI of 1949), the Saurashtra Prevention of Hindu Bigamous Marriage Act, 1950 (Saurashtra Act V of 1950) and the Saurashtra Hindu Divorce Act, 1952 (Saurashtra Act XXX of 1952) are hereby repealed.

SELECT BIBLIOGRAPHY

BOOKS

ALDOUS, JOHN, *Family Careers, Developmental Change in Families*, John Wiley & Sons, New York, 1978.

ANDERSON, MICHAEL (Ed), *Sociology of the Family*, Penguin Books Ltd., 1971.

BABER, RAY, E., *Marriage and the Family*, McGraw Hill Book Company Inc., 1953.

BURGESS, ERNEST W. AND LOCKE, HARVEY, J., *The Family, From Institution to Companionship*, American Book Co., New York, 1950.

BELL, NORMAN, W. AND VOGEL E.F., *A Modern Introduction to the Family*, Routledge & Kegan Paul, London, 1960.

CARTER, HUGH & GLOCK, PAUL, *Marriage & Divorce, A Social & Economic Study*, Harward University Press, Cambridge, 1970.

CHESTER, ROBERT, (Ed.), *Divorce in Europe*, Martinus Niz, Social Science Division, Leiden, 1977.

CHRISTENSES, HAROLD T., *Marriage Analysis, Foundations for Successful Family Life*, Second Ed., The Ronald Press Co., New York, 1958.

CORMACK, MARGARET, *The Hindu Woman*, Asia Publishing House, Bombay, 1961.

DERRETT, DUNCAN, J.M., *The Death of a Marriage Law, Epitah for the Rishis*, Vikas Publishing House Pvt. Ltd., New Delhi.

DESAI, KUMUD, *Indian Law of Marriage & Divorce*, Second Ed., N.M. Tripathi Private Ltd., Bombay, 1972.

ELLIOTT, M.A., & MERRILL, FRANCIS, E., *Social Disorganization*, Third Edition, Harper Bro. Pub., New York, 1950.

FLETCHER, R., *The Family & Marriage in Britain*, Penguin Books, Harmondsworth, 1966.

FONSECA, MABEL, *Counselling for Marital Happiness*, P.C. Manaktala & Sons., Ltd., Bombay, 1966.

GOODE, WILLIAM, J., *Woman in Divorce*, The Free Press, New York, 1965.

———, *The Family*, Prentice Hall of India, New Delhi, 1965.

GORE, M.S., *Urbanization & Family Change in India*, Popular Prakashan, Bombay, 1968.

KAPADIA, K.M., *Marriage & Family in India*, Second Ed., Oxf. Univ. Press, London, 1959.

KAPUR, PROMILLA, *Marriage & Working Women in India*, Abridged Ed., Vikas Publishing House Pvt Ltd., 1972.

———, *Love, Marriage & Sex*, Vikas Publishing House Pvt Ltd., New Delhi, 1973.

KEITH MELVILLE, *Marriage & Family Today*, Randon House, New York, 1977.

KENKEL, WILLIAM, F., *The Family in Perspective*, Third. Ed., Appleton Century Crafts, N.Y., 1973.

KOOS, EARL LOMON, *Marriage*, Henry Holt & Co., New York, 1958.

KUPPUSWAMY, B., *A Study of Opinion Regarding Marriage & Divorce*, Asia Publishing House, Bombay, 1957.

LANDIS, JUDSON T. & LANDIS, MARY I., Ed., *Readings in Marriage & the Family*, Prentice Hall Inc., N.Y., 1952.

LANDIS, JUDSON, *The Family & Social Change: A Positive View*, The Voice of America, Forum Lectures, 1964.

LEE, ALFRED MCCLUNG & LEE, ELIZABETH BRIANT, *Marriage & the Family*, Barnes & Noble Inc., N. York, 1961.

LEE, B.H., *Divorce Law Reform in England*, Peter Owen, London, 1974.

LESLIE, GERALD, R., *The Family in Social Context*, Fourth Ed., Oxf. Univ. Press, N.Y., 1979.

MCGREGOR, *Divorce in England*, Heinemann, London, 1957.

MEHTA, RAMA, *Divorced Hindu Woman*, Vikas Publishing House Pvt Ltd., New Delhi, 1975.

MELCRANTZLER, *Creative Divorce: A New Opportunity for Personal Growth*, M. Evans & Co., Inc., N.Y., 1973-74.

MERRILL, E.E., *Courtship & Marriage*, Henry Holt & Co., Inc., N.Y., 1959.

O' 'MOHONY J. (Ed.), *Catholics & Divorce*, Thomas Nelson, Ltd., London, N.Y., 1959.

PIETROPINTO, ANTHONY & SIMENAUER, JACQUELINE, *Husbands & Wives*, Berkley Books, N.Y., 1981.

POLLARD, ROBERT, S.W., *The Problem of Divorce*, C.A. Watts & Co., London, 1958.

PRABHU, P.H., *Hindu Social Organization*, Fourth Ed., Popular Prakashan, Bombay, 1963.

REED, ANGELA, *The Challenge of Second Marriage*, National Marriage Council, The Plume Press Ltd., London, 1973.

RUSSELL, BERTRAND, *Marriage & Morals*, George Allen & Unwin, 1929.

SAHA, A.N., *Marriage & Divorce*, Second Ed., Eastern Law House, Calcutta, 1981.

SANCTUARY, GERALD, & WHITEHEAD, CONSTANCE, *Divorce & After*, Victor Gollanez, London, 1970.

SEN GUPTA, NILAKSHI, *Evolution of Hindu Marriage*, Popular Prakashan, Bombay, 1965.

LEGISLATIONS (ACTS)

Hindu Marriage Act, 1955 (Act 25 of 1955)

The Special Marriage Act, 1954 (Act 43 of 1954)

Indian Divorce Act, 1869 (IV of 1869)

The Marriage Laws (Amendment) Act, 1976 (Act 68 of 1976)—An Act further to amend the Hindu Marriage Act, 1955, and the Special Marriage Act, 1954.

INDEX